[7—0]
Balsam Pear
(Momordica Charantia)

[7—0a]
Hoop Petticoat Daffodil
(Narcissus Bulbocodium conspicuus)

[7—0b]
Nemesia
(N. strumosa variety)

[7—0c]
Apostle Plant
(Neomarica Northiana)

[7-1]
Flowering Crab Apple
(Malus)

NEW ILLUSTRATED ENCYCLOPEDIA OF GARDENING

UNABRIDGED

EDITED BY T. H. Everett

Assistant Director (Horticulture) and Curator of Education
The New York Botanical Garden

WITH CONTRIBUTIONS FROM

TWENTY HORTICULTURISTS AND AUTHORITIES IN THE UNITED STATES AND CANADA

Growers, Breeders, Exhibitors, Plantsmen, Writers, Lecturers, Professors, Editors and Superintendents of Famous Estates, who are Experts in all Fields of Horticulture, including Pests and Their Control.

VOLUME SEVEN—Mah-Ora

GREYSTONE PRESS • NEW YORK

Copyright © MCMLXIV, MCMLXVII. By The GREYSTONE PRESS
100 Sixth Avenue
New York 13, New York
Library of Congress Catalog Card Number 60-7000
MANUFACTURED IN THE UNITED STATES OF AMERICA

Mahonia Bealei has sprays of handsome blue fruits.

MAHOBERBERIS NEUBERTII (Mahober'-beris). A hybrid between Mahonia Aquifolium and Berberis vulgaris. It is a hardy evergreen or semievergreen shrub that attains a height of about 6 ft. It is propagated by cuttings in late summer or fall and requires the same culture as Mahonia Aquifolium, which see. A variety of this interesting bigeneric hybrid named latifolia has broader leaves and is sometimes misnamed Berberis ilicifolia and B. latifolia.

MAHOGANY, RED. Eucalyptus resinigera.

MAHOGANY, SWAMP. Eucalyptus robusta.

MAHOGANY TREE. See Swietenia Mahoganii.

MAHONIA (Maho'nia). Evergreen shrubs with dark green leaves divided into a number of segments, the number, size and shape of the segments varying in different kinds. The yellow flowers are produced in rather dense clusters in spring, and are followed by dark purple or blue-black fleshy fruits covered by a definite bloom (waxy coating). The flesh of the fruits, though acid, is edible and can be used for making jelly.

The various kinds are natives of North America and Asia. Some are hardy in the North, a few can only be grown in the milder districts. Mahonia belongs to the Barberry family, Berberidaceae, and is very closely allied to Berberis. The name was given in honor of an American horticulturist, Bernard M'Mahon.

Methods of Propagation. All the Mahonias can be increased by means of seeds sown in sandy soil in a cold frame as soon as ripe. Seeds of the commonest kind, M. Aquifolium, may be sown in a prepared bed of soil out of doors; in fact, in favored localities young plants frequently develop from naturally sown seeds. Some kinds can be propagated by division, or by layering the branches in spring, but with such kinds as M. japonica and M. napaulensis it is almost essential to rely on seeds.

Hints on Cultivation. The different kinds of Mahonia vary a good deal in their requirements. All thrive in well-drained, loamy soil, but M. Aquifolium will flourish under varied conditions, in good soil and poor soil, in shade or in sunshine (except that, in the North, shade from winter sun and sweeping winds is important). It can be divided and the pieces transplanted with success; moreover it withstands regular and severe pruning, and it is useful for floral decorations. M. japonica and M. napaulensis, on the other hand, require good soil and a fairly open position; they resent root disturbance and do not require regular pruning. They are less hardy

The Holly Mahonia, Mahonia Aquifolium, is a native of the Pacific Northwest. It has attractive evergreen foliage and clusters of yellow flowers which are succeeded by blue-black berries.

Mahonia Bealei has handsome evergreen foliage and sprays of pale yellow flowers in late winter and early spring. It is hardy in sheltered places as far north as southern New York and southern New England.

than M. Aquifolium. Separate cultural directions are given with each kind mentioned.

Holly Mahonia. M. Aquifolium, often called Holly Mahonia, is a dense shrub 6-8 ft. high which grows wild from British Columbia to Oregon; the thick, leathery leaves are made up of five to nine large, spine-margined leaflets, which often assume a purplish-bronze tint in winter and occasionally turn scarlet before they fall. A number of varieties have been singled out for distinctive names, the differences being in the stature, and size and shape of the leaves and leaflets.

A Shrub for Shady Places. Holly Mahonia is invaluable for covering banks, for planting beneath trees in the garden, or for undergrowth in plantations. It withstands pruning well and can be kept to a height of $1\frac{1}{2}$ ft. by pruning annually either in summer or spring. It can be increased by division or by seeds and, if desired, the blue-black fruits may be used for jelly. The branches are often cut for decorative purposes in winter. The flowering time is April and May.

M. Aquifolium is hardy in sheltered places in Massachusetts and even as far north as Canada, where it is protected in winter by a good covering of snow.

M. Fremontii, 6-12 ft. high, is a shrub which grows wild in western Texas, Colorado and California, and is hardy about as far north as Virginia. From three to seven rather small, bluish-green spiny leaflets make up each leaf; the flowers are yellow and the fruits bluish-black. It appears to dislike root disturbance and requires little pruning except when young; the points of the shoots should then be removed on several occasions.

Handsomest of All. M. Bealei and M. japonica are very handsome shrubs with erect, rigid stems with few branchlets, each branch being crowned by a head of large leaves made up of, usually, nine to thirteen leaflets, each 2-5 in. long and $1\frac{1}{2}$-$3\frac{1}{2}$ in. wide. The fragrant, pale yellow flowers, which open in spring, are in erect clusters 6-9 in. long. The fruits are dark purple with a bluish bloom. These Mahonias should be planted in deep, loamy soil when quite small and then left alone. M. Bealei is from China, and M. japonica from Japan. They are hardy to southern New England.

M. napaulensis is a less hardy but closely allied kind which shares with M. japonica a dislike of root disturbance. It forms an erect bush with long, stout branches which are terminated by large heads of evergreen leaves 2 ft. long, made up of fifteen to twenty-five large leaflets. The heads of yellow flowers, which are out in April, are 9-12 in. long. This shrub is a native of the Himalayas.

Other Attractive Kinds. M. nervosa, Oregon Grape, is a small, graceful shrub 12-18 in. high, with leaves 18 in. long made up of eleven to nineteen leaflets. It is wild in western North America. M. Fortunei, a Chinese shrub with long, narrow leaflets, is also worth growing.

M. repens, a dwarf shrub, 9-12 in. high, of spreading habit, may be regarded as a dwarf M. Aquifolium. It grows wild from British Columbia to California. It is about as hardy as M. Aquifolium and can be grown in the same way.

MAIANTHEMUM—*Mayflower* (Mai'anthemum). Hardy herbaceous perennial flowering plants, natives of the cool regions of the Northern Hemisphere, including North America. These plants, which have leaves and flowers similar to those of the Lily-of-the-Valley, grow about 6 in. in height, have a slender creeping rootstock, heart-shaped leaves in pairs and white flowers. They belong to the Lily family, Liliaceae. The name Maianthemum is the Greek for Mayflower, from *Maios,* May, and *anthemon,* blossom.

For Shady Places. These plants are suitable for growing in shady borders or shrubberies and in wild gardens and woodlands. They will flourish in ordinary garden soil enriched with compost or leaf mold, and planting is done in September or October. Pieces of the slender rootstocks are planted 3 in. apart and 1 in. deep; they are laid flat. In April the soil is mulched with leaf mold or peat moss and the ground is watered in dry weather.

Propagation is by lifting the plants in autumn, separating the rootstocks into small pieces and replanting them in prepared soil.

The chief kinds are M. bifolium (M. Convallaria), 6 in., white, May; M. canadense, 6 in., white, May; and M. dilatatum, 8 in., white, spring.

MAIDENHAIR FERN. See Adiantum and also Notholaena.

MAIDENHAIR SPLEENWORT. Asplenium trichomanes, which see.

MAIDENHAIR TREE. See Ginkgo biloba.

MAIDEN PINK. See Dianthus deltoides.

MAIDEN'S WREATH. See Francoa ramosa.

MAIDEN TREE. A term used by gardeners to describe a fruit tree or Rose bush which has made one season's growth since it was budded or grafted. For example, a Rose, budded in July, will start into growth the following spring; during that year it is a "maiden" tree. In the following March or April the branch that grew the previous year will be pruned; subsequently the Rose bush is called a "cutback," because the first or "maiden" shoot has been pruned or cut back.

MAINE, GARDENING IN. See Regional Gardening.

MAJORANA—*Marjoram* (Majora′na). Perennial herbs, natives of Europe and the Near East, which belong to the Mint family, Labiatae. The leaves are used for flavoring, in sachets, and as a source of an oil used in perfumery.

Pot Marjoram (M. Onites) likes a sunny, well-

The herb Sweet Marjoram.

drained border, and will thrive in ordinary soil. A little decayed manure is dug into the ground when preparing the site in winter. The plants are set out in spring, 10 in. apart in rows 15 in. apart. The ground is made firm around the roots, and they are well watered in dry weather. The soil should be mulched each spring with decayed manure. They should not be disturbed for three or four years, when they are lifted, divided and replanted in freshly prepared soil.

Sweet Marjoram. Although Majorana hortensis is a perennial, it is not hardy and is best treated as an annual. Seeds are sown in flats of sandy soil in March and placed in a heated greenhouse. When the seedlings are 2 in. high, they are pricked out, 3 in. apart, in deep flats filled with light soil. They are watered and shaded until established, then hardened off and planted out of doors in April. A sunny, well-drained position is chosen. This is dug and manured and the seedlings are planted 6 in. apart in rows 12 in. apart. They are watered and shaded from hot sunlight until established.

The leaves are used when young for flavoring and the shoots are gathered when "spindling" for flower, tied in bundles and hung in a cool, shady shed or room to dry. The leaves are then stripped off and stored in packets or bottles for winter use.

MALACOCARPUS (Malacocarp′us). A group of South American Cacti that require the same care and culture as Echinocactus, which see. (See also Cactus.) They belong to the Cactus family, Cactaceae. The name is from *malakos*, soft, and *karpos*, a fruit, and has reference to the fleshy fruits. M. Sellowii has yellow flowers, is globular and measures about 6 in. across; M. Vorwerkianus also has yellow flowers, is nearly globular, and measures 3 in. across.

MALANGA. See Xanthosoma.

MALAXIS. See Microstylis.

MALCOMIA MARITIMA—*Virginian Stock* (Malcom'ia). A low-growing hardy annual, which grows wild in various parts of Europe, and belongs to the Mustard family, Cruciferae. The name commemorates William Malcolm, a London nurseryman of the eighteenth century.

This plant comes very quickly into bloom and is one of the most easily grown of all the hardy annuals. It thrives in ordinary cultivated garden soil, but must have a sunny place.

For growing in cool climates the Virginian Stock is a pretty annual.

Virginian Stock is grown as an edging for flower beds and borders. Seeds are sown in late March, or in April, as soon as the soil is so dry that it can be broken down and made friable, in the spot where the plants are to bloom in June and July. The seedlings make quick progress and must be thinned to 3 or 4 in. apart before they become overcrowded. Virginian Stock runs to seed rapidly, and the show of bloom is therefore not usually long-lived.

A good practice is to mix the seeds of Virginian Stock and Night-scented Stock (Mathiola bicornis); the latter is very fragrant in the evening, but dowdy by day, and the Virginian Stock serves the purpose of supplying color when the Night-scented Stock is unattractive.

Virginian Stock grows about 6 in. high; the color of the flowers of the typical kind is lilac-rose, but seedsmen supply varieties of distinct coloring—e.g., crimson, deep lilac and pale yellow—seeds of which can be purchased separately.

Other kinds of Malcomia are in cultivation, but they are little grown.

MALE BERRY. See Lyonia.

MALE FERN. See Dryopteris Filix-mas.

MALLOW. See Lavatera and Malva.

MALLOW, JEW'S. See Kerria japonica.

MALLOW, MUSK. See Malva moschata.

MALLOW, POPPY. See Callirhoë.

MALLOW, TREE. See Lavatera.

MALOPE TRIFIDA (Ma'lope). A hardy annual which grows wild in Spain and parts of northern Africa and belongs to the Mallow family, Malvaceae. The name is an old Greek one.

This plant reaches a height of about 2 ft. and bears crimson flowers in summer. It is easily managed if seeds are sown out of doors in March–April, where the plants are to bloom, in a place fully exposed to the sunshine, in well-tilled

Malope trifida, a showy annual which bears crimson, mallow-like flowers in summer.

garden soil. This annual flourishes best in well-drained ground; it is not a success on heavy, clayey soil. As the plants grow about 2 ft. high, the seedlings must be thinned out until they are from 9-12 in. apart to give them plenty of room for development. It is wasteful, therefore, to sow the seeds thickly. There are several varieties having crimson, rose-red, or white flowers. M. malacoides, 12 in., bears rose-colored flowers in summer.

MALPIGHIA (Malpigh'ia). Tender small trees and shrubs of tropical America, the West Indies and the southern United States. They belong to the Malpighia family, the Malpighiaceae. The genus is named in commemoration of Marcello Malpighi, an Italian naturalist.

Two kinds are commonly grown. M. coccigera, a pretty West Indian shrub with small holly-like leaves and delicate pink flowers, is widely cultivated in warm countries as an ornamental. M. glabra, the Barbados Cherry, which makes a good low hedge, is a native of tropical America to southern Texas; it forms a shrub 5-10 ft. tall and has rose-pink flowers and acid,

When covered with its delicate pink flowers, Malpighia coccigera is very attractive. It has tiny holly-like leaves.

cherry-like fruits that are edible and useful for making preserves. Both M. coccigera and M. glabra may be grown in pots in a warm greenhouse.

These plants grow without difficulty in any fairly good soil. They are easily propagated by seeds and cuttings.

MALTESE CROSS. See Lychnis chalcedonica.

MALUS: APPLES AND BLOSSOM AND FRUIT
Beautiful Trees and Shrubs for Gardens

(Ma'lus). The Apples and Crab Apples (or Crabs) are deciduous small trees and shrubs of the Northern Hemisphere. From one kind, Malus sylvestris, native of Europe and western Asia, has been developed, by selection and crossbreeding, all the varieties of orchard Apples and most of the Crab Apples cultivated for their edible fruits. Malus is the Latin name for the Apple tree. The genus belongs in the Rose family, Rosaceae. For the cultivation of orchard Apples, see Apple.

Among the species of Malus and their hybrids and varieties cultivated primarily for their blooms, are many of the loveliest of all flowering trees. They are suitable for both large and small gardens. Many assume rich foliage colors in autumn, and quite a number are attractive in fruit. The true species can be raised from seed, but this is a lengthy process compared with budding or grafting onto the stocks usually employed for orchard Apples. Varieties and hybrids must, of course, be propagated by the latter methods, as they do not come true from seed.

Soil Requirements and Pruning. The ornamental Crabs are not very exacting about soil requirements, but the best results are obtained in various kinds of loam, from light to heavy, and even clay. They are among the best flowering trees and shrubs for planting on alkaline (limestone) soils, and there the fruit usually colors very well.

Provided they have been regularly transplanted in the nursery, and long roots have been pruned, they will transplant with masses of fibrous roots, and no difficulty will be found in their re-establishment. Transplanting may be carried out in fall or early spring. A mulch of leaves, decayed manure or compost placed over

Flowering spray of the lovely white Malus Sargentii. This species develops as a large shrub rather than as a tree.

the soil the first summer will be an advantage.

Occasional attention to pruning will be necessary. With the more vigorous kinds, a definite length of trunk should be cleared of branches, and in all kinds the heads should be kept fairly open to admit light and air. This pruning may be carried out as soon as the flowers are over, after the fall of the fruit or in late winter or in spring.

The Common Apple. In its wild form, the Common Apple, Malus sylvestris, bears attractive flowers in spring, and these are followed by small green or reddish-green sour fruits. It is very effective in bloom. There are numerous varieties and hybrids between this and other kinds that are grown for their flowers and decorative fruits. These are increased by budding or grafting on the stocks used for Apples, the work being carried out in the same way and at the same time. (See Apple.)

Crab Apples For Jelly. There is a fine group of varieties or hybrids of M. sylvestris that pro-

The Tea Crab Apple, Malus hupehensis, has fragrant white or pale pink blossoms.

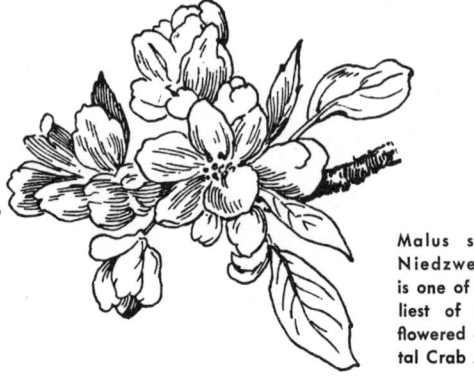

Malus sylvestris Niedzwetzkyana is one of the loveliest of the red-flowered ornamental Crab Apples.

The flowers of a variety of the Siberian Crab Apple, Malus baccata.

duce large and showy fruits, all of which can be used for making jelly. Good ones are Dolgo, Young America, Hyslop, Hopa and Columbia. These trees are also attractive in bloom.

The Remarkable Red-Vein or Purple Crab. M. sylvestris Niedzwetzkyana is a very distinct tree with large, reddish-purple flowers, large reddish-purple fruits and purplish leaves: the purplish color is also present in the wood and roots. It is attractive both in flower and fruit and is said to grow wild in the Caucasus and southwestern Siberia. Several handsome hybrids have been raised between this and other kinds.

Showy Red-flowered Hybrid Crabs. M. purpurea is a hybrid between M. sylvestris Niedwetzkyana and M. atrosanguinea. It is a very beautiful tree with dark purplish-green leaves, rose-crimson flowers and red fruits. This is an excellent kind for both large and small gardens and is very effective during late April and early May. A variety with deep red flowers is M. purpurea Eleyi. M. purpurea aldenhamensis has purplish leaves, deep-red flowers and red fruits. The best of all is M. purpurea Lemoinei, with its profusion of rich purplish-crimson flowers and bronzy foliage.

The Southern Crab Apple is M. angustifolia, a very fragrant-flowered kind that is found wild from Virginia to Florida and Missouri. Its blooms are pink or rose colored, about 1 in. or less across, and its yellow-green fruits are about 1 in. in diameter.

The Siberian Crab. M. baccata, the Siberian Crab, grows into a tree 25-30 ft. high with a large head of branches. It is improved by being trained as a tree with several feet of clean trunk. The white or slightly rose-flushed flowers are produced with great freedom in May, and are followed by round hard fruits, ¾ in. in diameter, that are red and yellow when ripe, and often remain on the trees throughout winter. The flowers are very fragrant. The fruits can be used for jelly. It is a native of Siberia, Manchuria and northern China.

Many varieties of the Siberian Crab Apple have been described. Among the more important are M. baccata variety columnaris, a tree of very upright growth, which is a rare character among Crab Apples; M. baccata variety Jackii, which has glossy red fruits and is one of the best of the Siberian Crab Apples; and M. baccata mandschurica, which is the earliest of all Crab Apples to bloom.

The Garland Crab Apple. M. coronaria, which grows wild from New York to Ontario and southward to Alabama and Missouri, is known as the Garland Crab Apple and sometimes as the Wild Sweet Crab. It grows to about 30 ft. high and has pink flowers that fade to white as they mature. The blooms measure about 1 in. across and the yellowish fruits (sour to the taste) are 1 in. in diameter. A number of varieties of this species have been described, including Charlottae and Nieuwlandiana, both double-flowered kinds.

The Showy Crab Apple. M. floribunda is possibly a native of Japan or China or may be of hybrid origin. It is one of the finest ornamental Crabs. It forms a large shrub or small tree and attains a height of 25 ft. or more. Its flowers are pink or deep rose, fading to white as they mature. They are about 1¼ in. in diameter. The red fruits measure about ⅓ in. in diameter.

Malus Halliana, sometimes called the Hall Crab Apple, is a native of China. It is an attractive kind that at maturity is a large bush or small tree 15-18 ft. tall. The blooms are deep rose-pink, the leaves purplish. The fruits are purple and about ⅓ in. across, and not particularly ornamental. A very beautiful double-flowered variety is M. Halliana variety Parkmanii. Its blooms, each of which has about 15 petals, are carried in drooping clusters.

Bechtel's Crab, Malus ionensis plena, is a variety of the Prairie Crab Apple. It is the latest of all Crab Apples to bloom.

The Tea Crab Apple. M. hupehensis, formerly known as M. theifera, is a small, vase-shaped tree with stiff branches that is a native of eastern Asia. Its blooms are white or pale pink and are delightfully fragrant. They are succeeded by red-flushed, greenish-yellow fruits that are about 1/3 in. in diameter.

The Prairie Crab Apple is M. ionensis, which grows wild from Indiana to Minnesota and Missouri. The double-flowered variety named M. ionensis plena, Bechtel's Crab, is most commonly grown. These kinds attain a height of 20-30 ft. and have white or pale pink blooms. The fruits are greenish. Bechtel's Crab is very handsome and late-blooming.

A Shrubby Kind. The smallest of all Crab Apples is M. Sargentii. This native of Japan does not grow taller than 6-8 ft., is low, bushy and much branched. Its flowers are pure white and are borne in great profusion. The fruits are about 1/2 in. in diameter and are dark red. In fall the foliage turns yellow or orange yellow. This is a most valuable kind for small gardens.

Some Other Good Crab Apples. Among other decorative Crab Apples that are well worthy of planting are M. prunifolia, which has white blooms and yellow or red fruits and is a native of eastern Asia that becomes a small tree; M. Sieboldii, the Toringo Crab Apple, a Japanese shrub 15 ft. tall with blush or pink flowers and red or yellowish fruits; M. spectabilis, probably a native of China, to 25 ft. tall, with large pink flowers and yellow fruits; M. spectabilis variety Riversii, similar but with large pink double flowers; M. toringoides, a most lovely Chinese kind that forms a shrub or small tree up to 25 ft. tall and has clusters of white or pinkish blooms and red-checked, yellow fruits about 1/2 in. in diameter (this is one of the most decorative kinds when in fruit). M. Zumi, which originated in Japan, may be a hybrid; it grows to 20 ft. tall or somewhat higher and has blooms that are pink when in bud but open white. The fruits, which are usually borne profusely, are red and about 1/2 in. in diameter.

A Handsome Hybrid. M. Arnoldiana is a reported hybrid between M. floribunda and M. baccata. It has much merit as an ornamental kind. It becomes a large shrub or small tree up to about 25 ft. tall. Its blooms are at first pink but fade to white as they mature. The fruits are larger than those of M. floribunda and are yellow rather than red.

The Carmine Crab Apple, M. atrosanguinea, is one of the most handsome. It is a hybrid between M. Halliana and M. Sieboldii. The Carmine Crab Apple becomes a large shrub or small tree and bears a profusion of rosy purple blooms that do not fade to white as they age. The fruits are red and not very showy. This Crab Apple has very dark green foliage.

Red Jade, a seedling of Exzellenz Thiel (a selected form of a hybrid of M. prunifolia pendula and M. floribunda), has drooping branches, blush-white flowers and a profusion of small red fruits.

Brilliant Autumn-tinted Leaves. M. Tschonoskii is a Japanese tree, growing 30-40 ft. high, producing white flowers and small orange and red fruits. Its best time, however, is in autumn, for the leaves turn brilliant red and orange-scarlet before they fall.

Other notable kinds are M. kansuensis, white flowers and red fruits; and M. yunnanensis, up to 40 ft. tall, with large clusters of white, pink-tinted flowers.

The perennial Mallow, Malva Alcea fastigiata.

MALVA—*Mallow* (Mal'va). Hardy annual, biennial and perennial plants which grow wild in European countries and belong to the family Malvaceae. Several species have become naturalized in North America. The name is an old Latin one for the Mallow.

For the Wild Garden. The Mallows are useful for the wild garden and a few of them are worth a place in the perennial border. They are very easily managed and thrive in ordinary soil in a sunny or slightly shady place. The perennial kinds can be increased by lifting the plants in October or November and separating them into rooted pieces for replanting.

White-flowered Malva moschata alba is an especially lovely kind.

Raising Seedlings. It is best, however, to leave Mallows undisturbed and to raise a fresh stock of plants by sowing seeds out of doors, in May, transplanting the seedlings to their permanent places as soon as they are well developed. The annual kinds are raised from seeds sown out of doors in spring, where the plants are to bloom in summer.

The Musk Mallow (M. moschata), 18 in., rose, and M. sylvestris, 2-3 ft., reddish-purple, are perennials suitable for the wild garden. The white Musk Mallow is an attractive plant and comes true from seed. They may be planted in autumn or spring, and thrive in ordinary or poor soil.

Good Border Plant. The kind of chief value in the garden is M. Alcea, a perennial which reaches a height of about 4 ft., and bears purplish-rose flowers in summer. Variety fastigiata is a good red-flowered form. M. crispa is an annual, 3 ft. or more high, with white flowers tinged with purple; it is grown by sowing seeds out of doors in spring, where the plants are to bloom in summer; the seedlings should be thinned to about 12 in. apart.

MALVASTRUM—*False Mallow* (Malvas'trum). Hardy and tender perennial plants, belonging to the Mallow family, Malvaceae, which grow wild in the United States and in South America. The name is a variation of Malva.

These plants need a well-drained sandy, loamy soil; they are low-growing and should be planted near the front of the border or in the rock garden.

The best method of propagation is by sowing seeds in a greenhouse or cold frame in May, growing the plants in pots and keeping them in a frame for the winter, and planting them out the following spring.

The chief kinds are Malvastrum coccineum, 6 in., bright red; M. lateritium, 6 in., red, and M. campanulatum, 15 in., rose-purple.

MALVAVISCUS (Malvavis'cus). Tender trees and shrubs that are natives of tropical America, Mexico and parts of the southern United States, and which belong to the Mallow family, Malvaceae. They are grown in tropical and subtropical countries as ornamentals and are sometimes cultivated in greenhouses. One, M. arboreus variety penduliflorus, is very freely planted in Florida and other parts of the far South, and is much admired for its bright crimson flowers, which are borne over a long period—in fall, winter and spring. The name is derived from Malva, a genus of plants, and *viscosus,* sticky, and refers to the sap.

Malvaviscus thrives without special care in a wide variety of soils and needs full sun for its best development. It is easily propagated by cuttings of leafy shoots planted in sand or vermiculite in a close propagating case in spring or summer. Seeds also afford a means of raising new plants. Pruning should receive attention in spring, after flowering. At that time old flowering shoots may be pruned back, and the crowded, unwanted ones removed.

When grown in greenhouses, these plants make handsome winter-flowering subjects in pots 7 in. in diameter or larger. They need a minimum winter temperature of 55-60 degrees; at lower temperatures they live but will not bloom well. They also need as much sunshine as possible.

In late spring, prune back old plants. Remove them from their pots, and, with a pointed stick, pick away as much old soil as can easily be removed from the outside of the root ball; now, repot them in well-drained containers in a rich, loamy soil. The soil should be packed quite firmly.

After potting, water should be applied in moderation until new roots take possession of the new soil; the tops should be syringed freely on all bright days. As the summer advances and the pots become filled with roots, more frequent watering will be necessary; at no time should the plants be allowed to suffer from dryness.

Repotting into larger receptacles (except in the case of specimens that are already in very large containers) will be necessary in June or July. Care must be taken at that time not to disturb the roots at all in the potting operation. After the potting is completed, the plants should be well watered with a fine spray and kept in the shade for a week or so.

During the warm summer months, pot-grown plants benefit from being plunged outdoors in a bed of ashes or sand in a sunny location, but they must be transferred to the greenhouse before the weather turns cold in the fall. From the time when their final pots are filled with roots, a weekly application of dilute complete liquid fertilizer will prove very advantageous.

Malvaviscus makes a fine specimen when trained in "standard" (tree-form) shape; shoots radiating from near a common center from the top of a 3-ft. or 4-ft. unbranched stem display the drooping flowers to perfection. Cuttings rooted in spring and grown on without pinching make very desirable decorative plants from November onwards.

The kind most commonly grown is M. arboreus variety penduliflorus (sometimes known in gardens as M. grandiflorus). It forms a spreading shrub 6-7 ft. tall with deep green leaves and flowers that measure 1-2 in. long. M. arboreus is native from Mexico to Peru and Brazil; its variety penduliflorus occurs naturally from Mexico to Colombia. Several more or less distinct varieties of M. arboreus are recognized by botanists, and it is likely that some of these are in cultivation.

MAMMILLARIA: NIPPLE CACTUS
How to Grow and Propagate These Interesting Cacti

(Mammillar'ia). Tender succulent plants, chiefly natives of the southwestern United States and Mexico, which belong to the Cactus family, Cactaceae. This is a very large genus, consisting of between two and three hundred kinds; they vary in height from 1-12 in. and mostly consist of a single thick, fleshy stem, surrounded by closely set tubercles (fleshy lumps) which are crowned with hairs or spines. The flowers, which are produced principally near the apex of the stems, are tubular at the base but the numerous petals spread out at the top into a star-shaped formation. They measure up to 2 in. in diameter and are purple, pink, red, yellow or white. The flow-

The spines on Mammillaria elongata form a beautiful starlike pattern.

ers are often succeeded by scarlet, berry-like fruits, which are very attractive.

Plants Without Leaves. All Mammillarias are devoid of leaves and have a thick outer skin which enables these plants to live in dry, barren climates where most other plants cannot exist, because transpiration (giving off water) is reduced to a minimum. During rainy periods Mammillarias are capable of storing water, which is utilized during periods of drought. The name Mammillaria is derived from *mamilla*, a nipple, and alludes to the small tubercles. Many of the species previously included in this genus are now referred to Coryphantha.

For Warm Greenhouse or Room Window. These plants can be grown in a sunny greenhouse or window, where the winter temperature does not fall below 55 degrees. They require a compost of two parts sandy loam and one part of equal portions of sand and crushed bricks. The pots, which should be just large enough to hold them, are filled to one third their capacity with crocks. These are covered with leaves or moss to prevent the compost from washing into the drainage. Repotting is best done in March or April, when new growth is beginning. The plants are knocked out of the pots, and the crocks and any loose soil removed with a pointed stick; they are then set in the new pots and the compost is made firm.

Repotting is not necessary every year; once every three or four years is usually sufficient. After potting, the plants are placed on a sunny shelf or bench and no water is given to the soil until it becomes quite dry. A light syringing twice daily is beneficial as it keeps down red spider mites and encourages new growth.

Summer and Winter Management. When the soil becomes quite dry, it is thoroughly saturated, and subsequently, is kept moist throughout the summer. When growth has finished, in July or August, less water is given and the plants are exposed to the maximum amount of sunlight to ensure the production of flowers. From October until April very little water is required, sufficient only being given to prevent the stems from shriveling.

Taking Cuttings. The tops of the stems, or side branches if they are available, are cut off and laid in the sun for a few hours to enable a skin to form over the cuts. This prevents them from decaying when inserted in the soil. They are planted in sand, and not watered until the

Mammillaria multiceps is a favorite kind. It has pinkish yellow flowers.

Mammillaria elongata is an interesting Cactus that bears white flowers.

Malvaviscus arboreus penduliflorus has bright red flowers.

soil becomes quite dry. This treatment is continued until roots have formed, when they are potted separately in pots just large enough to hold them.

Raising Seedlings. Seeds may be sown during spring or summer, in pots of sandy soil. The seed pots are well drained and the seeds scattered thinly on the surface of the compost. They are lightly covered with finely sifted soil, the soil is moistened and a pane of glass is laid over the pot. The seed pot is set in a warm greenhouse or sunny window until germination takes place. The glass is then removed and the seedlings are exposed to full light and air. Sometimes germination is very irregular, but it is not wise to leave the glass on the pot once the majority of the seedlings are through. If some of them are up long in advance of the others, they may be pricked off into another pot, and the seed pot re-covered with the pane of glass. The transplanted seedlings must not be disturbed until they have made sufficient roots to fill small pots.

The seedlings of Mammillaria are very interesting to watch in their development. They appear first as little globular masses of green tissue. These are in reality little bundles of food-bearing cells which supply nourishment to the young plants. The growing point or shoot bud is at the tip of the globular structure, and, as this elongates, the "bag of food" is gradually absorbed by the developing plant.

The chief kinds are M. applanata, white tinged with red; M. barbata, rose-pink; M. Blossfeldiana, carmine; M. bocasana, red; M. compressa, purple; M. dealbata, carmine; M. echinaria, yellow; M. elongata, white; M. fragilis, Thimble Cactus, cream-colored; M. melanocentra, pink; M. spinossima, red; M. Pringlei, deep red; M. prolifera, yellow; M. pygmaea, cream; M. rhodantha, pink; and M. multiceps, yellowish salmon.

MAMONCILLO. See Melicocca.

MANDARIN ORANGE. Citrus nobilis deliciosa, which see.

MANDEVILLA—*Chilean Jasmine* (Mandevill'a). Tender deciduous climbing plants, with attractive flowers. They are natives of Argentina and belong to the Periwinkle family, Apocynaceae. These vigorous climbers, which grow 20 ft. in height, have heart-shaped leaves and small clusters of funnel-shaped, five-petaled white, fragrant flowers in summer. Being of vigorous habit, they do not thrive when grown in pots, and are therefore planted in a prepared bed of soil in a greenhouse having a minimum winter temperature of 60 degrees; they are also grown outdoors in the far South. The name Mandevilla commemorates Henry John Mandeville, a British minister at Buenos Aires.

Climbing Plants for a Hothouse. The site is prepared by taking out a hole to the depth of 3 ft. A layer of broken bricks, 9 in. in depth, is placed in the bottom and is then covered with pieces of fibrous turf to prevent the compost from washing into the drainage and blocking it. The remainder of the space is filled with a compost consisting of equal parts of peat and loam and a sprinkling of sand and crushed charcoal.

Planting and Details of Management. Planting is done in March, the roots being spread out laterally and the compost made firm around them. The soil is then well watered and the plants shaded from the direct rays of the sun, the foliage being syringed twice daily to assist root action. Wires or trellis are fixed to the roof, to which the shoots are trained.

Pruning is done after flowering, when the lateral shoots are shortened to two or three buds, and weak and dead shoots are entirely removed. During the summer the soil is kept moist by watering freely at least once a week, but throughout the winter very little watering is required.

Taking Cuttings. Propagation by cuttings is the most popular method. Side shoots 2-3 in. long are inserted in sandy peat, in early summer, in a warm propagating case, which is kept closed until roots are formed.

The rooted cuttings are potted separately in 3-in. pots, and returned to the closed case for 3 or 4 days. They are then placed on the open benches and the tips of the main shoots removed to make side branches form. As soon as new shoots appear, the plants are potted in 5-in. pots, and, when well rooted in these, they are planted in the prepared bed.

The chief kind in cultivation is M. sauveolens, 20 ft., white, fragrant, summer.

MANDRAGORA — *Mandrake* (Mandrag'ora). A few kinds of herbaceous perennial plants found in the Mediterranean region are included under this name. They have no great value as decorative plants but have a very considerable mystical interest. M. officinarum, the common Mandrake, has from ancient times been connected with witchcraft, magic and other dark practices. Shakespeare and other writers frequently made use of the legends connected with Mandrake in their writings.

The Legend of the Mandrake. One legend is that any interference with the roots causes the plants to give forth most terrifying shrieks. The plant was also invested with all kinds of virtues and was credited, if collected in the right way and at the right time, with aiding love affairs and healing all sorts of disorders. As a matter of fact it has little or no value as a drug plant.

Why was so much attention paid to the plant in ancient times? Apparently, because the thick fleshy roots present a crude representation of the lower part of the human body, and our forefathers surmised that there was some connection between the plant and human beings.

Pliny records that those who undertook to collect the plant were careful to stand with the wind at their back and, before beginning to dig, they made three circles around the plant with the point of a sword. At one period a person might dig around a plant without trouble, but instead of pulling it out of the ground he tied a dog to it and made the dog pull it out in order to divert bad luck from himself to the dog.

M. officinarum grows about 12 in. high and bears white or pale purple flowers in early summer. Another kind, M. autumnalis, is also from the Mediterranean region. These plants thrive in ordinary garden soil.

MANDRAKE. See Mandragora.

MANETTIA (Manett'ia). Tender, evergreen climbing plants with attractive flowers. They belong to the family Rubiaceae and are natives of Brazil. The shoots attain a length of from 10-15 ft., have ovate or lanceolate pointed leaves and tubular flowers, 1-2 in. long, with four spreading petal tips; they are white yellow or red, and in some kinds the tips of the petals are yellow. The name Manettia commemorates Xavier Manetti, of the Botanic Gardens, Florence.

Showy Climbing Plants. These twining plants are trained to wires or a trellis fixed to the wall or roof of the greenhouse or grown in large pots and the shoots trained to a tripod of stakes. A winter temperature of 50 degrees is required. The best potting compost consists of equal parts of loam and fibrous peat, with crushed charcoal and sand added freely. Plants grown in pots should be repotted in March. They may be planted outdoors in summer. In the far South they may be grown permanently outdoors.

Details of Management. Well-drained pots must be used, as a waterlogged condition of the soil is harmful. The plants are knocked out of the pots, the crocks and a little of the loose soil being removed, and they are then set in pots two sizes larger. After potting, they must be frequently syringed and shaded from sunlight until established. Plants which are trained to the roof or wall of the greenhouse should be planted in a prepared bed of compost. A hole 2½ ft. deep is taken out and 6 in. of broken brick or rubble is placed in the bottom. On this a 3-in.-thick layer of rough leaves or turf is laid, and the remainder of the space is filled with the same compost as advised for potting.

Plants, well-rooted in 5-in. pots, are then set in position; they must be frequently syringed until the roots have established themselves in the new soil. Pruning is done as soon as the flowers have faded, when the shoots are slightly shortened.

Propagation by Cuttings. Small side shoots, 2 or 3 in. in length, are inserted in a propagating case in a 60-70-degree temperature. The case is kept closed to maintain a humid atmosphere, which prevents the cuttings from wilting. When rooted, they are removed from the propagating case and set on the open benches of the greenhouse. After a week or ten days each plant is then potted in a 3-in. pot and subsequently into a 5-in. pot, from which it is set in its permanent position.

During the summer months water must be applied freely to the soil and the atmosphere kept moist by frequently damping the floor and benches. During the winter the soil is only moistened when it becomes quite dry, and less syringing is required, although it must not be discontinued altogether, as in a dry atmosphere red spider mites are liable to infest the plants.

The chief kinds are M. bicolor, scarlet and orange, spring and summer; M. coccinea, pink and red; and M. glabra, 10-15 ft., crimson-scarlet, winter and spring.

MANETTI STOCK. An understock, introduced from Italy, on which bush Roses are sometimes budded.

MANFREDA (Manfre′da). A group of plants closely related to Agave that are chiefly Mexican, although some species are found to the south and some to the north of that country. M. virginica extends in nature as far north as Maryland. Manfreda belongs in the Amaryllis family, Amaryllidaceae. The genus was named, we are told, after "an ancient writer on simples whose work is in the Parisian library."

Culture. These plants need the same general culture as Agaves. The soil should be porous, well drained, and not excessively rich in nitrogen. During the winter it should be permitted to become almost dry before it is watered, but moisture may be more freely applied in summer. Repotting or planting should be done in spring just before new growth begins. A minimum winter temperature of 45-50 degrees is suitable.

Propagation is easily effected by means of seeds sown in pots or pans of sandy soil in spring and by offsets removed at planting or potting time. Manfredas need full sun for the greater part of the year, but, when grown in greenhouses, they appreciate a little shade in summer as a protection from the strongest sunshine.

The Mango, Mangifera indica.

Kinds. M. brachystachys, a native of Mexico, grows to 6 ft. tall and has green flowers; M. maculosa, with fragrant, greenish or whitish flowers, grows about 3 ft. tall and is a native of southern Texas; M. variegata, which comes from southern Texas and northern Mexico, attains a height of 4 ft. and has brownish-green flowers; M. virginica, with fragrant, greenish-yellow flowers, is native from Maryland to Florida and Texas and grows 6 ft. high. All are summer bloomers.

MANGIFERA—*Mango* (Mangif′era). A group of evergreen, tropical Asiatic trees. Only one, M. indica, the Mango, is commonly known in the United States. This splendid tree, under favorable conditions, will attain a height of 90 ft. and a spread of 120 ft. or more. It is a native of northern India, Burma and Malaya, and is widely planted in the tropics for its delicious fruit. In the United States its outdoor cultivation is limited to southern Florida and the warmest parts of California.

Mangifera belongs to the Cashew family, Anacardiaceae, and thus is a relative of the Poison Ivy. Its name is derived from Mango, the Hindu name for the fruit, and *fero,* to bear.

Soil and Planting. Mangoes may be grown on a variety of soils, and they are notorious for succeeding better than most trees where the soil is shallow and impervious, provided subsurface drainage is good. In poor soils Mangoes respond to fertilizers, but excessive applications of nitrogen tend to reduce the crops of fruiting-sized trees and are to be avoided.

Planting is best done in spring, although it may also be carried out in late summer or fall. A spacing of 30-35 ft. between the trees will usually be adequate, although at such close spacing pruning will eventually have to be employed to keep the trees in bounds and prevent them from interfering with the growth of their neighbors. Before planting, it is advisable to improve the site by mixing with the soil a liberal amount of compost or decayed manure. After planting, the soil surface should be kept mulched through the early years of growth.

For the first five years or so after planting, every effort should be made to encourage strong shoot and leaf growth. Fertilizer should be applied from time to time, and the trees should not be permitted to suffer from lack of moisture during the growing season. Once the trees have reached a fair size and are expected to fruit, less effort should be made to induce vegetative growth, because excess in this direction will impair fruit bearing.

For good results, it is important that the growth of trees of fruiting size be checked for several weeks before the flowering season. At blooming time, dry weather will help to encourage good pollination—but dryness of the soil is harmful then. From flowering time on through the period when the fruits are developing, ample water supplies at the roots are essential; however, less moisture is desirable when the fruit approaches maturity.

Propagation. Fresh seeds of Mangoes, planted preferably in sterilized soil, germinate rather irregularly in about three weeks, or more quickly, if the endocarp (husk) is removed from the seed before planting. Seeds that have been allowed to dry usually fail to germinate.

Seedling trees give rise to trees that bear fruits of very variable quality, and usually are very much less desirable than those of recognized named varieties.

Named varieties are propagated by air-layering, inarching and, more frequently, by bud-

An interesting house plant may be raised from a seed taken from a ripe Mango and planted in a pot of soil.

In a few weeks a thin shoot develops from the top of the Mango seed and roots grow from its bottom. With the passing of time, the shoot thickens into a sturdy stem bearing leaves.

A young Mango plant grown in a window garden from a seed.

ding or grafting (which see) on seedling stocks.

Varieties. A great many varieties of Mangoes are cultivated in tropical regions. In Florida the variety Hayden is one of the finest, but, unfortunately, does not bear very dependably. New varieties raised locally are now gaining favor and are being planted. Among these are Edward, Fascell, Kent, Zill, Julie, Whitney and Brooks.

MANGO. The common name used for Mangifera indica, and for the fruit of this tree. See Mangifera.

Mangoes as House Plants. Young plants of Mango form attractive and interesting house plants that withstand conditions within the average home well. Their merit lies in their beautiful foliage which is glossy and deep green. The new leaves, for some time after they first unfold, are rich brownish-red in color and very beautiful.

For use as house plants Mangoes are easily raised from seeds taken from fresh fruits and planted immediately. The seeds should be set, with their tips just showing above the surface, in pots of well-drained sandy, fertile soil. If the soil is kept reasonably moist in a temperature of about 70 degrees the seeds soon germinate.

Mangoes in pots grow well in a temperature of 60-70 degrees. They need good light but not necessarily direct sun. The soil in which they grow should be watered sufficiently often to keep it always moderately moist but not constantly saturated. Plants that have filled their pots with healthy roots benefit from being given dilute liquid fertilizer every week or two. When repotting is needed it is best done in spring.

MANGOSTEEN. One of the most luscious of tropical fruits, produced by an evergreen tree, Garcinia Mangostana, a native of the Malay Peninsula. The fruit is not generally grown in the American tropics. See Garcinia.

MANGROVE. See Rhizophora.

MANIHOT. A considerable number of tropical trees and shrubs and occasional plants of herbaceous growth are included under this heading. Manihot belongs in the Spurge family, Euphorbiaceae. The name is Brazilian.

The two most important kinds of Manihot are M. dulcis variety Aipi, known as Sweet Cassava, and M. esculenta, Bitter Cassava. Both are shrubby plants which occur naturally in Brazil; they

The variegated-leaved variety of Manihot esculenta has its foliage conspicuously marked with creamy white.

are widely grown throughout the tropics for their large, fleshy roots, which are very rich in starch. There are a number of cultivated forms which differ in size, shape or color of the tuberous roots. In addition to the name Cassava, numerous other vernacular names are given to the plant in various countries.

The roots of both the Sweet and Bitter Cassava are used as food in various ways, although, when freshly collected, the roots of the Bitter Cassava contain poisonous properties. These properties are, however, driven off in the cooking, and properly cooked roots are perfectly wholesome. From these the Tapioca of commerce is produced. A variegated-leaved variety of M. esculenta is a handsome decorative plant. It is readily propagated by sectional stem cuttings.

MANILA HEMP. A strong, hard fiber extracted from the leaves of Musa textilis, which see.

MANILA PALM. See Adonidia Merrillii.
MANIOC. Manihot esculenta, which see.
MANNA ASH. Fraxinus Ornus, which see.
MANROOT. Echinocystis oregana, which see.
MANURES. See Fertilizers.
MANZANITA. See Arctostaphylos.
MAPLE. See Acer.
MAPLE, FLOWERING. See Abutilon.
MAPLEWORT. See Aceranthus diphyllus.
MARANTA—*Arrowroot Plant* (Maran'ta). Warm greenhouse ornamental-leaved plants

[7—2]
Holly Mahonia
(Mahonia Aquifolium)

[7—2a]
Canadian Mayflower
(Maianthemum canadense)

[7—3] *Flowering Crab Apple (Malus Arnoldiana)*

[7—3a] *Flowering Crab Apple variety Hopa*

Maranta leuconeura Kerchoveana, a variety of the Prayer Plant.

which grow wild in tropical America and belong to the family Marantaceae. They are suitable for growing outdoors in frost-free regions only. These plants form tufts of leaves which rise straight up from the soil: they vary in height from 1-6 ft. The leaves vary in size and shape, some being oval, others lance-shaped, round or heart-shaped; they are often nicely marked with streaks or blotches of contrasting colors. The leaves may be gray, purple, or rose beneath, and green or variegated with white, pink, purple or brown above.

Maranta leuconeura Massangeana has richly patterned leaves.

Arrowroot of Commerce. M. arundinacea is the principal source of Arrowroot. It is grown chiefly in Bermuda, St. Vincent and Natal. The tuberous roots are dug up, washed and pulped, and passed through several processes to extract the easily digested substance known as Arrowroot. The name Maranta commemorates B. Maranti, a Venetian physician.

Handsome Ornamental-leaved Plants. Marantas require a minimum winter temperature of 60 degrees and a shady moist position in the greenhouse. The best potting compost consists of one part loam, two parts peat, and half a part sand. Repotting is done in February or March. Well-drained pots are necessary, as the plants require abundance of water during the summer but resent waterlogged soil conditions. When the plants are repotted, the loose soil is removed with a pointed stick and they are set in slightly larger pots. The compost must not be rammed, but simply firmed by pressure of the fingers.

Water is carefully applied to the soil until the pots are well filled with roots; afterwards it must be given freely until the end of the summer. The supply is then gradually reduced, and throughout the winter the soil is watered only when it becomes quite dry. During the summer months, well-rooted plants should be watered with weak liquid fertilizer, the atmosphere kept humid, and the foliage syringed several times a day. Throughout the winter the atmosphere must be kept moist, but much less damping and syringing are required.

The principal method of propagation is by division in late winter. Old plants are removed from the pots and the soil is washed away from the roots. The rhizomes are then cut through with a sharp knife; care must be taken not to bruise them, as this is liable to set up decay, and the cut surfaces are dipped in sulphur. The pieces are then potted separately in pots just large enough to hold the roots comfortably without cramping them. After potting, they are assisted to root quickly into the new compost by being plunged in a propagating case with bottom heat.

Thrips and red spider mites attack the leaves. (See Pests and Diseases.)

The chief kinds are M. bicolor, leaves 12 in. in length, pale green, spotted dark green; M.

leuconeura (Prayer Plant), leaves 6 in. long, pale green, with white and dark green blotches, and purplish beneath; and its varieties Kerchoveana, leaves larger, edged with red, and Massangeana, leaves purple beneath. M. arundinacea, the Arrowroot, grows to 6 ft. high. Its variegated-leaved variety, variegata, with yellow-blotched leaves, is sometimes grown for ornament; it attains a height of about 3 ft. Maranta is related to Calathea, in which genus many kinds are now included.

MARATTIA (Maratt'ia). Tender Ferns found in the West Indies, tropical America and the tropics of the Old World. They are strong growing and need a large greenhouse to accommodate them. The fronds, which are from 5-12 ft. in length, arise from a large fleshy crown covered with brown leathery scales with feathered edges. The long frond stems are mostly blackish in color and the fronds are divided into a large number of pinnules (leaflets). They belong to the family Marattiaceae, and the name commemorates J. F. Maratti, an Italian botanist.

Large Greenhouse Ferns. The minimum winter temperature required for these Ferns, when grown indoors, is 50 degrees, and the best compost consists of equal parts of loam, peat and leaf mold. Repotting is done in February or March. Plants in large pots or tubs do not require repotting each year; they can be kept growing vigorously with an annual top-dressing of fresh compost. Well-drained pots must be provided, as these Ferns require abundance of water but cannot tolerate sour soil conditions.

Details of Management. The plants must always be shaded from the direct rays of the sun, as they quickly wilt in strong sunshine. As these plants grow wild in marshy districts, it is essential that they be well supplied with water; therefore, during the summer months, the soil must be kept constantly moist. Less water is required in the winter, but the compost must not be allowed to become very dry.

Propagation. Spores of these Ferns do not germinate very readily, so that vegetative propagation is adopted. This is accomplished by detaching the thick leathery scales which cover the crowns and laying them on sphagnum moss. A deep pan is filled with moss, the scales are pressed into it with the outsides upwards and the pan is placed in a warm, moist atmosphere. Roots and bulblike growths eventually form, from which young plants are produced. These are potted first in 4-in. pots, and by gradual stages they are repotted until they are finally set in large pots or tubs 20 in. in diameter.

The chief kinds are M. attenuata, 3 ft.; M. alata, 5 ft.; M. fraxinea, 12 ft.; M. Kaulfussii, 4 ft.; and M. laxa, 4 ft. The measurements refer to the length of the fronds.

MARBLED. A gardening term used in describing leaves in which various colors intermingle instead of being in defined spots or blotches.

MARE'S-TAIL. See Hippuris.

MARGUERITE. The Marguerite, Chrysanthemum frutescens, is a tender semishrubby plant which may be used for filling summer flower beds and for the decoration of greenhouses and window boxes. It is a native of the Canary Islands. During the winter months it must be kept in a greenhouse having a minimum temperature of about 50 degrees or in a frostproof cold frame.

Propagation is by cuttings taken from flowerless shoots on the old plants in August or September. They are inserted in a propagating bench in a greenhouse or in sandy soil in a cold frame which must be kept close for a few weeks and shaded from bright sunshine. When the cuttings are rooted, the frame must be ventilated freely.

Before the approach of cold weather the plants should be potted individually in small pots of sandy soil and placed in a greenhouse, there to remain for the winter. In January or February the young plants should be transferred to larger pots, those measuring 5 in. in diameter being satisfactory. If necessary, a further supply of cuttings can be inserted in February; these are made from the fresh shoots on old plants potted in the previous autumn and pruned in January.

If required for planting in flower beds or in window boxes in May, they must first be hardened off in a cold frame. If wanted for the decoration of the greenhouse, the plants should be potted in 6-in. pots, using a compost of loam to which a little peat moss or leaf mold, bone meal and sand have been added. The finest of all the Marguerites is the double white variety. There are both white and yellow single-flowered varieties. These plants are also called Paris Daisies.

MARGUERITE, BLUE. See Felicia.

MARGUERITE, GOLDEN. Anthemis tinctoria, which see.

MARGYRICARPUS SETOSUS—*Pearl Fruit* (Margyricar'pus). A compact and slow-growing evergreen shrub, found wild in Chile and other parts of South America. It is suitable for the rock garden and the front of the shrubbery but is not hardy in the North; it is perhaps best adapted for the Pacific Northwest. It takes many years to reach its full height of 3-4 ft., and requires loamy soil mixed with ample amounts of organic matter.

The leaves are small and divided into several narrow, awl-shaped leaflets; the flowers are small, green and insignificant, the fruits white and attractive. Propagation is by small cuttings in July; these are inserted in sandy soil in a cold frame kept close. The plant belongs to the Rose family, Rosaceae. The name Margyricarpus is taken from the Greek *margaron,* pearl, and *karpos,* fruit, and alludes to the white fruits.

MARICA. Neomarica, which see.

MARIGOLD, AFRICAN. See Tagetes.

MARIGOLD, CAPE. See Dimorphotheca.

MARIGOLD, FIG. Mesembryanthemum, which see.

MARIGOLD, FRENCH. See Tagetes.

MARIGOLD, MARSH. See Caltha.

MARIGOLD, POT. See Calendula.

MARIPOSA LILY. Calochortus, which see.

MARJORAM. See Majorana and Origanum.

MARL. This is a natural substance dug from clay soil, which contains from 5-20 per cent of carbonate of lime; it is sometimes called calcareous clay. After being dug, it is scattered freely over the ground and left to weather for a few weeks; it is then turned into the ground. This is generally done in winter, but ground may have marl treatment at any suitable time.

Marl is used chiefly because of the lime it contains. It improves sandy soils, increasing their coherence and water-holding capacity. It is also particularly good on peat land, and improves worn-out and exhausted garden soils. Owing to its bulk and weight, it is used chiefly in the locality where it occurs naturally, because transport charges make it expensive. Soil which is a natural marl is fertile but difficult to manage, being hard in dry weather and greasy in wet weather. It can be improved by digging in peat, littery manure, and bulky vegetable matter, and by leaving the surface rough in winter.

MARLBERRY. Ardisia paniculata, which see.

MARMALADE PLUM. Achras Zapota, which see.

MARRAM GRASS. See Ammophila arenaria.

MARROW OR VEGETABLE MARROW. A kind of Squash. See Squash.

MARRUBIUM — *Horehound.* (Marrub'ium). Hardy perennial herbs which belong to the Mint family, Labiatae, and are found growing wild in Europe and Asia. Some are naturalized in North America. They are many-branched perennials with herbaceous stems, wrinkled leaves with crenate (rounded-scalloped) edges, and small, inconspicuous white or purplish flowers. They are of little decorative value, but are grown in large quantities in herb gardens and herb farms for medicinal purposes. They are used for making medicines to treat coughs and colds. The name Marrubium is derived from *marrob,* a Hebrew word signifying a bitter juice.

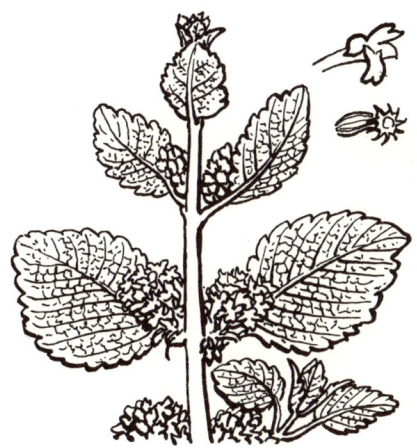

Marrubium vulgare, the herb commonly called Horehound.

Medicinal Herbs. These herbs like a sunny, well-drained position and flourish in ordinary garden soil. The roots are planted in spring, 2 ft. apart, and are not disturbed for several years. New plants are obtained by sowing seeds out of doors in early summer. The drills are made

Marsdenia erecta, a loose-growing, leaf-losing shrub, bears white, fragrant flowers in clusters.

½ in. deep and 6 in. apart, and the seeds are sown thinly. The seedlings are pricked out 6 in. apart in a nursery bed and transplanted to their final positions the following year.

Cuttings of young shoots may be rooted in sandy soil in July, in a cold frame, which is kept close until roots are formed.

The chief kind is M. vulgare, 1-3 ft., white, June.

MARSDENIA (Marsden'ia). A group of chiefly tropical shrubs and sub-shrubs. One species, M. erecta, occurs as a native in the eastern Mediterranean region and is hardy in the North. It is occasionally cultivated. Marsdenia was named in honor of William Marsden, an English historian. The genus belongs in the Milkweed family, the Asclepiadaceae.

Marsdenia erecta is a straggling deciduous shrub 3-6 ft. high, with more or less twining stems, grayish, heart-shaped leaves and, in summer, clusters of white, fragrant flowers. The flower clusters are borne in the axils of the leaves.

This plant thrives in any ordinary garden soil that is well drained. It requires a sunny location and is propagated by means of cuttings and seeds.

MARSHALLIA (Marshall'ia). Eastern North American hardy herbaceous plants belonging to the botanical family Compositae and useful for wild gardens, rock gardens and borders. This group of plants was named in honor of the American botanist Humphrey Marshall, who published the first list of American trees in 1785. They bear heads of flowers that have a general resemblance to those of Scabious.

Marshallias are easily raised from seeds sown either indoors or outdoors in spring, and they are also readily increased by division in spring or early fall. They prefer a well-drained soil; M. caespitosa appreciates one that contains lime. Most do well in light shade, but M. caespitosa prefers full sun.

Kinds commonly grown include M. caespitosa, 15 in., white or pale pink, late spring; grandiflora 2 ft., summer; M. trinervia, 2½ ft., white, late spring.

MARSH MALLOW. Althaea officinalis, which see.

MARSH MARIGOLD. See Caltha.

MARSILEA—*Pepperwort, Water Clover* (Marsil'ea). A group of aquatic plants belonging in the family Marsileaceae and useful for growing in pools, ponds and aquaria. They have four-parted clover-like leaves which provide a decorative attraction; they are fern allies and do not bear flowers.

These plants are easy to grow in any ordinary loam soil that is kept constantly wet, and are cultivated either in pots, pans or beds of soil covered with shallow water. They thrive in full sun or in light shade, and are very readily propagated by division in spring.

When grown in flowerpots or pans, the plants may be submerged, with the soil surface 1-3 in. under water, or the pots or pans may be stood in saucers that are kept always filled with water.

Of the kinds likely to be grown, M. Drummondii, from western Australia, is not hardy in the North and must be wintered indoors in a light position in a temperature of 55-60 degrees; it may be used in outdoor pools in the summer. M. quadrifolia, a native of Europe and Asia, is naturalized in eastern North America from Massachusetts southwards. It is hardy and is apt to become a weed if allowed to grow in outdoor pools.

MARTAGON LILY. See Lilium Martagon.

MARTYNIA (Martyn'ia). One annual flowering plant, a native of Mexico, Central America, the West Indies, and India to Malaysia; it belongs to the family Martyniaceae. This is a rather rank-growing, more or less trailing plant with roundish or heart-shaped leaves which are covered with sticky hairs. The flowers are five-lobed and white.

Ornamental Fruits. The fruits are cylindrical, the upper halves narrowing down into a long, curved, beaklike structure. They closely resemble those of Proboscidea. The plant grown in gardens under the name Martynia is usually Proboscidea Jussieui, which see. The thick fleshy root of this plant is preserved in sugar and eaten in some parts of the world. The name Martynia commemorates John Martyn, a professor of botany.

When to Sow Seeds. This plant is grown in gardens for its ornamental flowers and fruits, and not for food. Seeds are sown 1 in. deep in pots of sandy soil in March. The compost is thoroughly moistened and a pane of glass is laid over each pot until the seedlings appear above the soil. When the first pair of leaves has formed, each Martynia is potted separately in a 3-in. pot; the soil is watered, and the plants are shaded from sunlight until well rooted. They are then gradually hardened off and planted out of doors at about the time that Tomatoes are set out. A sunny position and a light, rich soil are necessary. The distance between plants is 18 in. They must be kept moist at the roots; it is a good plan to cover the surface of the soil with compost or well-decayed manure.

Treatment of Pot Plants. The seedlings are raised in the same way as for cultivation out of doors and are repotted from 3-in. pots to 5-in. pots, and finally set in 7-in. pots. When well rooted in these, they are set in a sunny, well-ventilated position, and the shoots are tied to sticks inserted in the pots. When growing freely, they require abundance of water and occasional applications of liquid fertilizer.

MARVEL OF PERU. See Mirabilis Jalapa.

MARYLAND, GARDENING IN. See Regional Gardening.

MASDEVALLIA (Masdevall′ia). Orchids which are found growing wild in Central America, Peru, Ecuador, Brazil and Costa Rica. They are without pseudobulbs but have evergreen leaves set closely together, from the bases of which the flower stems, generally single-flowered, are produced. Many of the Masdevallias are of botanical interest only, but a number have brilliantly colored flowers, while some are attractive by reason of their curious shape. In many kinds the extremities of the sepals are attenuated into tails as long as, and often longer than, the other parts of the flowers. Masdevallia, which belongs to the family Orchidaceae, commemorates Dr. Masdevall, a Spanish botanist and physician.

Orchids for a Cool Greenhouse. Masdevallias thrive in cool greenhouses; it is sufficient if, in winter, the night temperature is 55 degrees, or a few degrees lower in severe weather. A moist atmosphere is necessary. Cool summer conditions are essential for good results. Shading must be provided beginning early in the year, as strong sunlight is prejudicial to the plants. Throughout the warm weather the benches and floor of the greenhouse should be damped frequently and the plants may be syringed lightly.

Even in winter the atmosphere must be moist. Free ventilation is required in mild weather, and in summer the ventilators may be left open day and night. Water must be given at the roots throughout the year: abundantly in summer, and

The white-flowered Masdevallia tovarensis.

enough to keep the compost moist in winter.

Masdevallias are often affected by a black spot or blotch on the lower surface of the leaves. This may be taken as indicative of wrong conditions, a stagnant atmosphere, incorrect watering or drafts of cold air.

A suitable potting compost for Masdevallias consists of osmunda fiber, finely cut, or of Fir bark, Redwood bark or the fiber of the stems of Tree Ferns. Drainage must be free. Pots or pans may be used—the latter are better for the smaller-growing kinds. The Chimaera section of Masdevallia (described later) should be grown in pans which can be suspended from the roof of the greenhouse.

Repotting should be done early in the year, in February or March, if the plants are not in flower.

The showiest kinds are M. coccinea and its varieties. The flower stems, 6-9 in. high, bear only one flower each; the two lower sepals have short tails, the upper one is narrower with a longer, reflexed tail. The color varies from white to crimson, so much so that a large number are distinguished by names. Spring is the flowering season but blooms are often seen in late autumn. M. militaris (ignea) is similar in habit, but the flowers are cinnabar red.

An insect-trapping kind, M. muscosa, has small leaves and yellowish-green flowers; the lip is large in proportion, closes quickly on being touched, and will retain an insect for about twenty minutes. M. xipheres, of which the flowers are reddish-brown, exhibits similar action. In M. ephippium, often known as M. Trochilus, the lower sepals are cup-shaped, of chestnut-brown color: the tails are 3-4 in. long and bright yellow. It flowers in autumn and winter. M. elephanticeps, M. pachyantha, M. Mooreana and M. gargantua have large flowers on short stems and emit a fetid odor. M. tovarensis has white flowers, two to five on erect stems about 6 in. high; the old stems often produce flowers in the following winter.

The Finest of All. M. Veitchiana is the finest of all, with large open flowers, vermilion flushed with purple; the sepal tails are very short. It blooms chiefly during May but often at other seasons. Other notable kinds are M. caudata, M. corniculata, M. Schroederiana, M. inflata and M. torta. M. Chimaera has 3-in.-long tails to the sepals. The flowers, not counting the tails, are 3 in. across, yellowish in color and thickly spotted with dark red. There are numerous varieties. The blooms open chiefly in spring and summer. Others in this section, but with smaller flowers, are M. bella, M. trinema, M. Chestertonii, and M. vespertilio.

MASK FLOWER. Alonsoa, which see.

MASSACHUSETTS, GARDENING IN. See Regional Gardening.

MATHIOLA—Stock (Mathi'ola). Hardy annual, biennial and perennial free-flowering plants with fragrant flowers. They are natives of Asia Minor and Europe and belong to the family Cruciferae. The different kinds vary in height from 12-24 in., and all have narrow, oblong or lance-shaped leaves, which are 1-3 in. in length and are usually glaucous (bluish gray), but in varieties known as Wallflower-leaved Stocks are green.

The single flowers of all Stocks are cruciform (four petals in the shape of a cross), but the double-flowered kinds are the most popular. These have been evolved through the changing of the stamens into petals. Stocks are a most valuable race of garden plants, for they are easy to grow, and can be had in bloom during the greater part of the year; they are excellent pot plants for the greenhouse in winter and spring and provide good cut flowers. The name Mathiola commemorates Pierandrea Matthioli, an Italian botanist. Full details of the cultivation of Night-scented, Brompton and Ten Week Stocks are given under Stocks, which see.

MATILIJA POPPY. Romneya Coulteri, which see.

MATRICARIA — May Weed (Matrica'ria). Hardy annual and perennial flowering plants which are wild in the Mediterranean region, South Africa and the Orient, and are naturalized in North America. They grow from 12 in. to 2 ft. in height, have feathery leaves, and bear terminal clusters of small daisy-like flowers. Matricaria belongs to the Daisy family, Compositae, the name is derived from *mater*, mother, and refers to the soothing properties possessed by the plant. The plant listed by seedsmen as

Matricaria inodora.

Matricaria eximia is Chrysanthemum Parthenium, which see.

The only true Matricarias of any garden value are M. inodora, an annual 1-2 ft. tall, the double white-flowered form of which, plenissima, is useful for cutting, and M. Tchihatchewii, the Turfing Daisy, a mat-forming kind 6-12 in. tall. The former thrives in any average soil, and should be sown where it is to grow; the latter needs a sunny place and porous soil. The Turfing Daisy is propagated by seeds and division.

MATRIMONY VINE. Lycium, which see.

MAURANDIA (Mauran'dia). Tender climbing perennial plants which are free flowering and suitable for growing in pots in the greenhouse, or for planting out of doors. They are closely related to the Snapdragon (Antirrhinum), to whose family, Scrophulariaceae, they belong.

These plants, which are from Mexico, have slender stems up to 6 ft. in length and climb by means of their leafstalks, which twist around available supports. They have halberd-shaped leaves, 2-3 in. wide, and tubular flowers 3 in. in length, which are violet, purple, or rose in color. The name Maurandia commemorates Cartagena Pancratia Maurandy, a student of botany at Cartagena, Spain.

Climbing Plants for a Greenhouse. These plants require a minimum winter temperature of 45 degrees, and the most suitable potting compost consists of equal parts of loam and either peat moss or leaf mold, with sand added freely. The plants are grown in pots, the shoots being trained to stakes, or allowed to trail; or they may be trained to wires or a trellis fixed inside the greenhouse. They also are very effective when growing in hanging baskets.

Sowing Seeds. Plants are obtained by sowing seeds or taking cuttings. Seeds are sown in well-drained pots of sandy soil in March. The compost is moistened by immersing the seed pot in water, and, after the surplus water has drained away, the seeds are scattered thinly on the surface and covered very lightly with fine soil, which is damped with a fine spray. A pane of glass is laid on the pot, which is placed in a temperature of 45-55 degrees. When the seedlings appear above the soil, the glass is removed and they are set in a light position. As soon as they are 2 in. in height, they are potted separately in 3-in. pots, and subsequently are repotted in larger pots; finally they are transferred to pots 10 or 12 in. in diameter.

Suitable for Hanging Baskets. For growing in hanging baskets, young plants well rooted in 3-in. pots are removed from them and planted in baskets lined with moss and filled with a compost of loam and leaf mold in equal parts. They are well watered, shaded, and syringed until established, and are then placed in a light, well-ventilated position. Well-rooted plants require abundance of water and occasional applications of liquid fertilizer. Plants in large pots may be kept growing vigorously for several years by top-dressing with fresh compost in spring, a little of the topsoil being first removed.

Quick-growing Plants. Maurandias are such quick-growing plants, flowering freely in the first year, that it is usual to raise fresh plants annually. If the old plants are retained, however, they are carefully watered in the winter, sufficient water only being given to prevent the leaves from shriveling. From plants which have been kept through the winter, cuttings are obtained to provide new plants.

Taking Cuttings. Young shoots, 2 in. in length, are inserted in a propagating case which is kept close until roots have formed. The cuttings are then potted separately in 3-in. pots and afterwards treated as advised for the seedlings.

Planting Out of Doors. Small seedlings or cuttings well rooted in 3-in. pots may be transplanted out of doors in the North early in June, and set in a sunny position, where the shoots can be trained to wires or trellis. During the summer the soil is kept moist by frequent waterings in dry weather. In autumn the plants may be lifted and placed in large pots so that they can be wintered in the greenhouse and planted out in the garden in the following summer. In mild climates, such as that of California, they may be grown outdoors as permanent perennials.

The chief kinds are M. Barclaiana, violet-purple; M. scandens (Lophospermum scandens), purple and violet; and M. erubescens, rose and white.

MAXILLARIA (Maxilla'ria). Orchids which grow wild in the West Indies, Peru, Ecuador, Costa Rica and Brazil. As they are distributed so widely, they vary greatly, but all are epiphytal and evergreen and produce short flower stems from the base of the pseudobulbs, each stem bearing only one flower. Most of them bloom in spring and winter. The name Maxillaria is from *maxillae,* the jaws of an insect, from a fancied resemblance of the column and lip of some kinds to an insect's jaws.

Orchids for the Greenhouse. Most kinds require only moderate heat and may be grown in a greenhouse with a minimum winter night temperature of 50-55 degrees. The atmosphere must be kept moist and shade from bright sunshine is required. Ventilation must be given freely in warm weather. In spring and autumn care should be taken that water is not allowed to remain on the leaves. Water may be given freely in summer, but in winter less liberally. At no time should the potting compost in which the plants grow be allowed to dry completely.

Repotting should be done early in the year, in February or March, or as soon as the flowers are over. Those kinds with ascendent rhizomes, like M. tenuifolia, should be supported by sticks.

The best potting compost consists of cut osmunda fiber or of Fir bark, Redwood bark or Tree Fern fiber. In repotting, which need not be done annually, it may be necessary to divide large plants, for often the roots form a tangled mass, and the fresh material can be placed so that the new roots will enter it.

The Chief Kinds. M. grandiflora, a winter- and spring-flowering Peruvian Orchid, is a favorite on account of its large flowers, 3 or 4 in. across, with white sepals and petals, and white and yellow lip marked with crimson; these are pleasantly scented, but not so fragrant as those of M. venusta, with large flowers which are white, except for the yellow disc to the lip. M. Sanderiana has the largest flowers, often 6 in. across, very fleshy, with white or yellowish ground blotched with deep red. This plant should be set in an orchid basket as the short flower stems often grow downwards.

M. picta has flowers barely 2 in. in diameter; they are prettily marked with yellow and red, and deliciously fragrant. In M. tenuifolia the flowers are of medium size, rich red, marked with yellow.

Other kinds worthy of note are M. luteo-alba, M. Huebschii, M. Fletcheriana and M. striata.

MAY APPLE. See Podophyllum.

MAYFLOWER. See Epigaea repens and Maianthemum.

MAYPOP. Passiflora incarnata, which see.

MAZE. A labyrinth of walks, divided and enclosed by hedges, which set-the problem of finding the center and then finding a way out again. The most famous example is the Maze at Hampton Court in England, generally believed to have been made in William III's reign.

MAZUS (Maz'us). Dwarf, perennial herbs, natives of India, Australia, New Zealand and the Malayan Archipelago; they belong to the Snapdragon family, Scrophulariaceae. The name Mazus is from *mazos,* a teat, from the tubercled formation of the corolla.

Creeping Plants for the Rock Garden. Mazus Pumilio is a very pretty dwarf plant of creeping habit for the rock garden. The spoon-shaped leaves, with waved edges, are only about ½ in. high, and the comparatively large, pale violet flowers, almost stemless, are extremely attractive, and are produced abundantly in summer.

The plant forms a close mat, and is invaluable not only as a carpet in the rock garden for covering small choice bulbs, but for clothing the sides of rock-garden paths, and for planting in the crevices between the flagstones of paved paths. It is a native of New Zealand and is reasonably hardy in fairly light, rich soil, but is not dependably hardy at New York City.

Mazus Pumilio is very easily propagated by division of the roots. Portions of the plant may be dug up in spring, pulled to pieces, planted in light soil in a cold frame, and kept shaded until established, when they will be ready for planting out in their permanent quarters.

For the Crevices of Flagstone Paths. Mazus radicans (Mimulus radicans) is a close, dense creeper, its broad leaves lying flat upon the ground almost in the manner of Liverwort. The leaves are a curious brownish-bronze in color. The flowers, which are large for the size of the plant, are much like those of a Mimulus in shape, but greatly flattened; they are white and violet in color.

Mazus radicans is an excellent plant for clothing the sides of paths in the rock garden, as a close carpet over bulbs, and for the crevices in flagstone paths. It may also be used to good advantage in the alpine lawn, where it mingles well with the dwarf creeping Thymes and other turf-forming plants.

This plant, which flowers in June, will, in favorable climates, creep through the grass of an ordinary turf lawn if the situation is fairly moist, holding its own with the grasses, and, by reason of its very prostrate habit, escaping the lawn mower.

Mazus radicans is very easily propagated by simple division of the roots. Plants should be lifted in spring, pulled to pieces, planted in light sandy soil in a cold frame, and there kept shaded until established, when they may be transferred to their permanent quarters. They are not reliably hardy in the North.

Spreads Freely and Flowers Profusely. Mazus reptans (often wrongly called Mazus rugosus) is an extremely pretty dwarf carpeting plant with running stems, which root as they go, and light violet flowers, handsomely spotted with gold, in summer. The plant likes light, rich soil, and a fairly moist situation; it is a most valuable carpeter, never exceeding 1 in. in height, spreading freely without being too invasive, and flowering with the utmost freedom. It is excellent for clothing low-lying places in the rock garden, such as the sides of paths, and is a grand plant for running through the crevices of flagstone paths. This species, like M. radicans mentioned above, will invade lawns and maintain itself there, even in eastern North America.

Propagation may be done by division of the roots in spring, or soft cuttings may be taken in spring and rooted in a cold frame, kept close and shaded. The young plants may be potted in small pots, or put in a nursery bed of light, rich soil until large enough for their permanent quarters in the rock garden or elsewhere. M. reptans is a native of the Himalayas and is the hardiest species, living over winter satisfactorily at New York City and further north.

MEADOW BEAUTY. Rhexia, which see.

MEADOW FOAM. Limnanthes Douglasii, which see.

MEADOW RUE. See Thalictrum.

MEADOW SAFFRON. See Colchicum.

MEADOW SWEET. Filipendula (Spiraea) Ulmaria, which see.

MEALYBUG. See Pests and Diseases.

MECONOPSIS—*Poppywort, Blue Poppy* (Meconop'sis). An interesting group of hardy plants belonging to the Poppy family, Papaveraceae. The name is derived from *mekon,* a poppy, and *opsis,* resemblance, and refers to the resemblance of the plants to the true Poppies. These plants are chiefly natives of the Himalayas; one, the Welsh Poppy, occurs naturally in western

The beautiful Harebell Poppy, Meconopsis quintuplinervia, with soft lavender, drooping flowers carried gracefully on 12-18 in. stems.

Flowers of the Nepal Poppy, Meconopsis napaulensis. In its best blue form it is one of the loveliest of the race, flowering freely on 6-ft. stems.

Europe, including Great Britain. These plants are mostly biennial or short-lived perennials.

Difficult in Most Parts of America. In most parts of America these plants are difficult or impossible to grow; they do not take kindly to hot summers. The group may be cultivated in the Pacific Northwest and in other favored places where comparatively cool, moist summers are the rule. Only one kind, M. cambrica, seems to give fair results in the vicinity of New York City, although many have been tried.

Raising Plants from Seeds. Seeds of Meconopsis, both biennial and perennial, should be sown in autumn, as soon as ripe, in pots or pans of light, sandy soil with a liberal admixture of well-rotted leaf mold or peat moss. They must be kept in a shaded cold frame or cool greenhouse, and the pots covered with sheets of paper, or with sheets of glass with paper over them. It is usually found that the seeds germinate freely and evenly from autumn sowing, but irregularly if sowing is delayed until spring.

The seedlings are pricked off, about 2 in. apart, into flats of soil of the same nature as that in which they were sown; they must be kept shaded in a cold frame until large enough to

A group of Blue Poppies, Meconopsis betonicifolia, in open woodland.

The Welsh Poppy, Meconopsis cambrica, with flowers of yellow or orange, is a delightful plant for shady locations.

plant out of doors. The plants thrive best in light, rich soil in which there is plenty of humus, such as well-rotted leaf mold or peat moss. They like, too, a location sheltered from wind and shaded from strong sunshine.

The Best Kinds. Meconopsis betonicifolia, previously named M. Baileyi, is one of the most splendid of the group. It has undoubtedly received more attention than any other kind, yet, except in the most suitable climates, few American gardeners have had any real success with it. This perennial Blue Poppy, a native of Tibet, Yunnan and Upper Burma, grows 3-5 ft. tall and bears a considerable number of 2-in.-wide, flowers; in the best forms of the plant, these are

Flowers of the exquisite Blue Poppy, Meconopsis betonicifolia.

a rich sky-blue, but sometimes they are a less desirable rosy lavender color.

The Welsh Poppy, M. cambrica, is an easy-to-grow perennial that attains a height of 12-18 in., has bright green fernlike foliage and bears golden yellow or orange-yellow flowers, each 1½ in. in diameter. A double-flowered variety named M. cambrica flore pleno is cultivated.

Others worth attempting where cool summers make their cultivation possible are : M. aculeata, a biennial, 18-24 in. tall, flowers sky-blue; M. grandis, a perennial, 1-2 ft. tall, flowers blue, or blue marked with violet, 4-5 in. in diameter; M. integrifolia, usually biennial, 2-2½ ft. tall, flowers lemon-yellow or rarely white; M. napaulensis (M. Wallichii), a biennial, 4-8 ft. tall, flowers blue, red or purple; M. paniculata, a biennial, 4-6 ft. tall, flowers yellow; M. punicea, biennial or perennial, 12-18 in. tall, flowers bright red; M. quintuplinervia (the Harebell Poppy), a perennial, 12-18 in. tall, flowers soft lavender blue; M. superba, usually biennial, 2-3 ft. tall, flowers creamy white.

MEDEOLA VIRGINIANA—*Indian Cucumber Root* (Mede′ola; Medeo′la). A hardy herbaceous plant of little horticultural value. It is a native of eastern North America and belongs to the Lily family, Liliaceae. The white, fleshy rhizomes taste like Cucumber. The plant forms slender stems, 1-3 ft. in height, has two whorls of woolly, lance-shaped leaves and bears terminal clusters of small, inconspicuous flowers in June. It thrives in light, rich soil in a partly shaded position and may be increased by division of the rhizomes in spring. It is best suited for wild gardens.

MEDICAGO—*Calvary Clover, Medick* (Medica′go). Hardy annual and perennial flowering plants of little horticultural value. They are natives of Europe, but are naturalized in North America, and belong to the Pea family, Leguminosae. They grow from 1-2 ft. in height, have pinnate or trifoliate leaves, and axillary crowded spikes of small yellow or purple Pea-shaped flowers. Several kinds of Medicago are extensively grown as forage plants, particularly M. sativa, Alfalfa.

In addition to its value for feeding stock, Alfalfa, or Lucerne as it is known in some parts of the world, is a valuable soil-builder and is sometimes used as a green manure crop.

M. Echinus (Calvary Clover), a native of the Mediterranean region, has purple-black blotches on the leaves, and on this account it is sometimes grown in gardens. The seeds are sown ¼ in. deep in ordinary garden soil in April. When 2 in. high, the seedlings are thinned out to 6 in. apart. This plant is also grown in pots in a greenhouse or sunny window for the sake of its ornamental foliage. Seeds are sown ¼ in. deep in pots of sandy soil in March. When the seedlings are 1 in. in height, they are thinned out, leaving 3 in a 5-in. pot. They are not transplanted, but grown during the summer in the same pots. The soil must be kept moist and the plants given plenty of fresh air and exposed to full light. When the seeds have ripened, they are harvested for sowing the next season.

MEDICINAL PLANTS, EARLY BELIEFS. From time immemorial, plants have been used for their curative properties. Plants and their uses play a large role in the lore of the Druids, but we know very little of their teaching. Mistletoe, Holly, Birch, Ivy, Selago (generally identified with Lycopodium Selago) and Vervain (never satisfactorily identified) were regarded as almost sacred.

The Druids celebrated three great festivals: the first of May, the autumn festival and midwinter. At the midwinter festival Mistletoe was gathered with sacred ceremonies.

The European Mistletoe rarely grows on Oak trees, hence possibly the reverence of the Druids for Mistletoe Oaks. The Mistletoe, with its three white berries, was regarded as the symbol of the Druidic Trinity; its growth on the Oak was the symbol of the incarnation of Deity in man. It is noteworthy that in the Anglo-Saxon herbals little or no importance is attached to the plants which the Druids regarded as sacred.

Herbs Used in Saxon Times. Among the plants in commonest use in Saxon times were Betony, Yarrow, Mugwort, Peony and Plantain. Betony is described in one Saxon herbal as "good whether for a man's soul or his body." Yarrow has been used from very ancient times in Europe in incantations by witches. To this day country folk in England regard it as a valuable herb. Mugwort was specially venerated for its supposed power against the unseen powers of evil, and it is one of the nine sacred herbs mentioned in the *Lacnunga* (one of the earliest Saxon manuscripts treating of herbs). Peony roots were used as amulets not only in Saxon times but throughout the Middle Ages and to within living memory. Plantain, the weed that infests lawns, was one of the nine sacred herbs.

It is interesting to note the varied uses, both direct and indirect, made of herbs for medicinal purposes in Saxon times. They were administered in decoctions, used in baths and in fumigating the sick; they were worn as amulets and hung up in dwelling rooms. Herb drinks were usually made with milk, ale, vinegar or honey. Herb ointments were prepared with butter.

Herb Baths. The importance attached to herb baths, particularly vapor baths, in the Saxon herbals is striking. The herbs ordered in one prescription for this purpose include the rinds of Bramble, Elm, Ash, Sloe thorn, Apple tree and Ivy, and the following plants, Enchanter's Nightshade, Betony, Radish, Agrimony. Fumigating the sick with herbs was apparently as common in Saxon as in Babylonian times. The herbs were used thus for two purposes—to dull the senses of the patient and to drive away evil spirits.

Throughout the Middle Ages fumigating sick folk with herbs was practiced in most European countries and as late as December, 1921, a case was recorded in *The Times* of London, of an attempt made in Pomerania to cure a woman, believed to be possessed by a devil, by fumigating her with herbs. In Saxon times not only human beings but cattle also were fumigated.

Herbs were worn as amulets both to defend the wearer from the powers of evil and to cure him of illness. To this day white Heather and four-leaved Clover are carefully preserved by the superstitious. The use of red wool in conjunction with the herbs is noteworthy, for this custom is of very ancient eastern origin. Red was supposed to be a color abhorred by the evil spirits, and to within recent times belief in the efficacy of red wool prevailed.

Herbs were hung up over doors to preserve both human beings and cattle from evil. In the *Herbarium* of Apuleius it is stated of Mugwort: "If a root of this wort be hung over the door of any house, then may not any man damage the house." There are also traces in the Saxon herbals of the ancient and world-wide custom of transferring disease to plants and then throwing the plants into running water. For instance, in the *Leech Book of Bald* we find a prescription "for a salve to be made for one suffering from nocturnal goblin visitors," in which the herbs used (Wormwood, etc.) were to be boiled in butter and sheep's grease, with much "holy salt" added, and then thrown into running water.

The various incantations and charms to be sung or said when administering herbs are to be found in the herbals, and many of them are associated with Christian prayers. Some of the charms resemble children's nonsense rhymes, and others nursery rhymes. As an instance of the former there is a charm in the *Leech Book* which runs thus: "Gonomil, orgomil, marbumel, marbsai, tofeth." In the *Lacnunga* there is a counting-out charm which says: "Nine were Nodde's sisters, then the nine came to eight, and the eight seven, and the seven six, and the six five, and the five four, and the four three, and the three two, and the two one, and the one none."

It is also interesting to note the frequent instructions to pick the herbs at dawn, or when day and night divide, and to look towards the east when doing so. These are traces of the worship of Eostra, the Saxon goddess of the dawn. Sun worship is indicated in the instruction to gather plants with horns (emblems of the sun's rays). The teachings of Christianity had not altogether ousted the old heathen beliefs dating back to an immemorial past.

Use of Herbs in Cosmetics. Apart from their uses in medicine, herbs were frequently used in the making of cosmetics, even in Saxon times. Prescriptions for the cure of baldness also are numerous, Sowbread and Watercress being the herbs used. There are even prescriptions for helping hair which is too thick.

Throughout the Middle Ages monastic herb gardens were of the utmost importance, for they supplied the enormous quantities of herbs needed by the monks and nuns in their ministrations to poor sick folk.

Drying and Storing Herbs. Sixteenth-century gardening books show that herb gardens were usually divided into two parts, one part for the pot herbs and the other for the physic herbs. Thomas Hyll is the earliest writer to give full directions for the drying of herbs, and he advises hanging them up "in some Garrette or open roome and high, being sweete and dry through the Sun's dayly shining on the place at noone." He advises keeping dried herbs in leather bags or in boxes made of the Box tree, "to the eynd the Hearbes may not lose theyre proper moisture." He condemns the apothecaries for exposing herbs to cobwebs and "much other filth."

In his famous *Five Hundred Points* Thomas Tusser takes it for granted that the herb garden is the special province of the housewife, and he lays down that it is her duty to collect seeds from her own plot and exchange with neighbors. His list of physic herbs is lengthy.

Other Uses of Herbs. It is interesting to note in the *Grete Herball* (1526) a considerable number of references to the use of herbs as amulets, the effect of herbs on the mind, and the fumigation of the sick with herbs. "To make folk merry," for instance, "take the water that buglos [Bugloss] hath been soden in and sprynkle it about the hous or chamber and all that be therin shall be merry." For "weyknesse of ye brayne" it is enjoined to seethe Rosemary in wine and "let the patient receive the smoke at his nose." In Turner's *Herbal* cosmetics are never mentioned without condemnation. For instance, he states that some women wash their faces in distilled Cowslip water "to make them fayre in the eyes of the worlde rather than in the eyes of God, whom they are not afrayd to offend."

The Herbs Grown More Than 300 Years Ago. Even in the first half of the seventeenth century, "kitchen gardens" were as lavishly planted with medicinal as with pot herbs. The list of physic herbs in *The Countrie Farme* (1600) includes Mallows, Hollyhocks, Eyebright, Elecampane, Dittany, Celandine, Valerian, Angelica, Blessed Thistle, Scabious, Betony, Water Germander, Comfrey, Coltsfoot, Cinquefoil, Periwinkle, Agrimony, Paeonies, Mullein, Mercury, Adder's Tongue, Goosegrass, Solomon's Seal, Shepherd's Purse, Stinging and Dead Nettle, Pellitory of the Wall, Germander, Honeysuckle, Tobacco and Centaury.

Even Parkinson, a seventeenth-century writer whose *Paradisus* is the first book to treat of the pleasure garden as distinct from the herb garden, gives the medicinal uses of nearly all the plants he mentions in the "Garden of pleasant flowers."

"It is very rarely," he states, that "these flowers serve only to decke up the Gardens of the curious." Parkinson is to some extent scornful of the uses of herbs as amulets to ward off disease and evil, yet he does not question the efficacy of Borage and Bugloss to promote happiness. In common with other herbalists of his own and earlier times, he believed in the use of herbs to strengthen the memory and to help weak brains and to soothe "frenzied" people. His *Theatrum Botanicum* contains more cosmetic recipes than any other herbal.

The influences of the stars on the efficacy of herbs used as medicine was apparently universally believed. Even as late as the seventeenth century, John Archer (one of the Physicians in Ordinary to Charles II) states in his *Compendious Herbal* (1673) that "the Sun doth not draw away the vertues of herbs, but adds to them," and he gives full astrological directions for the picking of herbs.

The only herbal containing a section devoted entirely to herbs useful for animals is William Coles' *Art of Simpling* (1656). This section is full of curious folklore, some of it dating back to classical times.

Home Remedies Still in Use. Many plant products, such as digitalis, belladonna, quinine, and penicillin, are used in present-day medicines, but to treat of even a few would take us well beyond the scope of this article. (The reader should consult the articles on the specific herbs he wishes information about.) It is of interest, however, to note the survival of a number of the old home remedies. Such products as Dandelion tea, Pennyroyal tea, Sassafras tea, Boneset tea, Witch Hazel lotion, Horehound lozenges and Wild Cherry cough medicine owe their virtues to the plants from which they take their names.

The North American Indians, like all primitive peoples, employed a considerable number of native plants for healing. In the light of modern knowledge it seems certain that many of these possessed no particular medicinal virtues, but some undoubtedly did. Among the latter were Wild Cherry, Slippery Elm, Bearberry, Witch Hazel, Lobelia and Cascara.

The early colonists made use of many of the medicinal herbs favored by the Indians as well as kinds that were familiar in Europe and were brought to North America and grown in gardens.

MEDICK. One of the popular names of Medicago, which see.

MEDINILLA (Medinill'a). Tropical ornamental, evergreen foliage and flowering plants, from Malaya, Java, Sumatra and the Philippines. They belong to the family Melastomaceae, and are

A well-flowered, pot-grown specimen of the tropical Medinilla magnifica.

among the most handsome of hothouse plants. The principal kind, M. magnifica, forms a woody plant or shrub, with stout, winged branches, 4 ft. in height, and has large, broad, ovate or oblong, shining, leathery leaves, 12 in. long and 8 in. wide. The rose-pink flowers, which are about 1 in. in diameter, are produced on a pendulous panicle (branching spike) about 12 in. in length. In addition, the flower stalks and the bracts (small leaves at the base of the flowers) are also pink. The name Medinilla commemorates Jose de Medinilla of Pineda, a governor of the Ladrones.

Handsome Hothouse Flowering Plants. These plants require a minimum winter temperature of 60 degrees, and the best potting compost consists of equal parts of loam and leaf mold or peat moss, with a little well-decayed manure and a sprinkling of sand and crushed charcoal. Repotting is done in February. The plants are taken from the pots, and the crocks and any loose soil removed with a pointed stick; they are then set in pots two sizes larger. The pots must be filled to one third their depth with crocks, as these plants require abundance of water during the growing season, but soon deteriorate if the soil becomes waterlogged. The compost must be made moderately firm, as this ensures short-jointed growth, which is conducive to flower production.

Details of Management. After potting, the

plants are shaded from sunlight, and syringed two or three times daily to assist them to root into the new compost. It is necessary to syringe the lower as well as the upper surfaces to keep down red spider mites, which quickly breed on the leaves and spoil their appearance. While the plants are making new shoots, the atmosphere is kept moist by damping the floor and benches, and the plants must also be shaded from bright sunlight. Well-rooted plants are watered freely, and dilute liquid fertilizer is given once a week.

When growth has finished, less water is necessary, and the plants must be exposed to more light and air to ripen the shoots for flower production. When the flower buds are swelling, the plants are watered more freely again, and dilute liquid fertilizer is given once a week. After flowering, the plants should be lightly pruned into shape.

When to Take Cuttings. The principal method of propagation is by cuttings. Half-ripened side shoots are removed with a "heel" of old wood in March, and, after the "heel" has been pared cleanly, they are inserted in a propagating case with a bottom heat of 75-80 degrees. The case is closed to keep the atmosphere moist, which prevents the leaves from wilting, but it must be opened each morning to admit fresh air, and so prevent the accumulation of stagnant moisture.

When roots have formed, more air is given gradually, and in a few days the plants are potted singly in small pots. When they are well rooted in these, they are transferred to 5-in. pots, and subsequently into larger ones. The main shoots and subsequent side branches must be stopped to ensure well-branched plants.

The chief kinds are M. magnifica, rose-pink, 4 ft.; M. Teysmannii, rose-pink (without rose-colored bracts); and M. Curtisii, white flowers, purple anthers.

MEDIOCACTUS (Mediocac'tus). South American tree-perching (epiphytic) Cacti that have long, trailing, usually three-winged branches. They belong to the Cactus family, Cactaceae. The name is derived from *medius,* middle, and Cactus, the genus being intermediate between two others.

M. coccineus is sometimes grown. It has foot-long flowers that are white except for their outsides which are pinkish, brownish or yellowish. The flowers open at night. For culture see Cacti.

MEDIOLOBIVIA (Mediolobiv'ia). A small group of South American Cacti, family Cactaceae. The name is derived from *medius,* middle, and Lobivia, the name of a genus of Cacti. For their culture see Cacti.

Kinds include M. aureiflora, golden-yellow with white throat; M. Boedekeriana, pale orange with white throat; M. Duursmaiana, orange-yellow with white throat; M. elegans, bright yellow. All are of small size.

MEDITERRANEAN HEATH. See Erica mediterranea.

MEDLAR. A hardy, leaf-losing tree (Mespilus germanica) which is a native of Asia Minor, Greece and Persia. It belongs to the Rose family, Rosaceae. The Medlar is little known in North America.

Even in Europe, Medlars are nowadays grown more for their decorative effect in the garden

Young fruits of Medlar.

than for the fruits they bear, but by some the thoroughly ripened fruit is valued for dessert, and for making preserves, jellies, etc. The Medlar usually makes gnarled, twisted growth and develops into a tree of rambling habit and picturesque appearance; the solitary, large, white flowers which appear in May and June are very beautiful.

The Medlar thrives in ordinary, well-cultivated garden soil, providing it is not too dry; it prefers moist loam that is well drained and an open, sunny position.

Medlars are propagated by budding and grafting on Pear, Quince or Hawthorn stock, or on seedling Medlars.

MEDUSA'S-HEAD. See Euphorbia Caput-Medusae.

MEGACLINIUM (Megacli'nium). Orchids which are found wild only in Africa, and there principally on the west coast. They are remarkable for their extraordinary inflorescences. All are epiphytal, have evergreen foliage, and comparatively small pseudobulbs set at intervals on a creeping rhizome. The flower stem springs from the base of the pseudobulb and is at first stemlike, but the flower-bearing portion is greatly enlarged and flattened, the small flowers being set in a row on both sides. Nearly all of these Orchids bloom in spring.

The name, from *megas*, large, and *kline*, a bed, alludes to the curious shape of the flower stem. Megaclinium belongs to the family Orchidaceae.

Orchids for a Hothouse. A greenhouse with a tropical atmosphere is required; the minimum winter temperature should be 60 degrees by night. A moist atmosphere is necessary throughout the year, but the plants must not be watered frequently during the winter. Many have hard bulbs and thick leaves, and are the better for a rest. The smaller kinds should be placed in flower pans which can be suspended near the glass, and the larger ones in orchid baskets, as none of them like too much compost.

The potting compost should consist of osmunda fiber cut into small pieces, Fir bark, Redwood bark, or Tree Fern fiber. The plants must not be disturbed at the roots until young growths or roots are seen. Shading should be removed in autumn.

A remarkable kind is M. purpureorachis, which has a very large flower stem, sometimes 2 ft. high, spiral in shape; the flowers are yellow and purple-red, and open in April–May. The flowers of M. bufo, which blooms at about the same time, are brownish, with purple spots and blotches. M. falcatum and M. Clarkei are much smaller plants.

MEGASEA. Bergenia, which see.

MELALEUCA—*Bottle Brush* (Melaleu'ca). Tender, evergreen, flowering shrubs and trees from Australia which belong to the Myrtle family, Myrtaceae. They are similar in appearance and are closely related to Metrosideros (Callistemon), which is the most popular of the Bottle Brush shrubs. The Melaleucas form woody branching shrubs or trees up to 80 ft. in height and have ovate or lance-shaped leathery leaves, 2-4 in. long and ½-¾ in. wide.

The inflorescences are formed in the axils of the leaves. They are densely packed in the form of a spike, composed chiefly of long, conspicuous stamens which resemble a bottle-cleaning brush, hence the common name. The plant is distinguished from the Callistemon principally by its united filaments (stamen stalks). The name Melaleuca is derived from *melas*, black, and *leukos*, white, and refers to the black and white branches of one of the species.

Outdoors in Mild Climates. Melaleucas are favorites for outdoor cultivation in California and are grown to some extent in Florida and in other warm-climate states. They thrive in a variety of soils and are used as lawn specimens and as street trees; some are employed to hold the soil near the sea. For this last purpose M. Leucadendra is valuable.

Flowering Shrubs for a Greenhouse. When Melaleucas are grown indoors, a minimum winter temperature of 45 degrees is required. The best compost consists of peaty soil with sand added freely. Pruning, which consists of shortening the vigorous shoots by half, and the weaker ones by two thirds, is carried out as soon as the flowers have faded. After pruning, the plants are syringed, two or three times daily, until new growths appear, when repotting is carried out. The plants are removed from the pots, the crocks extracted, and a number of the roots loosened with a pointed stick, so that they stand out horizontally and therefore enter the new soil more readily.

Details of Management. The new pots should be one size larger than the old ones and provided with crocks for drainage. Over the crocks a thin layer of coarse leaves is placed to prevent the compost from washing into and blocking the drainage. The plant is then set in position and the compost rammed firmly around it with a wooden potting stick.

After potting, syringing must be continued and the plant shaded from bright sunlight until the roots enter the new soil; afterwards they are given more light and air, and drier atmospheric conditions. In summer the plants are plunged in a bed of ashes out of doors, to ripen the shoots for flower production.

Taking Cuttings. Propagation is chiefly by cuttings. Half-ripened shoots, 2 in. in length, are removed with a heel of old wood in July; some of the lower leaves are cut off and the heel is pared clean with a sharp knife. The prepared cuttings are then inserted in a mixture of equal parts of sand and peat moss under a bell jar in the greenhouse; the glass is wiped inside every morning to remove surplus moisture, which, if allowed to condense, would eventually drop on the cuttings and cause damping off.

When the cuttings are rooted, the bell jar is removed and, after a week or so, the rooted cuttings are potted separately in 2½-in. pots and subsequently in larger ones. Bushy plants are obtained by pinching out the points of the main shoot, and the resultant side branches are similarly treated.

The bark of M. Leucadendra is used by the Australians for thatching, and the leaves yield Cajeput Oil, which is used in medicine.

The chief kinds are M. Leucadendra, 15-20 ft., white; M. hypericifolia, 10-15 ft., scarlet; M. decussata, 10 ft., lilac; M. armillaris, 25-30 ft., white; M. elliptica, 6-10 ft., red; M. ericifolia, 18 ft., yellowish-white; M. lateritia, 8 ft., scarlet; M. nesophila, 10 ft., pink; M. styphelioides, 80 ft., creamy white; M. tenella, 6 ft., white; M. Wilsonii, 10 ft., red.

MELASTOMA (Melas'toma). Tropical, evergreen, flowering shrubs, which are rarely cultivated in North America except in botanical collections. They are found wild in India, China and certain Pacific Islands and belong to the family Melastomaceae. The name Melastoma is derived from *melas,* black, and *stoma,* mouth, and refers to the black stain which is left in the mouth when the berries are eaten.

These shrubs grow 6 ft. in height, have opposite, ovate or lance-shaped leaves with thick veins; the veins in the leafstalks of some kinds are red. The rose or purple flowers are generally produced singly, on the ends of the branches, and they are succeeded by fleshy berries.

For a Warm Greenhouse. These shrubs require a minimum winter temperature of 55 degrees, and a soil compost of equal parts of peat and loam with sand and crushed charcoal freely added. The annual repotting is done in February. The shoots are shortened by two thirds, and syringed until the buds break into growth. The plants are then taken out of the pots, the crocks and all loose soil are removed with a pointed stick, and the plants are potted in slightly larger pots into the bottoms of which new crocks have been put. After potting, the plants are syringed twice daily to assist them to root into the new soil and to encourage new shoot growth.

Summer and Winter Management. During the summer the soil must be kept moist and the foliage shaded from sunlight. The atmosphere of the greenhouse should be kept moist by frequently damping the floor and benches. When syringing, special attention must be paid to the lower surfaces of the leaves, as they are subject to the attacks of red spider mites. Well-rooted plants are given a biweekly application of dilute liquid fertilizer until the flowers show color.

During the winter months the soil should be moistened only when it becomes quite dry, and much less damping is required.

When to Take Cuttings. Young plants are raised from cuttings in March. Firm shoots, 2-3 in. in length, are removed, the lower leaves are cut off and a cut is made close beneath the lowest node (joint). They are then inserted in sand and peat in a propagating case with a bottom heat of 70-75 degrees. The frame is kept close, except for a daily airing for a few minutes each morning to allow excessive moisture to escape. Shade must be provided from bright sunlight.

When roots have formed, more and more air is admitted to the propagating case each day, and finally the cuttings are potted separately in 2½-in. pots and returned to the propagating case until the roots have entered the new compost, after which they are set on the greenhouse benches and repotted as becomes necessary. They form bushy plants if the tips of the main shoots and side shoots are pinched out.

The chief kinds are M. malabathricum, 4 ft., purple, and M. villosum, 3-4 ft., rose-pink.

MELIA—*Bead Tree* (Mel'ia). Tender deciduous (leaf-losing) and evergreen trees with ornamental flowers and foliage. Natives of Asia and Australia, they belong to the family Meliaceae. Melia is the Greek name for Ash. The leaves of Melia resemble those of Ash.

The commonest kinds, M. Azedarach and its varieties, form branching trees with furrowed bark and grow up to 40 ft. in height; they have feathery leaves, sometimes 3 ft. in length, and produce panicles 4 in. long, composed of small purple, lilac or white fragrant flowers. The flowers are succeeded by yellow berries containing "stones," which are used in some countries for making rosaries, hence the common name of Bead Tree. M. Azedarach is also known as China Berry, Indian Lilac and Pride of India.

Cultivation. In mild climates M. Azedarach and its varieties thrives in sunny places; they should be planted in a deep sandy loam, and must be kept moist at the roots during the summer.

Propagation may be effected by cuttings, which consist of well-ripened side shoots, detached with a heel of old wood, and inserted in July-August. The cuttings are placed under a hand light outdoors or in a greenhouse. When rooted, they are potted separately in 3-in. pots and subsequently in larger ones. A more usual method of propagation is by seeds, sown when ripe.

The chief kind is M. Azedarach, lilac flowers, fragrant. M. floribunda, white, a variety of M. Azedarach, blooms when 2-3 years old. M. Azedarach umbraculiformis, the Texas Umbrella Tree, has radiating branches and drooping leaves. M. Azidirachta, the Neem Tree, a native of the East Indies requires tropical conditions. It has white, honey-scented flowers and grows 20-50 ft. high.

MELIANTHUS—*Honeyflower* (Melianth'us). South African shrubby plants with handsome compound leaves which are often glaucous or blue-green in color. They require greenhouse cultivation in colder regions; in warm regions they are useful outdoor decorative plants. The name Melianthus is derived from the Greek *meli*, honey, and *anthos*, a flower, and refers to the nectar-laden blossoms. The plant belongs to the family Melianthaceae.

Out of doors, M. major grows to 10 ft. tall and bears leaves 1½-2 ft. long and nearly 1 ft. wide. The terminal spikes of brownish, fragrant flowers are carried in foot-long racemes.

M. minor is very like the last named, but smaller in all its parts. Both kinds, when grown in pots in the greenhouse, thrive in a mixture of three parts fibrous loam, one part leaf mold and one part sand. Propagation is by cuttings taken in summer and placed in a glass case in the greenhouse and by seeds sown in spring.

MELICOCCA—*Mamoncillo, Spanish Lime, Genip* (Melicoc'ca). Two trees of tropical America that belong in the Soapberry family, Sapindaceae. One, M. bijuga, is cultivated in southern Florida and similar warm climates. In Florida it thrives best in the Key West area. When well established, this tree will survive light frosts. The name is derived from *meli*, honey, and *kokkos*, a berry, and has reference to the sweet fruits.

M. bijuga attains a height of 50-60 ft. It bears small, greenish-white fragrant flowers and yellow-fleshed fruits that are about an inch in diameter and are agreeably flavored. To ensure fruiting it is important to plant male (staminate) trees near female (pistillate) trees to serve as pollenizers, although some trees bear both sexes on the same tree and will bear fruit even if not near others of their kind.

This tree can be propagated by cuttings, by air layering, and by grafting or budding, but more often it is raised from seeds. Seedlings vary considerably in their fruit-bearing qualities, and the flavor of the fruit also varies with different individuals; in some it is too tart to be pleasant.

M. bijuga is rather slow growing. In addition to its value as a fruit producer, it is an attractive ornamental.

MELIOSMA (Melios'ma). Evergreen and leaf-losing trees and shrubs, natives of Asia and tropical America. Several kinds are hardy in the South; these are natives of China and Japan, and most have been introduced to cultivation during the present century. They can be separated into two distinct groups by means of the leaf characters, one group having simple leaves, the other compound leaves. The flowers are generally in large, graceful panicles, though individually the blooms are very small, and usually yellowish or white. Meliosma belongs to the family Sabiaceae; the name is derived from the Greek *meli,* honey and *osma,* odor, and has reference to the honey-scented flowers.

Propagation and Cultivation. The simple-leaved kinds root fairly well if short cuttings of side growths are inserted in a close and warm propagating frame in summer. The compound-leaved kinds may also be rooted in the same way, but are difficult, and use should be made of seeds whenever possible. The difficulty of procuring seeds and rooting cuttings has caused several of the more decorative kinds to remain very rare.

A position well exposed to sun and air should be chosen for these trees or shrubs. Deep, well-drained loamy soil is suitable, and a little peat should be placed about the roots at planting time in autumn or spring.

The Most Striking Kind. M. Veitchiorum is the most striking of the kinds with compound leaves. It is a tree of erect growth 40-50 ft. high, with a rather narrow head of stout, short branches, bearing handsome leaves up to 2-2½ ft. long, made up of 9-11 large leaflets. The summer flowers are white, in terminal inflorescences up to 18 in. long and 12 in. in diameter at the base. This fine tree was introduced to Europe from China in 1901. It is probably hardy as far north as New Jersey.

M. Oldhamii, from western China, is another kind with compound leaves, but it is usually less than 40 ft. high; the branches are more slender and the leaves smaller than in M. Veitchiorum. The flowers are white in terminal inflorescences. Another attractive kind is M. Beaniana, a tree of medium size with compound leaves; it differs from those before mentioned by the inflorescences of white flowers appearing from the leaf axils. It is probably as hardy as M. Veitchiorum.

Of the simple-leaved kinds, M. cuneifolia forms a spreading bush, 10-12 ft. high. The leaves are 3-7 in. long and 1½-3 in. wide, and the small flowers are creamy white at first, changing to white. They open in June and are followed by small black fruits. This bush is probably hardy to about Virginia.

M. myriantha is a shrub or small tree, up to 20 ft. high, bearing leaves 8 in. long and 3 in. wide. The flowers are yellowish-white, very small, and borne in terminal inflorescences 6-8 in. long. This shrub, too, is probably hardy as far north as Virginia. All these kinds are deciduous.

MELISSA—Balm (Meliss'a). Hardy herbs, with aromatic leaves, which are natives of the Mediterranean region and Asia but have become naturalized in North America. They belong to the Mint family, Labiatae.

The principal kind, M. officinalis, has slender rhizomes (underground stems) and soft herbaceous shoots, clothed with rough oval leaves, 2 in. in length, 1½ in. broad, heart-shaped at the base, and crenate around the margins. When crushed, the leaf emits a delicious odor, suggestive of that of the Lemon-scented Verbena.

This herb is grown in gardens for its scented leaves, which are sometimes used in the concoction of claret cup. There is also a variegated form which is used as an edging for flower borders. The flowers, which are Salvia-shaped, are white, small and inconspicuous. The name Melissa is derived from *melissa,* a bee. Bees obtain large quantities of honey from the flowers.

Balm requires a sunny, well-drained position and will flourish in ordinary garden soil.

The stems are sometimes cut just before the flowers open, dried and hung in clothes closets.

For ordinary purposes the plants can remain undisturbed for several years, but when extra-vigorous shoots are required the plants are lifted annually in autumn or spring and divided into small pieces, each piece containing not more than six shoots. They are then planted in newly prepared soil. This is the principal method of propagation. The variegated kind is increased by division only. This has golden-variegated leaves and requires the same treatment as the green-leaved kind.

M. officinalis is 2 ft., green leaved, lemon-scented. M. officinalis variegata has leaves of green and yellow.

MELITTIS MELISSOPHYLLUM — *Bastard Balm* (Melitt'is). A perennial flowering plant, found wild in Europe and Asia and belonging to the Mint family, Labiatae. It is similar in appearance to the true Balm (Melissa officinalis). It has slender perennial rhizomes (underground stems), grows 18 in. in height, and has rough ovate leaves which are short-stalked and 1 in. in length. The foliage is not scented, but the flowers are somewhat ornamental. They appear singly in the axils of the leaves, towards the tips of the shoots, in May; they are tubular, 2 in. long, cream-white and pink. The name Melittis is derived from *melitta*, a bee, and refers to the fact that bees extract quantities of honey from the flowers.

For a Shady Border. Melittis thrives in ordinary garden soil and is suitable for semishaded borders or the edge of the shrubbery. Propagation is by division of the rhizomes in autumn or spring. Seeds may also be sown in the open ground in summer.

MELOCACTUS—*Melon Cactus* (Melocac'tus). Succulent plants from the West Indies, Brazil and Mexico, which belong to the Cactus family, Cactaceae. The generic name of Cactus is favored by some botanists for this genus. The plants form cylindrical masses of tissue with conspicuous longitudinal ridges, armed with clusters of short, strong spines. At the top there is a cushion-like head, surrounded by reddish bristle-like spines. The red flowers, which are produced from the cap, are small and inconspicuous; they are succeeded by red berries, having numerous black seeds. The name Melocactus is derived from *melos*, a Melon, and *Cactus*, and has reference to the shape of the stems.

For a Greenhouse. Melocactus requires a minimum winter temperature of 50 degrees, and the best compost consists of two parts of sandy loam and one of equal quantities of crushed brick, lime rubble and sand. Repotting is done in March or April, but the plants are only moved into larger pots when growth is unsatisfactory, for they do best when the roots are cramped in small pots.

When repotting becomes necessary, the plants are removed from their pots, and, if the soil is sour, every particle is removed and dead roots

A well-grown specimen of the Melon or Turk's-Cap Cactus, Melocactus communis, one of the oldest Cacti known to cultivation.

are pruned back to healthy portions. The plants are then repotted in pots just large enough to hold the roots. When repotting plants which have a compact ball of healthy roots, the crocks and a little of the loose soil only are removed and they are then set in pots one size larger. After repotting, the soil is not moistened until it becomes quite dry; then it must be saturated.

Well-rooted plants are watered freely from April until August; afterwards the supply of water is gradually lessened, and throughout the winter sufficient only is given to prevent the stems from shriveling. No shading is required and the plants should be ventilated freely on all favorable occasions.

Propagation. This is principally by seeds, which may be sown at any time between March and August (see Cacti).

One of the best-known is Melocactus communis, Turk's-Cap Cactus, which bears red flowers in summer and is one of the oldest Cacti in cultivation. Others include M. Antonii, with pale pink flowers; M. Broadwayi, flowers purplish; M. intortus, flowers pinkish, spines yellow or brown; M. Lemairei, flowers pink, spines wine-red; M. macrocanthus, flowers pinkish; M. melocactoides, flowers white to pale pink, spines white or gray; M. peruvianus, flowers pink, spines brown; M. Zuccarinii, flowers soft pink, spines yellow-gray.

MELON: A DELICIOUS SUMMER FRUIT
Details of Outdoor, Frame and Greenhouse Cultivation

The Melon or Muskmelon is botanically known as Cucumis Melo. It is native of southern Asia and is included in the Gourd family, Cucurbitaceae.

Cultivated Melons have long, slender, pliant stems that bear heart-shaped, rather rounded leaves which frequently have three to five lobes. The stems are creeping, and in garden culture the plants have no useful need for the tendrils they bear. Usually distinct male (staminate) and female (pistillate) flowers are produced on the same plant, but sometimes flowers bearing both male and female elements develop. When Melons are grown in a greenhouse or cold frame, hand pollination of the flowers is necessary to ensure a set of fruit. The fruit in some varieties have orange or salmon-pink flesh, while in others, as in the Honeydew, the flesh is green.

Classifications or Types. Melons, excluding Watermelons (which are a quite different fruit; see Watermelon), are classified into two main groups. One contains the netted-skinned Nutmeg Melon or Muskmelon (popularly known in North America as the Cantaloupe, although this name more properly belongs to a group of European hard-rinded, warty-skinned varieties that are scarcely known in America), the other the smooth-skinned or Honeydew Melon and the Cassaba Melon; both of the latter require a long growing season in which to mature, and are not generally suitable for outdoor culture in the North.

Growing Melons Outdoors

The Muskmelons are best for gardens in temperate regions. In the coldest sections of the United States and Canada it may be necessary to grow them in a cold frame.

Commercially this crop is raised in many states but its cultivation is restricted mostly to regions with a long growing season where the fruits will mature from seeds sown directly in the field, without the necessity for sowing the young plants indoors and transplanting them.

Culture. The usual custom in warm-temperate regions is to sow the seeds when the surface soil is warm and when the weather is quite settled, about 2-3 weeks after the first sowing of Corn is made, and about the time it is safe to plant Geraniums outdoors. The seeds should be planted in hills or stations 5-6 ft. apart. Set 3-4 seeds in each hill and, after the young plants are up and danger of loss from the cucumber beetle has passed, pull out all except the strongest and most promising one.

In the northern States and in Canada a better

The Muskmelon, a favorite fruit. The type of Melon best adapted for growing outdoors in the North.

start is assured when the seeds are sown indoors in pots or in pieces of inverted grass sods 4-5 weeks before it is safe to set the young plants in the garden. When sown on pieces of sod, seeds should be placed 6 in. apart to enable the grower to cut out each plant without damaging the roots. Melons need careful handling when transplanting is being done; if their roots are much injured or their stems damaged, they are likely to die.

Soil. Good Melons may be grown in almost any fairly moist soil that contains an abundance of organic matter and is well drained. Although quick growth is important, the soil should not be excessively rich in available nitrogen, since this tends to cause rank growth of vine and leaf and to result in fewer and inferior fruits. The plants must have ample direct sunlight and generous water supplies throughout the entire growing season.

Weeds must be controlled and regular shallow cultivation is important so long as there are any bare spaces of ground between the developing vines.

Melons are superior in flavor when allowed to ripen on the vine. Smooth-skinned types may be cut earlier than netted types and will yet develop their distinctive flavor. Varieties of the latter begin to change color as they ripen, but the ripeness in netted kinds is not so easy to detect in this way. When cracks appear at the point where the fruit is attached to the vine, maturity or approaching maturity is indicated.

Growing Melons in a Greenhouse

The best method of cultivating Melons in a greenhouse, which should be heated sufficiently to maintain a minimum temperature of 60 degrees, is to make up a hotbed of manure on the floor of the greenhouse, or on a bench. If, however, there are hot-water pipes beneath the benches, the hotbed of manure can be dispensed with.

Making a Hotbed. The best material with which to make a hotbed is fresh stable manure which has been turned several times to allow the rank "steam" to escape. It is then made up on the floor of the greenhouse, or on a bench, until it reaches to within about 18 in. of the trellis beneath the roof, after it has been trodden down firmly. For several days following the making of the hotbed the top ventilators of the greenhouse should be left slightly open to allow the rank gases or "steam" to escape.

As soon as the hotbed is made up, small mounds of loamy soil are placed on it, in each of which one Melon plant will be set; the mounds, about 10 in. high and 18 in. wide, should be set near the front of the greenhouse, and 2½ ft. apart.

Planting the Seedlings. A wire trellis, on which the shoots of the Melon plants will be trained, is fixed beneath the roof at a distance of about 12 in. from it. When the seedlings are nicely rooted in the small pots in which the seeds were sown, they are planted out, one in each mound of soil. Care should be taken to moisten them thoroughly before they are transplanted. The measure of success obtained in the cultivation of Melons depends very largely on the quality of the soil in which they are planted; it is useless to attempt to grow the plants in poor soil.

The Best Soil for Melons. Professional gardeners who grow these fruits to perfection plant them in turf loam, and no other kind of soil is so suitable. This loam is turf which has been stacked for a year or more: by then the grass will have decayed completely and the heap will consist of soil and fibrous material—the dead roots of the grass. Such soil, if of a fairly heavy character, will grow Melons to perfection, and amateurs who wish to obtain really good fruits should purchase a few bushels of this material if they have no stack on which to draw.

It is unnecessary to mix other materials with the loam unless it is rather clayey; a little leaf mold and sand may then be added.

Melons flourish in a warm though not too moist atmosphere. The minimum temperature during the spring and summer months is 60 degrees. It must not fluctuate: a steady uniform temperature is essential to success. Naturally, the higher the minimum temperature the earlier will the fruits ripen. Daytime temperatures of 70 degrees and higher are beneficial.

For the first week or two after the small plants are set in the mounds of soil, they will need no watering, provided the roots are moistened thoroughly before planting is done. The soil and the plants must, however, be syringed to encourage free growth.

Details of Management. When the thermometer registers 10 degrees above the minimum night temperature the top ventilators should be opened slightly; if the day is warm and sunny, ventilation must be increased as the day advances. Early in the afternoon, before the sun has ceased to shine on the roof of the greenhouse, the ventilators must be closed. This will have the effect of increasing the temperature considerably and if the wall and floor are syringed, a warm, moist atmosphere which encourages the growth of the plants will be assured. This method of management lessens the need for much artificial warmth.

Pruning and Training the Shoots. The young Melon plants are allowed to grow unchecked until they reach the wire trellis placed beneath the roof. The point or tip of each plant is then pinched off or cut off. This treatment has the effect of causing the development of several side shoots, which, as they grow, must be tied to the trellis. It is on these fresh shoots that the flowers will be produced.

Any shoots which develop after the crop of fruits is set should be stopped as soon as they have made one leaf, or cut out altogether; otherwise, the trellis may become crowded with a mass of small leaves which will prevent air and light from reaching the plants, and so interfere with the ripening of the fruits.

Pollinating the Flowers. Now comes one of the most important details in the management of the Melon—the pollination of the flowers to ensure a satisfactory crop of fruits. The Melon bears two kinds of flowers, male and female. The latter are easily distinguished by the swollen part at the base of the bloom; the female flower, when fertilized, will develop and provide the fruit.

Pollination is effected by pulling off a male flower, removing the petals, and placing it on the fruiting bloom so that the pollen falls on the stigma of the latter. Pollination should be carried out preferably near the middle of the day, and, if possible, in warm, bright weather.

Several Blooms Must be Pollinated on the Same Day. It is most important that all the female or fruiting blooms be pollinated at the same time on the same day. If one bloom is pollinated one day and two or three blooms are pollinated the next day, the former will provide a large fruit, but the fruits from the later pollination will be small—they will not reach their full development. A disappointing crop will result if this detail is neglected.

It is often necessary to remove the earliest fruiting or female flowers if only one or two are open together: by waiting a few days it is certain that the grower will find five or six female blooms which are open at the same time. If all are pollinated the same day, the fruits will develop evenly and all will be of about the same size.

It is not usually possible to obtain more than five or six fruits of good average size from one Melon plant; if any develop after the five or six chief fruits are set and making progress, they should be cut off, for they will be valueless and will interfere with the development of the other and better ones.

Top-Dressing with Soil. When the roots of the Melon plants are seen to have penetrated to the outside of the small mounds of soil, further soil of the same kind should be added. Several further additions will be needed during the season of growth. The best material to use is the fiber from old turf; the roots penetrate this quickly and freely, ensuring vigorous stem and leaf growth. It is a better practice to add further soil from time to time in the way advised than to make up a complete bed of soil in the first place, for in sour or sodden soil Melon plants quickly perish.

When the Melons are in bloom, it is necessary that the greenhouse be kept dry and airy so that the pollen will be dry and easily transferred from the anthers to the female or fruiting bloom.

When it is seen that the fruits are set and are increasing in size, a warm and moist atmosphere in the greenhouse will assist their development.

When the fruits begin to change color, drier and more airy conditions are again necessary to enable the fruits to become thoroughly ripe.

Watering is a detail of considerable importance in the successful management of Melons.

A magnificent greenhouse crop of Melons. Note the netting support.

The soil must not, of course, be allowed to get dry while the plants are in full growth, but it is essential that the soil be not overwatered. When the soil is moderately dry, it should be given sufficient water to moisten the mound thoroughly; water ought not to be given until the soil is again moderately dry. More Melon plants are spoilt through overwatering than by any other means.

Supporting the Fruits. As the fruits of the Melon increase in size, it becomes necessary to support them; if support is not provided, the fruits are so heavy that they pull down the shoots and break them. The simplest form of support is provided by several strands of raffia tied to the trellis and passing beneath the fruit. Pieces of wood, on which the fruits may rest, attached to the trellis by string, are sometimes used, but they are not recommended; moisture collects on the board on which the base of the fruit rests, and the latter often starts to decay where it touches the board.

The best method of supporting Melons is by using small nets which are placed around the fruits and suspended from the trellis; these keep the fruits safe and do not interfere with their development.

As soon as a Melon is almost ripe, it should be cut and placed in a cool room; in the course of a few days it will be in perfect condition for eating. If the fruits are cut, one by one, as they become ready, those remaining on the plant will ripen more quickly.

After the fruits begin to change color, the soil must be watered less frequently, and when the fruits are almost ripe the soil should be allowed to become dry. The greenhouse must also be ventilated more freely and the atmosphere must be kept perfectly dry by discontinuing syringing and "damping down."

The Melon is essentially a fruit for warm weather, and it is scarcely worth while attempting to produce fruits which ripen earlier than June in amateurs' greenhouses. By sowing seeds in a warm greenhouse, having a minimum temperature of 60 degrees, in early February, and following the procedure already described, it is possible to ensure ripe fruits in early summer.

Melon Growing in a Frame

As Melons can only be successfully grown in a cold frame during the summer months it is not wise to make a start before the middle of March. A hotbed of fresh stable manure, which has been turned several times, should be made up in the frame in the way already described. (See Hotbed.) Mounds of soil are placed on the manure as soon as the hotbed is made. For three or four days after this is done the frame must be ventilated slightly throughout each of the days.

The seeds may then be sown separately in small pots of loamy soil, the pots being plunged to the rim in the hotbed. When well rooted, the seedlings are planted out, one in each mound of turfy loam. One plant is enough to plant in a frame 6 ft. by 4 ft. It should be set in a mound of soil placed in the middle of the frame.

Training the Shoots. When the plant is about 6 in. high the top must be pinched off to cause the development of side shoots, and if, when the latter are 10 in. or so long, they also are "stopped" by pinching off the ends, sufficient branches will form to fill the available space. It is important to ensure the growth of a number of vigorous shoots with large leaves before the plants bloom, for small shoots which develop subsequently are valueless and should, in fact, be stopped at the first leaf, or cut off.

When a sufficient number of fruits has set, the shoots which bear them ought to be stopped just above the first or second leaf; this practice helps the progress of the fruits and prevents superfluous growth. In growing Melons in a frame it is important that the bed be not overcrowded with small shoots which hold moisture and keep out sunshine and air.

As the plants make progress, further loamy soil must be added to the mounds so that the roots shall be well nourished.

A hill of young Melon plants. At this stage of growth all except the strongest plant in each hill are pulled out.

Until the Melon plants begin to flower, the frame must be kept warm and moist by closing it early in the afternoon before the sun has ceased to shine on it.

This is a most important detail of cultivation when Melons are grown in a cold frame, and should not be neglected.

When the plants are in bloom, free ventilation should be given in warm weather. After the fruits are set and are noticed to be increasing in size, warm and moist conditions are suitable, but as soon as the fruits begin to change color, the soil should be watered less frequently and syringing should not be practiced.

Every day during warm weather the frame should be ventilated, for Melons do not flourish in an atmosphere that is continually close and moist. They like warmth and moisture, too, but the air in the frame must be what the gardener calls "sweet," and that can be achieved only by ventilating whenever conditions out of doors are suitable.

MELON CACTUS. Melocactus, which see.

MELON, CHINESE PRESERVING. Benincasa hispida, which see.

MELOTHRIA (Melo'thria). A group of fast-growing, slender, nonwoody vines, two of which are cultivated, chiefly in warm-climate areas. They belong to the Gourd family, Cucurbitaceae. The name is presumably from *Melothron*, the Greek name for Bryony. They possess decorative value, chiefly in their fruits.

Culture. These plants thrive in any good soil but prefer one that is fairly loose and rich in organic matter, and that is well drained but always fairly moist. They grow in full sun.

The plants are readily raised from seeds, which, in warm climates, may be sown directly outdoors in spring. In colder climates the plants can be raised in pots indoors, the seeds being sown about a month before they are needed for planting outside; the young plants are transplanted to their stations in the outdoor garden when the weather is warm and settled. Supports around which their tendrils can twine should be provided; they may be of twiggy brushwood, strings, wires or other suitable material.

Kinds. M. punctata is a thick-rooted perennial, a native of Africa, that may be grown permanently outdoors in the very warmest parts of the United States; elsewhere the roots may be dug before frost and stored over winter in a cool, dark, frost-free place. The fruits of this kind are brown, about ¼ in. in diameter and slightly pitted. Its flowers are small, white and fragrant.

In addition to its value as an outdoor subject, M. punctata also makes a very good house plant and thrives without difficulty in a temperature of 60-70 degrees, provided it receives good light. If desired, plants lifted from the garden in the fall can be potted and carried over winter in a sunroom or window in a growing state rather than dormant in a cellar or similar place. In spring, after all danger of frost has passed and the weather is quite warm and settled, plants so wintered may be cut back severely and planted in rich soil outdoors, where they will quickly recover and develop into splendid vines.

M. scabra is usually grown as an annual. It has larger fruits than M. punctata; these are not pitted but are green-spotted. They measure 1 in. long by half as wide. This kind is a native of Mexico.

MENISPERMUM — *Moonseed* (Menisper′mum). Hardy climbing plants of considerable vigor, with soft, woody stems and slender branchlets bearing round leaves shaped rather like those of a Nasturtium. The greenish-yellow flowers, which open in summer, are inconspicuous, and are followed by small black fruits arranged several together on long, slender stalks. Menispermum belongs to the family Menispermaceae, and the name is derived from the Greek *mene*, moon, and *spermo*, seed.

M. canadense grows wild from Quebec to Georgia and Arkansas. It is more conspicuous by reason of its distinct leaves, which fall in autumn, than it is for either its flowers or fruit. It spreads by underground stems and forms a dense tangle of shoots which will cover a support 15 ft. high. A second kind, which does not differ very materially from the American kind, is M. dauricum, widely distributed in northeastern China.

Both kinds thrive in ordinary garden soil and are increased by seeds sown out of doors in May, or by suckers dug up from the old plants in autumn. The long, loose ends of the shoots should be cut back in spring.

MENTHA—*Mint* (Men′tha). A group of hardy perennial herbs which are widely spread in the temperate parts of the globe. The name is the old Latin name. Mentha belongs to the family Labiatae.

The nomenclature of the Mints appears to be a matter of considerable confusion and difficulty, largely due no doubt to the numerous natural hybrids which occur. Several Mints are attractive subjects for planting to run wild by the waterside, though they are not really showy.

Kinds of garden importance are Mentha Pulegium, Pennyroyal, a medicinal herb; Mentha spicata, the Spearmint or common garden Mint; M. rotundifolia, sometimes grown as Apple Mint; M. piperita, Peppermint; and Mentha Requienii, which is a valuable carpeting plant in the rock garden, and for the crevices of flagstone paths. For cultivation of the culinary kinds, see Mint. For cultivation of Peppermint, see Peppermint.

The Smallest Flowering Plant in Cultivation. Mentha Requienii is probably the smallest flowering plant in cultivation, with perhaps the tiniest individual flowers. Nor are the flowers produced in such masses as to make any show. This Mint, which is a native of Corsica, is a minute creeping plant, the stems rooting as they go, and forming a dense carpet of pinhead leaves of a fine fresh green. In early summer the flowers appear; they are of light lilac color and extremely small. Intermixed with the leaves, they give a pretty "shot" effect.

A Fragrant Plant for Garden Paths. The chief charm of this interesting little plant, apart from the fresh green, mosslike carpet that it makes, is its refreshing, peppermint-like fragrance when bruised. Planted among the stones of the rockgarden paths, or in the crevices of flagstone paths it fills the air with this scent whenever it is trodden under foot. It prefers a cool, moist situation and, although tolerant of a fair amount of sunshine, it will not withstand real drought. It is not reliably winter-hardy at New York City, but, even though the old plants are killed, new ones from self-sown seeds appear.

Propagation. Mentha Requienii is very easily

propagated by seeds and by the simple method of digging up turfs of the plant, pulling them into small tufts and replanting. This may safely be done at almost any time of year, especially in spring.

MENTZELIA (Mentze'lia). A small genus, consisting chiefly of annuals and biennials originating in North and South America and belonging to the family Loasaceae. The name commemorates Christian Mentzel, a German botanist.

An Attractive Annual. The kind most frequently grown by gardeners is Mentzelia Lindleyi, commonly listed as Bartonia aurea. This

The showy golden-yellow-flowered annual Mentzelia Lindleyi, commonly called Bartonia aurea.

showy annual is a native of California, 15-18 in. high, with ornamental, deeply divided leaves and large, yellow, five-petaled flowers in summer.

The plant needs a sunny place and well-drained soil; ordinary garden soil can be made suitable by adding compost and sand. Seeds may be sown out of doors in spring, where the plants are to bloom, the seedlings being thinned out to 8 or 9 in. apart. An alternative method is to sow the seeds in a pot of light, sifted soil in March in a greenhouse—temperature 50 to 55 degrees—and to plant the seedlings out of doors in May.

MENYANTHES TRIFOLIATA—*Bog Bean* (Menyan'thes). An aquatic plant found wild in many parts of North America. It belongs to the Gentian family, Gentianaceae, and has smooth, green, semiprocumbent stems, ½ in. in diameter. These elongate rapidly and new roots are formed all along the stems, which penetrate into the mud. The leaves are smooth and green, and trifoliate (consisting of three leaflets), the leaflets being 2-3 in. in length and 1½-2 in. broad, and obovate.

During early summer, racemes of flowers are produced in the axils of the leaves; these consist of from 12-20 small, white, fringed, bell-shaped flowers. The leaves have been used in medicines as a tonic and to add bitterness to beer. The name Menyanthes may have been derived from *men,* a month, and *anthos,* a flower, with reference to the plants' being in flower for about one month.

Suitable for the Margins of Ponds. Being of such vigorous growth, the plant is not suitable for small ornamental ponds, but needs a large pond or lake where it has ample room for development. The tips of the shoots, from 2-3 ft. in length, are inserted in the mud at the edge of the lake, and, once planted, need no further attention; however, if they encroach beyond their allotted space, the shoots are cut back after flowering. The principal method of propagation is by inserting pieces of shoot as described above. This is done in early fall or in spring.

MENZIESIA (Menzies'ia). Deciduous shrubs, often of small stature, though sometimes attaining a height of 5-8 ft.; natives of North America and eastern Asia, they belong to the Heath family, Ericaceae. Menziesia was named in honor of Archibald Menzies, a Scottish surgeon and naturalist of the late eighteenth and early nineteenth centuries. Few are of garden value.

These shrubs thrive under conditions suitable for the hardy Heaths and are increased by seeds sown on the surface of sandy peat under glass in September or March, or by cuttings of short shoots planted in sandy peat out of doors under a bell jar in July.

M. pilosa, a shrub 3-6 ft. high which grows wild in eastern North America, is one of the best. Its leaves are 1-2 in. long and up to 1 in.

wide, and its drooping yellowish-white flowers are produced in May. M. ferruginea is a West Coast native, to 8 ft. tall, with greenish-yellow flowers. M. purpurea, 3-6 ft., from Japan, with nodding clusters of red-purple flowers in May–June, is an attractive kind.

MERATIA. Chimonanthus, which see.

MERCURY. Chenopodium Bonus-Henricus, which see.

MERENDERA—*Pyrenean Meadow Saffron* (Merende′ra). Hardy bulbous plants from the Mediterranean region; they are closely allied to Colchicum and Bulbocodium, and belong to the Lily family, Liliaceae. They grow from 3-4 in. in height, have strap-shaped leaves, which appear in some kinds after the flowers have withered, and have lilac or purple six-petaled, funnel-shaped flowers in spring or autumn. The name Merendera is derived from the Spanish name for Colchicum, *Quita meriendas*.

For the Rock Garden. These plants require a semishaded location and deep, moisture-holding soil. The position should be prepared by digging holes 18 in. in depth and sufficiently wide to accommodate the bulbs when set 3 in. apart. The holes are then filled with a soil consisting of equal parts of loam and peat moss, compost or leaf mold. This is pressed in firmly and the bulbs are planted 3 in. deep in early autumn. They should not be disturbed until they show signs of deterioration; then they are lifted, the soil removed and the best bulbs replanted.

Propagation. The smaller bulbs are planted in a nursery bed until they attain flowering size. They may also be increased by sowing seeds in flats of light soil sifted through a ¼-in. sieve. The seedlings are pricked out into other flats when large enough to handle, and finally they are transferred to the nursery bed. Seedlings take four or five years to flower.

The chief kinds are M. Bulbocodium, rosy-lilac; M. trigyna (caucasica), rose; and M. robusta, fragrant, pale lilac or white.

MERTENSIA—*Bluebells* (Merten′sia). These are hardy perennial flowering plants of North America and the Himalayas, which belong to the Borage family, Boraginaceae. They grow 12-24 in. in height, have oval to oblong leaves and terminal clusters of tubular flowers about 1 in.

Mertensia virginia, the Virginia Cowslip.

in length in early summer. The name Mertensia commemorates Karl Mertens, a German botanist.

For a Shady Position. These plants are suitable for planting on the shaded side of the rock garden, under deciduous (leaf-losing) trees, at the edge of the shrubbery and in partially shaded borders. They do best in a sandy, peaty soil but will flourish in most soils containing plenty of humus or decayed vegetable matter. Planting is done in October or March–April. After planting, Mertensia should not be disturbed for several years, but when growth becomes unsatisfactory the clumps are lifted, divided and replanted.

Raising Seedlings. Propagation is best effected by sowing seeds in autumn or spring. Deep seed pans are used. These are well drained with crocks, which are covered with the rough siftings from the compost, and the pans are then filled with finely sifted sandy, peaty soil. The seeds are sown thinly and covered lightly with fine soil.

The soil is moistened by immersing the pans in a pail of water; they are set in a cold frame and covered with pieces of glass and are kept shaded. When germination takes place, the glass is removed and the seedlings are exposed to the light; when 1 in. in height, they are pricked off, 2 in. apart, in flats, and, when large enough, are planted in their permanent quarters.

The chief kinds are M. echioides, deep blue; M. primuloides, purple; M. virginica, the Virginia Cowslip, blue; and M. sibirica, pale blue, and its variety alba, white. Several species occur as natives in the Rocky Mountain region, but these are generally difficult to cultivate except in most-favored climates. They may be tried in rock gardens. The same remarks apply to a number of species that are natives of the Pacific Northwest. Of these Western American kinds the most important are: M. laevigata, M. longiflora, M. nutans, M. oblongifolia, M. paniculata, and M. platyphylla.

MESEMBRYANTHEMUM — *Fig Marigold* (Mesembryanth'emum). A large group of succulent plants, mostly of trailing habit. Except in mild climates, they require the protection of a greenhouse during the winter. They are natives principally of South Africa, and belong to the family Aizoaceae.

These plants vary greatly in habit; most kinds have trailing, succulent stems, some are semi-woody and are of shrubby growth, 2 or 3 ft. in height. The leaves vary from ½ in. to several inches in length; some are triangular, others cylindrical. Many are covered or tipped with fine hairs, while some are smooth and hairless.

The flowers of Mesembryanthemums are daisy-like in shape, and measure from ½ to 2 or 3 in. in diameter. They are red, pink, magenta, yellow or white, and are composed of numerous narrow petals and equally numerous narrow stamens. Most of the flowers open in full sunlight, but a few expand in the evening. The present spelling of Mesembryanthemum is derived from *mesos,* middle, *embryon,* fruit and *anthemon,* flower, though the earlier name, Mesembrianthemum, was from *mesembria,* midday, and *anthemon,* flower, as the then known species flowered only around midday.

Modern Names. Many of the plants previously called Mesembryanthemums have been regrouped by modern botanists into a large number of newer genera. Because many that have been so transferred are still commonly grown in gardens as Mesembryanthemums, and because these require essentially the same culture as the plants that botanists still regard as Mesembryanthemums, some are mentioned in the following discussion. In such cases the preferred modern name is placed in parentheses after the older name that applied. Additional information regarding these plants will, in most cases, be found under their new names in this Encyclopedia.

Cultivation in the Greenhouse. These plants require a minimum winter temperature of 40 degrees. The best soil consists of two parts sandy loam and one of equal quantities of sand, crushed bricks and limestone chips. No shading is required and the greenhouse must be ventilated freely at all seasons of the year, except in frosty weather. Repotting of the vigorous kinds is done annually in March. The shoots of the trailing or shrubby kinds should be shortened when necessary. The soil is made firm with a potting stick, but no water is given until it becomes quite dry.

Well-rooted plants are watered freely during the summer months, but throughout the winter the soil is only moistened when it becomes quite dry. When grown in window gardens and sunrooms, these plants require the same care as when greenhouse-grown.

For Summer Flower Beds. M. cordifolium variegatum (Aptenia cordifolia variegata), which forms a compact mat of variegated foliage, and is used in carpet-bedding designs, for carpeting flower beds, or as an edging, is planted

Mesembryanthemum tricolor, which has flowers in various colors, is commonly grown as an annual, especially in seaside gardens.

outdoors after the weather is warm and settled. In the autumn some of the plants should be lifted, trimmed slightly and potted or placed in boxes of soil. During the winter they are kept in a frostproof greenhouse and given just sufficient water to prevent the stems from shriveling.

When young shoots are developing in the spring, they should be taken off and inserted in pots or boxes of sandy soil; when rooted, they are gradually hardened off for planting in the summer flower beds.

Annual Kinds. M. tricolor (Dorotheanthus gramineus); the Ice Plant, M. crystallinum (Cryophytum crystallinum); M. pomeridianum (Carpanthea pomperidiana); and other annual kinds, or kinds treated as such, are grown in pots in the greenhouse or window garden or sown out of doors for summer flowering. If they are to be grown in pots, the seeds are sown in early spring in well-drained 5-in. pots filled with a soil of two parts sandy loam and one of equal parts sand and crushed bricks. They are lightly covered, and the soil is moistened by immersing the pots in a pail of water. A pane of glass is placed over the pot, and this glass is wiped on the underside each morning to remove condensed moisture.

When the seedlings appear, the glass is removed and they are exposed to full light. They are thinned to 1 in. apart, when large enough to handle, and left to flower in the same pots. The maximum amount of fresh air is required, and the soil must be kept moist until the plants go out of flower, when they are discarded.

Sowing Out of Doors. The annual kinds may also be grown out of doors. The seeds are sown in spring in the locations in which the plants are to flower. They are scattered thinly on the surface, raked in, and the seedlings thinned to 2 in. apart, when large enough to handle. They require a sunny place and light, well-drained soil.

In Mild Climates. In California and other mild, dry climates, especially near the sea, many are hardy and some have become naturalized. The Hottentot Fig, M. edule (Carpobrotus edule), yellow or purple, and M. uncinatum (Ruschia uncinata), pink, should be planted in light, well-drained soil in spring. They do best when planted at the top of a steep bank or among rockwork, where the long trailing shoots have ample room for development.

Propagation of all perennial kinds is effected by cuttings at any time from March to September. Shoots 2-6 in. long, according to the vigor of the plant, are prepared by removing some of the lower leaves. Like those of all other plants of a succulent nature, the cuttings, after being prepared, are laid on a shelf or bench for a few hours, to allow a protecting skin to form over the cut portions before they are inserted in the sand or sandy soil they require. The pots of cuttings are placed on a shelf or set in a cold frame until roots are formed, when they are potted separately in 3-in. pots and subsequently in pots of larger size.

Seeds provide a very ready means of propagating Mesembryanthemums. They germinate quickly when sown in well-drained pots of sandy soil and kept in a light location in a minimum temperature of about 55 degrees.

The Principal Kinds. M. tigrinum (Faucaria tigrina), the Tiger's Mouth, yellow, 6 in.; M. crystallinum (Cryophyton crystallinum), the Ice Plant, white, leaves covered with glistening white lumps resembling ice; M. cordifolium variegatum (Aptenia cordifolia variegata), small ovate variegated leaves and purple flowers (used for summer bedding), and M. tricolor (Dorotheanthus gramineus), red, white, and other shades, 3 in., a half-hardy annual suitable for pots or the flower border.

Noteworthy kinds for the greenhouse include M. acinaciforme (Carpobrotus acinaciformis), red, trailing; M. aureum (Lampranthus aureus), golden-yellow; M. blandum (Lampranthus blandus), pink; M. roseum (Lampranthus roseus), pale pink; M. coccineum (Lampranthus coccineus), 12 in., scarlet; M. floribundum (Drosanthemum floribundum), 12 in., red; M. spectabile (Lampranthus spectabilis), 12 in., red; M. violaceum (Lampranthus emarginatus), 2 ft., purplish, July.

MESOCHIL. A term used in describing the central part of the labellum (lip) of an Orchid when three divisions are present, as in Stanhopea.

MESPILUS GERMANICA—*Medlar* (Mes'-pilus). A hardy, leaf-losing tree, a native of Eu-

rope and Asia Minor, rarely more than 20 ft. high, frequently less than 15 ft., with a rather dense spreading head of branches which may or may not bear stiff spines. It is closely related to the Hawthorn, but the leaves are much larger, 2-5 in. long and up to 2 in. wide, and the margins, instead of being deeply lobed, have only rather inconspicuous teeth. The solitary white flowers, produced in May, are about 1½ in. across, sometimes flushed with pink on the outer side of the petals. The flowers are followed by brown fruits which are often more than 1 in. in diameter.

The seeds are rather like those of Hawthorn. The Medlar can be grafted upon Hawthorn and can also be raised from seeds which, however, are a long while in germinating. The curious graft hybrids referred to under Crataego-Mespilus originated after grafting Medlar on the Hawthorn. Mespilus belongs to the Rose family, Rosaceae, and the name is the ancient Latin one for the tree.

METASEQUOIA (Metasequoi'a). A genus of only one species, M. glyptostroboides, whose origin, like that of Taxodium, to which it is related, dates back millions of years. Metasequoia was first described from fossil remains. It belongs to the Pine family, Pinaceae. The name is derived from *meta,* with, and Sequoia, and refers to its close relationship to Sequoia. Metasequoia is sometimes called Dawn Redwood.

Three living trees were discovered in Szechuan, China, by an expedition organized in 1945, and seeds were collected in 1947 from trees discovered by the Fan Memorial Institute of Biology, Peiping, with financial assistance from the Arnold Arboretum of Jamaica Plain, Massachusetts. About 1,000 trees were then discovered in northeastern Szechuan; the largest of these was over 100 ft. tall and 11 ft. in diameter.

Seeds brought to the United States in 1948, soon gave rise to flourishing plants. These have been tested under outdoor conditions in various parts of the United States and elsewhere. In ten to twelve years specimens growing under favorable conditions attained heights of 30-35 ft. and some bore seed cones.

For its satisfactory growth Metasequoia requires moist soil and light shade. It appears to succeed best where winter temperatures do not drop below −15 degrees farenheit. Metasequoia is easily raised from seeds and also roots very readily from leafy cuttings taken during the summer.

Metasequoia, like its relative the Taxodium or Bald Cypress, a deciduous conifer. It has much the general appearance of Taxodium. In fall its foliage turns golden yellow before it drops.

METROSIDEROS (Metrosider'os; Metrosid'eros). Tender, evergreen trees and shrubs mostly natives of New Zealand and Polynesia. Their chief value is for planting outdoors in frost-free or nearly frost-free climates such as that of California. They may also be grown in greenhouses under the same conditions as recommended for the culture of Callistemon, which see. Metrosideros is closely related to Callistemon, and some botanists include it in that group. It belongs to the Myrtle family, Myrtaceae. The name is derived from *metra,* middle, and *sideros,* iron, and alludes to the hardness of the heartwood.

The Metrosideros group thrive best in a well-drained, peaty soil of acid reaction, but they will flourish in a wide variety of soils. They need full sun. They may be pruned in spring.

The Dawn Redwood, Metasequoia glyptostroboides.

Propagation is effected by seeds sown in sandy, peaty soil in spring and by means of cuttings of firm growths inserted in a greenhouse propagating case in summer.

Kinds include M. diffusa, a high-climbing shrub, flowers red with yellow anthers; M. florida, tall climber, flowers orange-red; M. lucida, tree 30-60 ft., flowers bright crimson; M. robusta, tree, 60-80 ft., flowers dark red; M. scandens, tall climber, flowers white; M. tomentosa, widespreading tree to 70 ft., flowers dark red; M. villosa, tree 20-60 ft., flowers scarlet.

METROXYLON—*Sago Palm* (Metrox'ylon). Tropical Palms from the Malay Archipelago, New Guinea and Fiji. They grow 50 ft. in height, have straight cylindrical trunks and a terminal tuft of suberect pinnate (feather-like) leaves. At maturity flowers are formed, and sometimes a few fruits, then the plants die.

Two kinds, M. vitiense and M. Sagu, are cultivated abroad for their easily digested and nutritious sago, which is obtained from the trunks. The name Metroxylon is derived from *metra,* the heart of a tree, and *xylon,* the wood, and refers to the large central pith.

Palms for Conservatories. These Palms are not popular as pot plants, owing to their large dimensions. Young plants are sometimes grown to decorate large conservatories. They require a minimum winter temperature of 50 degrees and a compost of equal parts of loam and leaf soil. Repotting is done in March; the plants are taken out of the pots, the crocks and loose soil are removed, and the plants are repotted in pots two sizes larger. After potting, water is given carefully until the roots have entered the new soil; it should be applied liberally throughout the summer. During the winter less water is required.

Propagation is by seeds sown in pots of sandy soil in spring or summer. They are plunged in a propagating case with a bottom heat of about 80 degrees; when the seedlings are 3 in. high, they are potted singly in small pots.

The chief kinds are M. vitiense and M. Sagu.

MEUM ATHAMANTICUM—*Bald Money, Spignel; Spicknel* (Me'um). A hardy perennial found wild in many parts of Europe and belonging to the Parsnip family, Umbelliferae. It grows 1-2 ft. in height, has ornamental, feather-like leaves and terminal umbels of small white flowers. The name Meum is derived from *meion,* small, and refers to the plant's decorative leaves.

For the Rock Garden or Dry Bank. This plant will grow in any well-drained soil in borders or on banks. The flowers are not showy, but the plant is sometimes grown for the sake of its feathery foliage. The roots are planted in autumn or spring and should not be disturbed until the plants show signs of deterioration. These are then lifted and divided and the strongest portions set in fresh soil.

Propagation is by division of the rootstock or by sowing seeds, in the places in which the plants are to grow, in April.

M. athamanticum, 1-2 ft., white flowers and feathery foliage, is the only kind cultivated.

MEXICAN BAMBOO. See Polygonum cuspidatum.

MEXICAN FIRE PLANT. See Euphorbia heterophylla.

MEXICAN LILY. This is Hippeastrum Reginae.

MEXICAN ORANGE BLOSSOM. See Choisya.

MEXICAN TULIP POPPY. See Hunnemannia fumariaefolia.

MEZEREON. See Daphne Mezereum.

MICE. See Pests and Diseases.

MICHAELMAS DAISY. Aster, which see.

MICHAUXIA—*Michaux's Bellflower* (Michaux'ia). Hardy perennial flowering plants, of which two kinds are occasionally cultivated. They are found wild in Asia Minor and belong to the Bellflower family, Campanulaceae.

M. campanuloides grows 4-5 ft. in height, has lanceolate, hairy leaves and a pyramidal, candelabra-like head of white flowers, which have 8-10 narrow petals, divided right to the base. M. Tchihatcheffii is taller and more pyramidal in habit, and also has white flowers. The name honors André Michaux, a French botanist.

These plants are usually treated as biennials, seeds being sown one year to provide flowering plants the following year. They may, however, take 3 or 4 years to reach the flowering stage. They are excellent for the back or middle of the herbaceous border. Seeds are sown in April or May in flats of sandy soil.

[7—4]
Maxillaria picta

[7—4a]
Moonseed
(Menispermum canadense)

[7—4b]
Mesembryanthemum

[7—4c]
Miltonia hybrid

[7—5]
Stocks
(Mathiola incana variety)

[7—5a]
Malvaviscus arboreus penduliflorus

[7—5b]
Four-o'Clock
(Mirabilis Jalapa)

[7—5c]
Melons in Greenhouse

Miconia pulverulenta has white flowers with pink stamens.

MICHELIA (Michel'ia). Tender evergreen trees and shrubs, closely allied to Magnolia, which belong to the same family, Magnoliaceae. They are natives of subtropical and tropical Asia. Michelia was named in honor of a Florentine botanist, Pietro Antonio Micheli, who lived during the latter part of the seventeenth and early part of the eighteenth centuries.

The hardiest kind is M. compressa, a native of Japan. It is an evergreen tree, 30-40 ft. high in Japan. The magnolia-like flowers are white or cream-colored and 1½-2 in. across. A better-known species is M. fuscata, a Chinese tree or large bush. This is popular in the South and, because of its distinctive fragrance, is called Banana Shrub. It has attractive glossy leaves and brown-purple flowers borne in spring and early summer.

Spice-scented Flowers. A curious point connected with this plant is that the characteristic spicy odor of the flowers is not apparent early in the morning. This shrub should be given well-drained soil. Seeds form the best means of propagation; they should be sown in a frame in spring. Cuttings inserted in a greenhouse in late summer are also satisfactory.

M. Champaca is found in India, Java and the Philippine Islands, where an essential oil used in perfumery is obtained from the flowers. Several kinds form large trees in tropical forests; their wood is used for building purposes.

MICHIGAN, GARDENING IN. See Regional Gardening.

MICONIA (Mico'nia). Tropical evergreen ornamental foliage plants, from Argentina to Mexico, which belong to the family Melastomaceae. The cultivated kinds have ovate leaves, measuring up to 2 ft. in length, which are wavy-edged, crinkled, the upper surface green, the lower surface red, and have prominent whitish veins. The flowers, which are inconspicuous, are white, purple, or yellow, and are produced in a spreading cluster. The name Miconia commemorates D. Micon, a Spanish botanist.

Greenhouse Plants with Ornamental Leaves. A minimum winter temperature of 55 degrees is required and a soil of equal parts of peat, loam and leaf mold, with sand added freely. Repotting is done in February, when the plants are set in slightly larger pots.

Taking Cuttings. The best results are obtained by raising plants annually. This is chiefly accomplished by inserting cuttings in March or April. Side shoots, or tips of the stems, 4 in. long, are taken off, the lower leaves are removed and a cut is made below the lowest joint. They are then inserted in a mixture of sand and peat moss in a propagating case with a bottom heat of 80 degrees. The case is kept closed, with the exception of a few minutes each morning, when it is opened to admit fresh air.

As soon as sufficient roots have formed, the glass case is ventilated more freely, and eventually the rooted cuttings are potted in 3-in. pots and, when rooted in these, are transferred to larger pots. In the early stages of growth, water must be applied to the soil only when it becomes dry, but well-rooted plants should be watered freely during the summer. In winter much less moisture is required, sufficient only being given to prevent the leaves from wilting.

Raising Seedlings. Seeds, when obtainable, are also sown in spring. Well-drained seed pans or 5-in. pots are used, and these are filled with a finely sifted compost of sandy, peaty soil. The vessels are watered by immersing them up to their rims in a pail of water, then set aside to drain; the seeds are scattered thinly on the surface and covered with a little sand. A pane of glass is laid over the seed pan and the underside of this is wiped every morning to remove condensed moisture.

When the seedlings show above the soil, the glass is removed and, after a week or two, they are pricked out 2 in. apart, in deep pans.

The chief kinds are M. flammea, 18 in., leaves green; M. Hookeriana, 2 ft., leaves olive-green; M. pulverulenta, leaves green; and M. magnifica, 18 in., leaves bronze-green.

MICROCACHRYS TETRAGONA (Microcach'rys). A low-growing, straggling, evergreen bush with four-angled branchlets thickly covered with tiny, scalelike leaves arranged in four regular ranks. Male and female flowers are found in different parts of the same plant, the latter being followed by fleshy, bright red fruits (cones).

This very rare Conifer belongs to the Yew family, Taxaceae; a native of Tasmania, it is hardy only in the warmer parts of the United States. The name Microcachrys is taken from the Greek *mikros,* small, and *kachrys,* a cone, and refers to the very small cones.

MICROCITRUS (Microcit'rus). Tender, spiny shrubs or small trees from Australia and New Guinea that belong to the Rue family, Rutaceae, and are related to the Orange. The name is from *mikros,* small, and Citrus.

The best-known kind is M. australasica, the Finger Lime. The fruit is useful for preserves. As the plant is hardier than the Lemon and the Lime, it may have value as an understock. It attains a height of 30-40 ft.

MICROCYCAS—*Corcho* (Microcyc'as). One Cuban Cycad, resembling Zamia. Its name is derived from *mikros,* small, and Cycas, a genus of plants. It belongs to the Cycad family, Cycadaceae.

M. calocoma attains a height of 30 ft. and may be either single-stemmed or with a few branches. It requires the same culture as Cycas, which see.

MICROGLOSSA ALBESCENS (Microgloss'a). A hardy subshrub or shrub with soft, woody stems, closely allied to Aster and belonging to the Daisy family, Compositae. A native of the Himalayas, it grows about 3 ft. high, and bears masses of lilac-blue flower heads from the tips of young shoots in July. Propagation may be by cuttings of young shoots set in a sand bed in a cold frame in August, or by division of the rootstock in fall. Plant in a sunny position in well-drained, light, loamy soil and cut back the dead ends of the shoots in early spring. The name Microglossa is derived from the Greek *mikros,* small, and *glossa,* a tongue, and refers to the segments of the corolla.

MICROMERIA (Micromer'ia). Small subshrubs or herbaceous plants of thyme-like appearance, with small, fragrant, rounded leaves and tiny purplish or white flowers produced in summer. They have no merits as flowering plants, but are interesting for the rock garden, where they should be planted in light, loamy soil in a sheltered place at the foot of a rock exposed to sun. Cuttings about 1½ in. long, inserted in a cold frame in summer, will form roots in a few weeks. They should be grown in a cold frame during the winter where winters are very cold.

A large number of kinds distributed in many parts of the world have been described, but a few only are in cultivation. Among the best known of these are M. Chamissonis, from western North America; M. croatica, from Croatia; M. graeca, from Greece; and M. Piperella and M. rupestris, from southern Europe. Micromeria belongs to the Mint family, Labiatae; the name is taken from the Greek *mikros,* small, and *meris,* a part, and refers to the size of the flowers.

MICROSTYLIS (Micros'tylis). Orchids of Europe, tropical Asia and North and South America. These terrestrial Orchids grow up to 15 in. in height, have solid pseudobulbs, oval, plicate (crinkled from top to bottom) leaves, and slender spikes of small yellowish or purple pouch-shaped flowers in summer. They belong to the family Orchidaceae, the Orchid family. The name Microstylis is derived from *mikros,* small, and *stylos,* a column or style. By some botanists these plants are named Malaxis.

Hothouse Orchids. The more tropical kinds require a minimum winter temperature of 55 degrees. They should be repotted annually in early spring, as soon as new growth commences.

They are taken out of the pots in which they have rested during the winter, and all loose soil is removed from the roots. They are then repotted in pots large enough to hold the roots comfortably; the pots must be well drained. A compost of three parts fibrous loam, one part leaf mold and equal parts of chopped sphagnum moss and dried cow manure is used, and is made moderately firm. After potting, water is applied very sparingly.

Summer and Winter Management. The atmosphere must be kept moist by frequently damping the floor and benches, and the plants are shaded from strong sunlight until growth has finished. Afterwards they are exposed to full light to ripen the pseudobulbs.

In the autumn the water supply is gradually reduced, and the soil is kept dry during the winter. Propagation is by division of the pseudobulbs at potting time.

Hardy Microstylis. A kind suitable for planting in wild gardens and rock gardens is M. unifolia (Malaxis unifolia). This species is a native of eastern North America, Mexico and the West Indies. It grows about 12 in. high and has a dense raceme of tiny greenish flowers. Like other hardy kinds, this Microstylis grows best in moist, woodsy soil in partial shade.

The tender kinds are M. calophylla, 9 in., yellow; M. discolor, 9 in., yellow, leaves reddish-purple; M. Lowi, 9 in., purple; M. metallica, 9 in., rose-purple; and M. Wallichii, 9 in., yellow.

The hardy kinds include M. monophylla, 10 in., greenish; M. unifolia, 12 in., greenish; M. spicata, 12 in., yellow and orange; and M. Paludosa, 6 in., yellowish green.

MIDRIB. The middle or main vein of a leaf.

MIGNONETTE. This fragrant perennial plant is usually treated as an annual, and seeds are sown out of doors in spring. If grown under glass from seeds sown in July–September, Mignonette will bloom in winter in a greenhouse. The botanical name is Reseda odorata, which see.

How to Grow Mignonette. Mignonette is one of the most delightful of annuals; the flowers are not showy but they are deliciously scented. In many gardens some difficulty is found in the cultivation of this plant, while in others it flourishes with little attention. To ensure successful results, its needs must be carefully provided for. It must be grown in a sunny place in firm, well-drained soil which is not deficient in lime.

Clayey soil can be made suitable by digging and raking to make it friable, and by adding sand and a scattering of lime. When the soil is reasonably dry in spring, it should be trodden down firmly, for Mignonette does not flourish in loose soil. A final raking to ensure a fine surface will complete the preparation.

Light land is made suitable by mixing in some thoroughly decayed manure or compost and a scattering of lime.

When to Sow Seeds. Seeds are sown out of doors in spring where the plants are to bloom in summer, as soon as the ground is so dry that it can be prepared in the way advised. It is useless to sow in wet, ill-prepared soil.

The seeds are very small, and care is needed to avoid sowing too thickly, for that necessitates a good deal of thinning of the seedlings and is wasteful. They need but the slightest soil covering.

The seedlings must be thinned to about 5 in. between individuals, or to a greater distance if that should be found necessary. If the plants are crowded, they will bloom sparsely, and the display will be poor and short-lived.

As a Pot Plant. Mignonette will bloom in winter and early spring if grown in flowerpots in a cool greenhouse; one in which a night temperature of 45-50 degrees is maintained is suitable. Five-inch pots are drained with crocks, and filled with a compost of loam, two thirds; leaf mold, one third; and a free scattering of sand and lime. The compost must be made firm before the seeds are sown and, when pressed down, should reach to within half an inch of the rims of the pots. A few seeds are scattered on the surface and covered very lightly with sifted compost.

If kept moist and shaded from bright sunshine, the seeds will soon germinate. When well developed, and before they become crowded, the seedlings should be thinned out, until only three remain in each flowerpot. They must not be transplanted.

Some growers leave only one seedling in each

pot, and obtain a well-branched, bushy plant by pinching off the top and treating the subsequent side branches similarly; this treatment delays the blossoming.

The Best Varieties. There are many varieties of Mignonette having much larger flowers than the species or wild types; the flowers are of various colors: reddish, pale yellow and greenish-white. These varieties are listed in seedsmen's catalogues. All are richly scented.

One of the wild types, named Reseda glauca, which has gray-green leaves, and bears greenish-white flowers, is a perennial which is sometimes grown in the hardy flower border or wild garden in European gardens and, occasionally, in botanical collections in North America.

Tree Mignonette. Although gardeners usually grow the Mignonette as an annual by raising plants from seeds every year—in spring out of doors, and in late summer and fall under glass—it is really a perennial, and can be kept growing from year to year to provide "tree" or standard Mignonette in pots for the decoration of the greenhouse; the plants will live for several years. These are not to be confused with the Mignonette Tree, Lawsonia inermis.

The quickest way to grow the Mignonette in "tree" form is to take cuttings in summer; shoots 2-3 in. long are taken off with a slight heel or piece of the old stem attached, and are inserted in a close propagating case. When rooted, they are potted separately in small pots and subsequently repotted in 6-in. pots. During the summer the plants should be grown in a frame which is ventilated very freely, and they must be watered carefully until well rooted or they may damp off. All side shoots are taken off the plants until the desired height of stem has developed, and the latter is supported by a stick. The stem is usually allowed to reach a height of 2-3 ft. If the top is then pinched off, side shoots will form and in due course will bear flowers.

During the winter months the Mignonette "trees" must be kept in a greenhouse with a night temperature of 45-50 degrees.

The most suitable potting compost is that recommended for Mignonette in pots.

MIGNONETTE TREE. Lawsonia inermis, which see.

MIGNONETTE VINE. Boussingaultia baselloides, which see.

MIKANIA (Mikan'ia). Mostly tender, perennial flowering plants, the most popular of which are evergreen climbers. They are found wild in North and South America, and belong to the Daisy family, Compositae. They climb by means of their twisted leafstalks, have heart-shaped leaves, pointed at the tips, and in summer bear axillary clusters of small yellow and white flowers similar in appearance to the Eupatoriums, to which they are closely related. The name Mikania commemorates Professor J. G. Mikan, of Prague.

A Hardy Kind. M. scandens, the Climbing Hempweed, grows wild from Maine to Florida and Texas, and into South America. It is a twining plant suitable for limited use in wild gardens. It prefers a moist soil.

Climbing Plants for the Greenhouse. For the tender kinds a minimum winter temperature of 45 degrees is required, and a potting compost of two parts loam, one part leaf mold and a little well-decayed manure and sand. The plants are grown in large pots or tubs and the shoots are trained to wires or trellises fixed to the roof of the greenhouse. Potting is done in March and the soil is made moderately firm. After potting, no water is applied to the soil until it becomes moderately dry, when it is thoroughly moistened; thereafter, during the summer, it is kept moist. The plants should be shaded from sunlight until established, and then exposed to full light. During the winter, water is applied to the soil only when it becomes fairly dry. Pruning consists of thinning out the weak shoots and shortening the extra vigorous ones, after flowering.

When to Take Cuttings. Propagation is by inserting cuttings in spring. Shoots 3 in. long are selected, the lower leaves removed and a cut made below the bottom node or joint. They are inserted in a warm propagating case until roots have formed, and then potted separately in small pots. When established in these, they are transplanted to larger pots or tubs, and are kept growing vigorously for several years by being top-dressing annually in spring with fresh soil.

Planting Out of Doors. Specimens, well rooted

in 5-in. pots, may be planted in spring in well-drained light soil out of doors. Wires or a trellis should be fixed to the wall to support the climbing shoots, and the soil should be well watered in dry weather. Where winters are cold, in October the roots are lifted and stored in pots in a frostproof greenhouse for the winter. In frostless climates tender kinds may be left outdoors all winter.

In South America the leaves of M. amara (Guaco) are used as a cure for snakebite.

The chief kinds are M. scandens, Climbing Hempweed, yellow and white; and M. apiifolia, yellow. They reach a height of 6-15 ft.

MILDEW. See Pests and Diseases.
MILFOIL. See Achillea.
MILK AND WINE LILY. See Crinum.
MILKBUSH. See Euphorbia.
MILK THISTLE. See Silybum Marianum.
MILK VETCH. See Astragalus.
MILKWEED. See Asclepias.
MILKWORT. Polygala, which see.
MILLA. Brodiaea, which see.
MILLET. Panicum miliaceum, which see.
MILLET, AFRICAN. See Eleusine coracana.
MILLIPEDE. See Pests and Diseases.
MILTONIA (Milton'ia). Orchids which grow wild chiefly in Brazil and Central America. All are epiphytal, with persistent foliage and comparatively small, smooth pseudobulbs set closely together or at intervals on the rhizomes. The flower spikes are produced from the base of the bulbs, and usually bear several flowers each. M. vexillaria, M. Roezlii, M. spectabilis and M. Phalaenopsis, with a few others, are distinguished by their large and rather flat flowers, which have been likened to those of Pansies in shape. All are very handsome.

From M. vexillaria and M. Roezlii chiefly, a series of most beautiful hybrids have been obtained which vary in color from white to deep crimson, and flower at various seasons of the year. Hybrids have also been obtained between

The beautiful rose-colored Orchid, Miltonia vexillaria, of which there are many variations of rich and varied colorings. The spray beneath is of an Odontioda.

A single bloom of Miltonia Roezlii.

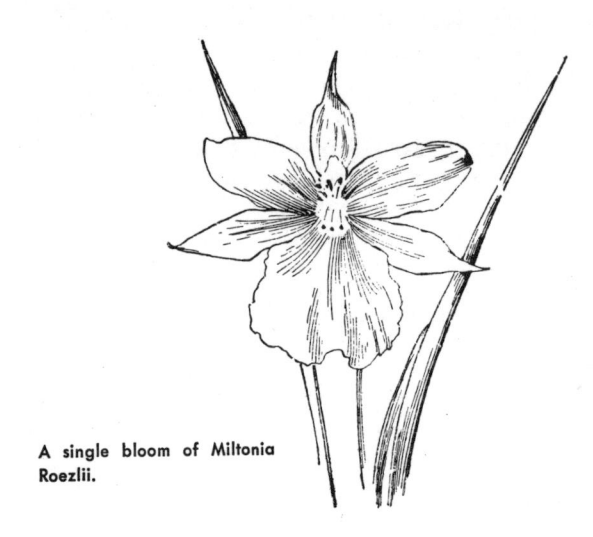

Miltonia and Oncidium, Miltonia and Odontoglossum, and Miltonia and Cochlioda. Miltonia was named after Viscount Milton, not Milton the poet.

M. vexillaria and its hybrids should be grown in a warm, moist atmosphere in summer, and in a winter temperature of not less than 55-60 degrees. M. vexillaria itself has little root action during the winter, and should be very carefully watered at that season, just sufficient water being given to keep the roots moist but not wet.

Those kinds with hard pseudobulbs—e.g., M. cuneata and M. candida—will withstand a slightly lower temperature. Too dry an atmosphere is conducive to attacks by thrips; these insects are particularly fond of the flowers, attacking them while they are in bud. For control of these pests see Pest and Diseases.

Like other epiphytal Orchids, Miltonias may be grown successfully in cut osmunda fiber, in Fir bark, Redwood bark or in the fiber of the trunks of Tree Ferns.

All need well-drained pots. M. vexillaria is potted early in September, or in March; others are potted in spring when young growths are seen.

The Chief Kinds. M. vexillaria has gray-green leaves and slender arching spikes bearing several large, flattish, rose-colored flowers in May. This Orchid is most variable, and in some varieties the basal part of the lip is marked with a deep crimson, butterfly-like blotch; in others the lip is white or the sepals and petals may be white, and the lip deep rose. M. Roezlii has similar but larger flowers, white with a purplish blotch at the base of each petal; it usually has only two

A magnificent variety of Miltonia vexillaria, showing the typical butterfly-like markings.

Miltonia flavescens has straw-colored flowers, each with a purple-marked lip.

or three flowers on a stem. M. Phalaenopsis has white flowers, the lip beautifully marked with rose-purple or purple. M. Roezlii and M. Phalaenopsis need a higher temperature than the other kinds.

M. spectabilis, from Brazil, has erect spikes of rose-colored flowers, and the variety Moreliana is rose-purple. M. candida, which blooms in the autumn, has reddish-brown sepals and petals and white lip. M. Clowesii has a pointed lip with a flush of violet-purple on the basal portion; M. cuneata is somewhat similar. Other kinds are M. Endresii, M. flavescens, M. Regnellii, and M. Warscewiczii.

MILTONIODA. A group of very attractive

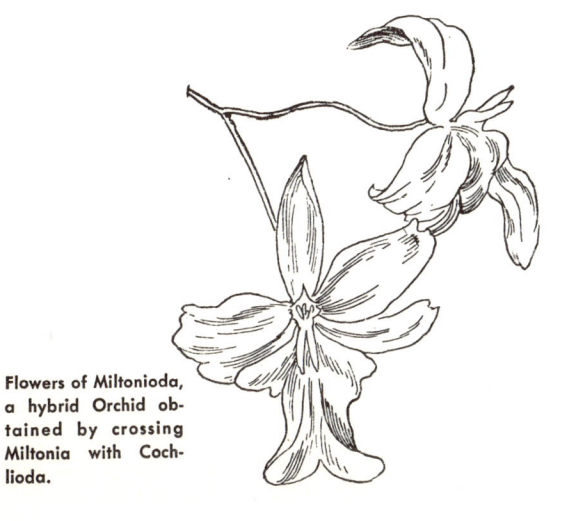

Flowers of Miltonioda, a hybrid Orchid obtained by crossing Miltonia with Cochlioda.

Orchids resulting from crossbreeding between Miltonia and Cochlioda. Cultivation is the same as for Miltonia.

MIMOSA. As a common name, Mimosa is used for some Acacias and also for Albizzia Julibrissin. See Acacia and Albizzia. For the botanical genus Mimosa, see below.

MIMOSA—*Sensitive Plant* (Mimo'sa). Tender shrubby plants from Brazil, India and Ecuador which belong to the Pea family, Leguminosae. There are numerous kinds, but few are in cultivation in North America. The name Mimosa is derived from the Greek *mimos,* mimic. It refers to the fact that the leaves of some kinds are sensitive.

The most popular kind is M. pudica, a perennial shrubby plant with prickly stems and bipinnate leaves. It is commonly grown as the Sensitive Plant, although this name has been applied to all sensitives. The flowers are produced in little fluffy balls. Most of the Mimosas have pink or purplish flowers.

Leaflets Fold Up When Touched. The Sensitive Plant is so called because the leaflets fold up when touched, or when blown by the wind. When a lighted match is held near the tip of one of the leaves, the leaflets fold up in a most spectacular manner; commencing at the top, they close in pairs with clocklike precision, and as soon as the stimulus reaches the base of the leafstalk the whole leaf drops suddenly as if on a hinge. The movements are quickest in young plants and in bright sunlight, and if made to droop when the sun is shining, they return to their normal condition in a few minutes.

If the plants are placed under an airtight bell jar, and subjected to a dose of chloroform, they become insensitive and the leaves cannot be made to move while under its influence.

When to Sow Seeds. Mimosa pudica is best treated as an annual. The seeds are sown in March in a compost of equal parts of peat moss and sand, or in sandy soil. Two-inch pots are used, and these are half-filled with crocks, which are covered with a small quantity of rough leaves or fiber. The pots are filled with the compost and three seeds are sown in each pot. After the soil has been moistened, the pots are packed close together in a box on a layer of damp moss.

When the leaves of the Sensitive Plant, Mimosa pudica, are touched they quickly react.

The reaction: the leaflets fold close together. The same effect may be achieved by blowing on the leaf.

The box is covered with a pane of glass and set in a greenhouse with a minimum temperature of 55 degrees.

Managing the Seedlings. As soon as the seedlings are above the surface of the soil, the glass covering is removed; when the plants are 1 in. tall, the pots are set on the greenhouse benches. To ensure vigorous plants, the two weakest seedlings in each pot should be discarded, and the good plant repotted in a 4-in. pot. A compost of equal parts loam, peat, leaf mold and sand is used. When you repot, the balls of soil must be kept intact, as these plants resent root disturbance. After this the plants must be shaded for a week or two from sun, and the atmosphere kept moist by frequent damping of the floor and benches. No water is applied to the soil until it becomes fairly dry; then it is saturated and kept moist throughout the summer.

When established in 4-in. pots, the plants are

kept in a well-ventilated sunny greenhouse for the remainder of the summer; afterwards they are discarded, as they are not easy to keep alive during the winter, and young seedlings raised each spring are the most vigorous.

Most failures with the cultivation of Mimosa are due to overwatering. When the soil is kept constantly saturated, air is entirely excluded. As a result, acids accumulate and make the soil sour, causing the roots to decay quickly.

A Shrubby Kind. M. Speggazzinii forms a low shrub and can be kept for many years. It is raised and treated in the same manner as M. pudica in the first year. However, instead of being discarded in the autumn, it is kept in a greenhouse with a minimum winter temperature of 55 degrees, and the soil is watered only when it becomes fairly dry during the winter. The shoots are cut back by one half early in March, and the plants are frequently syringed until side growths appear; they are then repotted in pots one size larger, and afterwards given the same treatment as advised for the seedlings.

Propagation by Cuttings. M. Speggazzinii and other perennial kinds can also be increased by cuttings in spring. The side shoots, with a "heel" or piece of the old branch attached, are selected when 2 in. long; a few of the lower leaves are removed and the "heel" is pared smooth with a sharp knife. The cuttings are then inserted in a propagating case having a bottom heat of 75 degrees. When rooted, they are potted and treated as advised for the seedlings.

The chief kinds are M. pudica, rose-purple; M. sensitiva, pale purple (this is the original Sensitive Plant, but it is less popular than M. pudica, as it is not so sensitive); M. Speggazzinii, rose-purple, and M. rubicaulis, red. M. pudica is naturalized as a roadside weed in the lower South.

MIMULUS: THE MUSK OR MONKEY FLOWER
Flowering Plants for Garden and Greenhouse

(Mim′ulus). This group of some seventy species of hardy and tender herbs, often with showy flowers, are natives of the Americas, Asia, Australia and Africa, and are most numerous in western America. They belong to the family Schrophulariaceae. The name Mimulus is derived from *mimus,* a buffoon, an allusion to the shape of the flower.

All are best grown in fairly rich, moist soil, and some are first-rate plants for the bog garden and the waterside. The seeds, which are very small, should be sown in spring in a cold frame and covered very thinly with fine soil. When large enough to handle conveniently, the seedlings should be placed in flats of light soil, a good mixture being two parts fibrous loam, one part leaf mold or peat moss and one part cow manure, with a sprinkling of sand.

Mimulus cardinalis is an attractive perennial for the flower border, 1-2 ft. high, with handsome scarlet flowers in summer. Variety grandiflorus is a specially good form.

Mimulus cupreus, a native of Chile, is a perennial, growing 6-9 in. tall. In the Pacific Northwest and other places where it is hardy it is excellent for the cooler, moister parts of the rock garden, or for the margins of ponds and pools in the garden. It is of neat habit and never encroaches in the way that M. luteus does. A number of varieties which have been raised and named in Great Britain may be of interest to American gardeners. Notable among these are Bee's Dazzler, crimson; Brilliant, purple-crimson; Cerise Queen, cerise; Fireflame, flame-red; Leopard, yellow, spotted mahogany; Red Emperor, crimson-scarlet; and Whitecroft Scarlet, scarlet, dwarf, small-flowered. Mimulus cupreus and its varieties are easily increased by division in spring, or by cuttings rooted in sandy soil in a frame in spring.

The Bush Musk. Mimulus aurantiacus, also known as Diplacus glutinosus, is a subshrubby plant that grows wild from California to Oregon. It has wiry stems which are woody at the base, sticky leaves, and large, handsome flowers which vary from buff or salmon to mahogany

A good seed strain of hybrid Mimulus or Monkey Flowers, with richly colored, heavily blotched flowers.

red. This elegant and showy plant is excellent for bedding out in summer borders, and as a greenhouse and sunroom pot plant; it may be had in flower almost all the year round.

The plants can be kept dwarf and bushy by pruning the shoots to one third their lengths in February. You may also train them to a trellis or to a pillar by allowing the shoots to develop to their full length and afterwards shortening the side shoots in spring. This plant can be grown out of doors in mild climates.

Propagation is by cuttings of young shoots inserted in sandy compost in a close frame or propagating case in spring and summer.

The Showy Yellow Musk. Mimulus luteus is a native of Chile. Where winters are not excessively severe, it is hardy and well adapted for planting by the waterside. Its large, handsome yellow flowers make a brilliant show. It is a perennial, increasing rapidly in suitable ground by means of its rooting stems, as well as by self-sown seeds. Because it spreads so quickly, this plant should be treated with caution in small gardens. In larger places, where room can be spared, it is excellent for naturalizing, especially as ground cover among taller, stronger plants, where it makes a great show in summer. There are varieties with mahogany-red spots or blotches on the petals.

Monkey Flowers. The well-known Monkey Flowers (Mimulus) of the seedsmen and the florists are probably derived from M. luteus crossed with M. cupreus and M. variegatus. The plants have large flowers, handsomely and curiously blotched and spotted with crimson, maroon or purple on a yellow or white ground. They are easily raised from seed sown under glass or in the open in spring. They are tender perennials but are often grown as annuals. Any especially fine varieties can be increased with ease by means of cuttings, in a cold frame, at almost any time in spring or autumn. Young, nonflowering shoots only should be chosen as cuttings. These plants do well in town gardens.

The Musk Which Has Lost Its Scent. Mimulus moschatus, which was discovered in western North America more than a hundred years ago, is a low-growing perennial of prostrate or creeping habit. The smallish, almost regular flowers are a clear yellow color, and appear from June until September. The leaves and stems are covered with a somewhat clammy "down." This pretty plant was for long a universal favorite on account of the pleasant musk scent which emanated from it, and was commonly grown as a pot plant in windows.

Some years ago the plant lost its scent completely. Diligent search has been made wherever Musk is grown, but no trace of a scented plant can be discovered. Plants growing wild in their native haunts have been examined, but with the same result; no specimen with scented flowers, either wild or cultivated, can be traced. This total loss of scent is something of a mystery, and learned scientists seem unable to offer any entirely adequate explanation of the phenomenon. The possession of its musk scent made Mimulus moschatus a general favorite, especially among home gardeners.

Mimulus moschatus is very easily propagated, either by simple division of the roots at almost any time of year, or by seeds, which may be sown in a pot in a cold frame, window garden or greenhouse in spring; the seeds should be kept shaded, and the seedlings pricked out when large enough. Raising the plants from seeds is to be recommended, as there is always the possibility that one plant with scented blooms may crop up among seedlings, whereas the chances of a scented specimen occurring among plants propagated vegetatively are much smaller.

The Rose-colored Musk. Mimulus Lewisii is a beautiful perennial plant, 12-18 in. high, of British Columbia to California and Utah. The large flowers are rose-colored and appear in July and August. This Musk is most suitable for the cooler, moister parts of the garden. It may be increased by seeds sown in a cold frame in spring or by cuttings taken in spring and rooted in sand in a frame. The variety albus is a distinct and striking form, with pure white flowers. It comes quite true from seed. This is a choice and extremely beautiful plant.

As Greenhouse Plants. Mimulus cardinalis and the hybrid Musks that the seedsmen sell are easily raised from seeds and make very attractive pot plants. Specimens that bloom in April–May in 5-in. to 7-in. pots may be had by sowing seeds in September and growing the plants in a sunny greenhouse, night temperature 45-50 degrees. From February on, well-rooted specimens should be fertilized freely. M. moschatus also makes an attractive greenhouse specimen. It requires the same culture, but 5-in. pots are large enough for finals.

Other Attractive Kinds. Mimulus luteus variety variegatus, from Chile, is very similar to M. luteus, but is shorter, and with larger, white-throated flowers which are variously colored. Bonfire is a good orange-scarlet variety; it is one of the parents of the seedsmen's strains.

Mimulus primuloides is a small, creeping perennial with pretty flowers carried singly on erect, threadlike stems, 2 or 3 in. high. It requires a cool position and moist soil, and is a charming and dainty plant for a choice place in the rock garden. It is easily increased by division of the root in spring. It is a native of western North America.

MINA. Quamoclit lobata, which see.

MINERAL DEFICIENCY. See Pests and Diseases.

MINIATURE GARDENS. Attractive miniature gardens for rooms can be made in earthenware dishes; with careful treatment, the plants will remain in good condition for months. Although it is possible to keep these small gardens attractive for some time without providing drainage holes at the bottom of the vessel, the plants will thrive better if drainage is provided. The soil compost should consist of loam, two thirds, and leaf mold or peat moss, one third, with a free addition of small pebbles, crushed brick and sand. If there are no drainage holes in the vessel the bottom ought to be covered with pebbles and crushed brick and, every time you water, you should tilt the vessel afterward, so that surplus water can drain away. Unless this is done, the soil will soon become sour and the roots of the plants will perish.

The miniature gardens must be kept in good light near the window in a sunroom or cool room. The chief care is needed in watering. If too much water is given, the plants will soon turn yellow and die. The secret of success is not to water the soil until it is moderately dry.

Small pebbles or gravel are used to represent walks, and a little grass seed, if sown thickly and if the grass is kept cut very short, will make a natural lawn. Those miniature rustic bridges and garden ornaments which are sold at stores add to the charm of the miniature garden. A piece of a mirror may be used to represent a small pool.

Small rooted slips of shrubs make good representations of trees; seedling Ferns, too, are useful, as well as low-growing rock plants. Miniature Orange trees, Oaks raised from acorns and other seedling trees are just right for a miniature garden. The little rock plants named Arenaria caespitosa, Acaena Buchanani (which has gray leaves), Cotula squalida, and small pieces of Thyme and Mentha Requieni are all suitable.

MINIATURE TREES. A fascinating hobby, and one which can be indulged in by even those who have no garden, is the cultivation of trees in small pots. Any of the common trees, such as Yew, Oak, Beech and Horse Chestnut, are suitable for the purpose.

It is remarkable how attractive these trees are after they have been confined in small pots for several years. The soil may become almost dry and remain so for days, but they do not appear to suffer. A small collection of dwarf trees forms

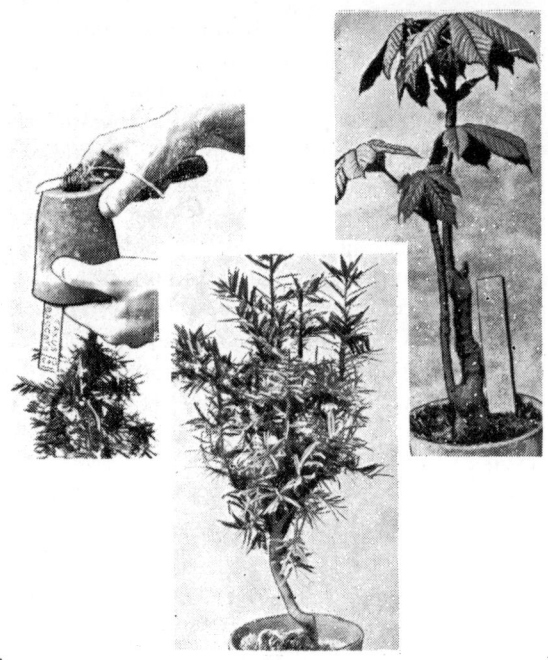

Home-grown miniature trees of Horse Chestnut *(upper right)* and Yew *(center).* Excess root growth is checked *(upper left)* by cutting off roots that have protruded through the drainage hole.

an interesting feature, especially in spring when the young leaves are unfolding. The plants may be grown entirely on the window sill of a cool sun room if no other space is available.

Seedlings can usually be gathered in the vicinity of the trees. They should be potted in 3-in. pots, using poor, sandy compost. Make the soil as firm as possible and stand them in a shady place until established. Afterwards, give them full sunlight, and water only when the soil is nearly dry. It is essential that they be stood on a hard base, such as a window sill, or a concrete path, to prevent the roots from growing through the drainage holes. If the roots are allowed to penetrate into rich soil, growth will become too luxuriant.

There is no need to repot the trees; simply trim off the roots as they appear through the drainage hole and prune straggling shoots. See also Japanese Dwarf Trees.

MINNESOTA, GARDENING IN. See Regional Gardening.

MINTBUSH. See Prostanthera.

MINT, HORSE. Monarda, which see.

MINT, LEMON. Monarda pectinata.

MINT, MOUNTAIN. Pycnanthemum, which see.

MINT OR SPEARMINT. The Mint commonly grown in gardens is Mentha spicata, though the downy-leaved M. rotundifolia has a better flavor.

This herb is easily cultivated if planted in ordinary soil of fair depth, which does not dry out quickly in hot weather. If, however, it is planted in a hot, sun-baked border, where the roots suffer from the effects of drought in summer, it will fail, or make such weakly, woody growth as to be useless. It need not be planted in full sunshine; a half-shady place will do. In fact, in gardens where the soil is light and soon becomes parched in hot weather, Mint ought to be grown in partial shade.

Mint spreads so rapidly that it may soon become a nuisance; the underground stems travel along the border, and the shoots push through the soil at some distance away, and may spoil neighboring plants.

It is a good plan to sink an old zinc vessel in the ground, fill it with soil and then plant the Mint. This method will prevent the Mint from spreading and becoming a nuisance.

The best Mint is obtained from single vigorous roots. It is thus advisable to lift the old clumps

Mint is a favorite herb. A patch in the herb garden, vegetable garden or near the kitchen door provides a constant supply for picking through the summer.

Apple Mint: this large-leaved woolly kind makes a handsome decoration as well as a flavoring for drinks. Its flowers are cream colored.

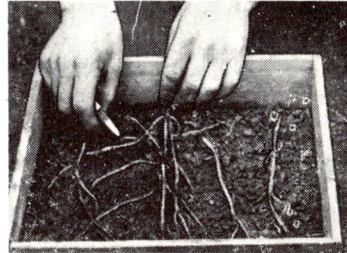

To obtain fresh Mint in winter, roots can be planted in flats of loamy soil and grown in a warm greenhouse, or even on the window sill of the kitchen or other warm room. After being forced in this way, the roots should be discarded.

every year or two, in autumn or spring, separate them into rooted pieces and replant the latter; the old central parts of the plant which have become woody should be discarded.

Mint in Winter. It is a simple matter to obtain a supply of Mint in the winter months.

In autumn some of the plants should be lifted and set close together in a box about 8 in. deep, filled with sandy, loamy soil. If they are placed

The simplest way to plant Mint is to spread the roots thinly in a flat-bottomed trench *(left)* and cover with 2 in. of soil *(right)*.

in a warm greenhouse having a temperature of 50-55 degrees, or even in a sunny window, and are kept moist at the roots, the plants will soon start into fresh growth.

Mint may be cut from plants out of doors in summer, before the growths come into flower, and hung in bunches in a cool, airy room to dry; the leaves should then be stripped from the shoots and placed in stoppered or corked bottles to keep them dust-free. They will then be available for use during the winter.

MINT, STONE. Cunila origanoides, which see.

MIRABILIS — *Marvel-of-Peru, Four-o'clock* (Mirab'ilis). Tender perennial herbaceous flowering plants, mostly natives of tropical America and North America, which belong to the family Nyctaginaceae. The most popular kind, M. Jalapa, has tuberous roots, from which soft succulent stems, 2-3 ft. in height, develop in summer. They are covered with ovate leaves and bear tubular flowers in summer in shades of red, yellow and white. The name *mirabilis* means wonderful, and refers to the colors of the flowers. The flowers of M. Jalapa open in late afternoon, hence its common name, Four-o'clock.

The most popular method of growing these plants is to raise them annually from seeds. These are sown in spring directly outdoors where the plants are to bloom; or else plants are raised indoors from seeds sown early, and are set out when the weather is warm. Indoors the seeds are sown in a pot filled with light, sandy soil and are covered with a thin layer of fine soil. The

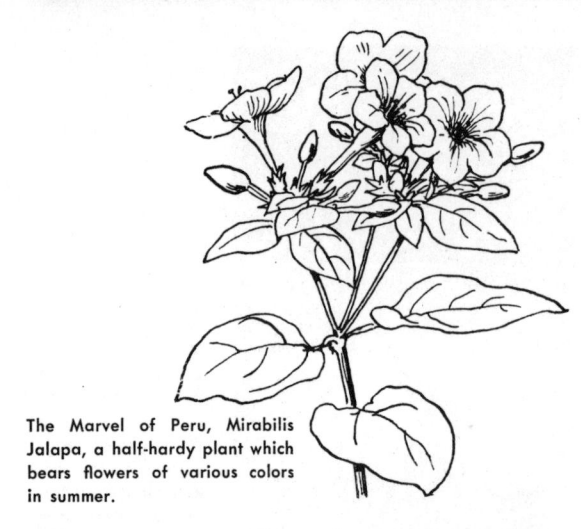

The Marvel of Peru, Mirabilis Jalapa, a half-hardy plant which bears flowers of various colors in summer.

seed pot is immersed to the rim in a pail of water to saturate the soil, and a pane of glass is placed over the pot, which is set in a temperature of 55-60 degrees. The underside of the glass must be wiped each morning to remove condensed moisture.

After the seeds have germinated, the glass should be removed and the seedlings exposed to the light. When 2 in. in height, they are potted separately in 3- to 4-in. pots, well watered and shaded until established. When well rooted, they are planted out of doors after the weather is warm and settled. They require a sunny position and light, well-drained soil.

Can Be Treated Like Dahlias. If desired, the plants can be kept for many years if treated in the same way as Dahlias. In the autumn the tubers are lifted and dried and stored in a frost-proof place for the winter. The clumps of tubers are divided and planted out of doors in May.

The chief kind is M. Jalapa (Marvel-of-Peru or Four-o'clock), 2-3 ft., with red, yellow and white flowers. Other kinds are M. longiflora, 2-3 ft., white, pink or violet, and M. multiflora, 2-3 ft., purple.

MISCANTHUS—*Zebra Grass, Eulalia* (Miscan'thus). Hardy, ornamental-leaved plants from Japan and China, which belong to the Grass family, Gramineae. They grow 6-10 ft. in height and have narrow, arching leaves which are green or striped with silver or yellow. The flowers are in plumes.

The plants flourish in ordinary garden soil which is deeply dug and enriched with leaf mold or compost, and may be planted in the herbaceous border, in the front of a shrubbery, or by the waterside. They are at their best during late summer and autumn. The dead stalks are cut down in spring and the soil is top-dressed with decayed manure or rich compost. Propagation is by division of the clumps at planting time, which is in spring.

Ornamental Pot Plants. The variegated kinds make ornamental pot plants. They are potted in 5- or 6-in. pots in March, and watered freely during the summer. Less moisture is required during winter, and the soil is only moistened when it becomes quite dry. They require a minimum winter temperature of 40 degrees.

The Chief Kinds. Among these are M. sinensis (Eulalia japonica), green leaves, and its varieties: variegatus, green and silver; zebrinus, Zebra Grass, green and yellow leaves (this kind and variegatus are the best for pots); and gracillimus, with slender leaves. Also noteworthy is M. sacchariflorus, with wide, green leaves.

MISCHOBULBUM SCAPIGERUM (Mischobul'bum). This low-growing Orchid is found wild in Borneo and Formosa. It is terrestrial and has a creeping rhizome; the leaves are heart-shaped and persistent, and are marked with dark green on a paler green ground. The flower stems are erect, about 4 in. high, and usually bear two flowers each, in May and June. The flowers are nearly 2 in. in diameter, with reddish sepals and petals. The front lobe of the lip is bright yellow while the side lobes are white, spotted with crimson. The name is probably derived from *miskos,* a stem, and *bulbon,* a bulb.

A flower pan is preferable to a flowerpot for this Orchid, as the greater area it provides suits the creeping habit of the plant, which requires a warm greenhouse with a tropical atmosphere. The winter temperature should be 60-65 degrees. Drafts must be avoided; the plant is often grown under a bell jar. Shade must be provided from bright sunshine, and the compost is kept moist throughout the year.

The compost should consist of two parts cut osmunda fiber and two parts sphagnum moss. Repotting, if necessary, should be done early in the year, or the compost can be replenished from time to time without disturbing the plants. As the rhizome branches freely, propagation is effected by taking the branches off when they have roots.

MISSISSIPPI, GARDENING IN. See Regional Gardening.

MISSOURI, GARDENING IN. See Regional Gardening.

MIST FLOWER. Eupatorium coelestinum, which see.

MISTLETOE. The name Mistletoe is applied to a number of semiparasitic plants that belong in the botanical family Loranthaceae. None are cultivated in the ordinary sense of the word, although some gardeners encourage them to grow by sticking seeds on the undersides of the branches of suitable host trees. This is particularly true in Europe, where Viscum album, the native European Mistletoe and the Mistletoe of classical history and legend, is often encouraged to grow on Apples in this way.

In America the most common Mistletoe is Phoradendron flavescens, a native of the eastern part of the continent from New Jersey to the Gulf Coast. In the Western states other species are known as Mistletoe.

MISTLETOE CACTUS. Rhipsalis, which see.

MITCHELLA REPENS — *Partridgeberry, Twinberry, Squawberry* (Mitchell'a). A dwarf plant with creeping stems and small, opposite, rounded leaves. It has white flowers tinged with purple which appear during summer and are followed by bright red fruits. This native of the eastern half of North America is an interesting plant for the rock garden or wild garden, where it should be given a moderately moist and not too sunny position, in light soil rich in leaf mold. It can be increased by division of the clumps in spring and by seeds sown when ripe in sandy, peaty soil.

Mitchella belongs to the family Rubiaceae, and was named in honor of an American botanist, Dr. John Mitchell, a correspondent of Linnaeus.

MITE. See Pests and Diseases.

MITELLA DIPHYLLA—*Bishop's-Cap, Mitrewort* (Mitel'la). North American hardy herbaceous perennials of which only one kind, Mitella diphylla, is generally cultivated, although others are sometimes brought in from the wild and planted in gardens. These plants belong to the Saxifrage family, Saxifragaceae. The name is from *mitra,* a mitre, and alludes to the form of the young seed pods.

Mitella diphylla reaches a height of about 9 in. It is suitable for planting in the rock garden, where it thrives in soil with which leaf mold or peat has been mixed, together with sand, if necessary, to ensure free drainage. Planting may be done in autumn or spring. The small, white, fringed flowers open in early spring. If an increased stock is required, the plants should be divided in autumn.

MITRARIA COCCINEA—*Mitre Flower* (Mitra'ria). A tender evergreen, shrublike flowering plant, from Chile, which belongs to the family Gesneriaceae. It has slender, woody trailing branches, which bear evergreen, ovate leaves, ¾ in. long, toothed at the margins and tinged with red beneath. The flowers are scarlet, tubular, and 1¼ in. in diameter, and are produced during the summer. The name Mitraria means mitre, and refers to the shape of the seed pod.

This plant can be grown in a greenhouse having a minimum winter temperature of 45 degrees; in mild climates such as that of California it is grown out of doors.

Cultivation in the Greenhouse. A compost of two parts peat and one part leaf mold, with sand added, is required. Repotting is done in March, the plants being set in pots two sizes larger. Crocks are put in for drainage, and these are covered with a layer of rough siftings from the compost. An inch or two of soil is put in the pot and made firm; before the plant is placed in the pot the loose roots at the base of the ball of soil should be spread out. The compost is added, a little at a time, and made firm with a potting stick. Sufficient space should be left at the top for water.

After potting, the plants are set in a cool, shaded position. The atmosphere is kept moist by frequently damping the floor, walls and benches, and the leaves should be syringed daily. When the roots have entered the new compost, the plants are placed in a light position, but shaded from the direct rays of the sun. They must be kept moist at the roots during the summer, but from September to April much less water is required; then the soil is moistened only when it becomes fairly dry.

Cultivation Out of Doors. This plant can be grown out of doors in warm parts of the United States. It requires a compost similar to that used for potting; planting is done in spring. When the plant is grown against a wall, the shoots are tied to wires or a trellis, but in the rock garden they are allowed to sprawl over a large boulder.

When to Take Cuttings. Propagation is by cuttings inserted at any time from April to August. Side shoots 2 in. in length are taken off with a heel of the old branch attached. The lower leaves are removed with a sharp knife (not torn off, as this damages the stems and causes decay) and the "heel" is pared smooth.

The cuttings are inserted 1 in. apart in a mixture of peat moss and sand in a propagating case and are then well watered. The case is kept close to prevent the shoots from wilting. Each morning the case is ventilated for a few minutes and the moisture is wiped from the undersides of the glass.

When roots have formed, they are given more air each day, and in a week or ten days they are potted separately in 3-in. pots and afterwards treated as advised for the older plants. To make bushy specimens, pinch the tips of the main shoots when they are 4 in. in length, and treat the subsequent side shoots similarly. Well-rooted plants in 5-in. pots are most suitable for planting out of doors.

MITRE FLOWER. See Mitraria coccinea.

MITREWORT. See Mitella.

MITREWORT, FALSE. Tiarella, which see.

MITRIOSTIGMA—*Citron-scented Gardenia* (Mitriostig'ma). Tender evergreen flowering shrubs, from South Africa, which belong to the family Rubiaceae. These plants closely resemble the Gardenia and are placed in that genus by some botanists. The principal kind, M. axillaris, is known also as Gardenia citriodora. It may be grown outdoors in warm climates.

The Mitriostigmas form woody shrubs, 5 ft. in height, have ovate to lance-shaped glossy green leaves, and bear white, fragrant, tubular flowers, in early summer; the tips of the petals spread out salver-shaped. The name is from *mitra*, mitre, and *stigma*, and refers to the shape of the stigma.

Mitriostigma, when grown indoors, requires a minimum winter temperature of 55 degrees. The best potting compost consists of equal parts of peat, loam and well-decayed manure, with sand freely added, and a small quantity of crushed charcoal.

Repotting of the old plants is done in February or as soon as new growth commences. The shoots are shortened by one half, and the plants are frequently syringed to induce new shoots to form. The plants are taken out of the pots, and the crocks and all loose soil are removed; they are then set in pots two sizes larger.

A layer of crocks is placed in the pots and covered with rough siftings from the compost to prevent the soil from washing into the drainage. An inch or two of compost is then placed in the pots and made moderately firm with a wooden potting stick. The plant is set in the center of the pot and the compost, as it is added, is made firm, sufficient space being left at the top for watering.

Details of Management. After potting, the plants are shaded from strong sun. A moist atmosphere is maintained by frequently damping the floor and benches, and the foliage is kept syringed. When established, the plants are only shaded from the fiercest rays of the sun, and water is applied freely to the soil. Dilute liquid fertilizer should be given to well-rooted plants twice a week. Syringing is discontinued when the plants are in flower, as the moisture discolors the blooms.

Less watering is done in winter, but neither the atmosphere nor the soil must be allowed to remain dry for long.

When to Take Cuttings. Two-year-old plants produce finer flowers than older ones, and new plants are therefore raised each year. Young shoots, 3 in. in length, are taken from the old plants in March, some of the lower leaves are removed and a cut is made beneath the lowest joint.

The cuttings are inserted in a propagating case in the hothouse. The case is kept close, except for a few minutes each day, when the cover is raised to change the air, and the moisture is

[7—6]
Matricaria inodora variety

[7—6a]
Oswego Tea
(Monarda didyma variety
Cambridge Scarlet)

[7–7]
*Grape Hyacinths
(Muscari) naturalized*

[7–7a]
*Grape Hyacinth
(Muscari armeniacum)*

wiped from the undersides of the glass. It is very important that this condensed moisture should be removed daily, as it is liable to drip on the cuttings and cause them to decay. As soon as roots have formed and growth becomes active, more air is given each day for a week or so; the rooted cuttings are then potted separately in 3-in. pots. For a few days they are replaced in the propagating case; then they are gradually hardened off and set in the open greenhouse. Subsequently, they are repotted in 5-in. pots and treated as advised for older plants. The plants are made bushy by removing the tips of the main shoots when these are 5 in. in length, and the resultant side shoots are similarly treated.

The chief kind is M. axillaris (Gardenia citriodora), 5 ft., white, fragrant.

MOCCASIN FLOWER. Cypripedium spectabile, which see.

MOCKERNUT. Carya tomentosa, which see.

MOCK ORANGE. See Philadelphus, also Prunus caroliniana.

MODIFIED LEADER. See Pruning.

MOHRIA CAFFRORUM (Moh'ria). A greenhouse evergreen Fern, from South Africa, which belongs to the family Schizaeaceae. It grows about 18 in. in height, and has pinnate (featherlike) fronds similar to those of the Cheilanthes. The name Mohria commemorates Daniel Mohr, a German botanist.

Fern for a Greenhouse. This Fern requires a minimum winter temperature of 45 degrees, and the best potting compost consists of two parts of peat and one part of equal quantities of sand, crushed lime rubble and charcoal. Repotting is done in March or as soon as the new fronds commence to uncurl. The pots are half-filled with crocks, and these are covered with a thin layer of fibrous material sifted from the peat. The plants are then knocked out of their pots and the crocks and all loose soil removed from the "ball" with a pointed stick. Compost, 2 in. in depth, is then placed in the pot and made firm; upon this the plant is placed and the new compost is filled in around it.

After potting, the plants are placed in a shaded part of the greenhouse and the atmosphere is kept moist by damping the floor and benches. The fronds must not be wetted, however, as this causes them to damp off. During the summer the compost is kept uniformly moist, but from September to April it is watered only when it becomes fairly dry.

Propagation is by spores, for the treatment of which see Ferns.

M. caffrorum, with fronds 18 in. long, is the only species. The variety achilleifolia has more finely cut fronds.

MOLE. See Pests and Diseases.

MOLINIA CAERULEA (Molin'ia). A hardy Grass, a native of Europe, naturalized in the eastern United States. It belongs to the family Gramineae. It grows about 3 ft. in height, has rather rigid, slender leaves, and purplish flower spikes. The variety M. caerulea variegata, with white-striped leaves, is the kind chiefly cultivated; this is used for forming tufts of variegated foliage in herbaceous borders. The name Molinia commemorates J. Molina, a botanical author of Chile.

The roots may be planted in October or in March or April. The plant requires a sunny position, and ordinary garden soil will grow it to perfection. Once it is established, very little attention is needed until the clumps become overgrown, when they should be lifted and divided.

MOLTKIA (Molt'kia). Previously included in the genus Lithospermum, the Moltkias are delightful subshrubs or perennial herbs for the rock garden, but are not easy to grow where summers are hot. Cultivation is the same as for Lithospermum. The shrubs are natives of southern Europe and Asia, and the name commemorates Count Joachim Gadake Moltke, of Denmark.

Moltkia suffruticosa (graminifolia) is one of the best and most beautiful kinds. It forms wide tussocks of long, narrow, grasslike foliage, and, on 6- to 9-in. stems, carries heads of brilliant blue flowers in early summer. It enjoys a lime soil and a sunny, well-drained position. It may be increased by seeds sown in pots in spring and kept in a cold frame; by cuttings taken with a "heel" in early summer, or by layering in July.

Beautiful and Easily Grown. Moltkia intermedia is one of the most beautiful and most satisfactory of the family. It is subshrubby in habit, forming fine, rounded plants, woody at the base, branched, with tufts of narrow, dark green leaves, from which, in early summer, spring numerous 6-in. stems carrying heads of tubular, bright, deep blue flowers. This fine plant should be grown in ordinary loamy soil in full sun, and looks best in a well-raised position among the rocks. It seems indifferent as to the presence or absence of lime in the soil.

It is best propagated by soft cuttings taken with a "heel" in early summer; the cuttings should be placed in sand in a cold frame, which must be kept close.

A Blue-flowered Dwarf Shrub. Moltkia (Lithospermum) petraea is a definitely shrubby kind, growing 12-24 in. in height, with dark green foliage and showy heads of brilliant blue flowers in early summer. This beautiful little shrub is worthy of a choice position in the rock garden, in a slightly raised pocket among the rocks facing south, in rich, light soil. It may be raised from seeds—which, however, are not easily obtainable—sown in spring in a pot or pan in a cold frame.

MOLUCCA BALM. Molucella laevis, which see.

MOLUCELLA (Molucell'a). Two aromatic annuals, or plants grown as annuals, that are natives of the eastern Mediterranean region and nearby western Asia. They belong to the Mint family, Labiatae, and are grown in flower borders for garden decoration and for cutting. The name is derived from the Moluccas, where one of the species was, wrongly, believed to originate.

The best-known kind is M. laevis, which is called variously by the common names Molucca Balm, Shellflower, Bells of Ireland, and Irish Bells. The latter two names are given because of the predominantly green coloring of the flower spikes and the bell shape of the enlarged calyces, which form their most conspicuous parts. The flowers proper are small, white and fragrant. This kind is a true annual and grows 2-3 ft. tall.

The second kind, M. spinosa, is often biennial and perhaps perennial, but for garden purposes is usually best treated as an annual. It attains a height of 6-8 ft. Its flowers are white. This kind

Bells of Ireland is one of the common names applied to Molucella laevis. The plant is actually a native of the eastern Mediterranean region.

is much less commonly grown than M. laevis.

The culture of Molucella presents no difficulty. The seeds may be sown directly out of doors in early spring where the plants are to bloom, and the resulting seedlings are thinned to stand 9-12 in. apart; or plants may be raised by sowing indoors in March and transplanting the seedlings to flats or small pots and setting them in the open garden when the weather is settled and all danger of frost has passed.

These plants need a well-drained, moderately fertile soil that is inclined to be dryish rather than wet and a position in full sun. From a September sowing made indoors, plants may be raised that, in a sunny greenhouse, with a night temperature of about 50 degrees, will produce a good crop of flowers in late winter and spring.

MOMORDICA—*Balsam Apple, Balsam Pear* (Momor'dica). Tender annual climbing plants which are cultivated for their ornamental fruits. They grow wild in tropical countries and belong to the Gourd family or Cucurbitaceae. The name Momordica is derived from *mordeo,* to bite, and refers to the seeds, the edges of which have the appearance of having been bitten.

The Balsam Pear, M. Charantia, is an annual which grows about 10 ft. in height and resembles the Cucumber except in its fruits. The slender stems are slightly pubescent (hairy), and the Cucumber-like leaves are 3 in. long and 3 in. broad, with seven lobes. The edges of the lobes are wavy and bear minute spines. Opposite each leaf is a long, slender tendril, and from the axils of the leaves the flowers are produced. They are solitary, dioecious (male and female organs in separate flowers), yellow, five-petaled and 1 in. in diameter.

Plants with Ornamental Fruits. The fruits are oblong, pointed, furrowed from end to end, and covered with tubercles (small lumps). When ripe, they are yellow and contain large flat seeds covered with bright red pulp. As soon as the seeds are ready for dispersal, the fruits split open at the tip into three segments. These curl backwards and the red seeds displayed against the yellow of the seed coats are very attractive. In tropical countries, the pulp surrounding the seeds is eaten by the natives and the fruits are used for medicinal purposes.

The Balsam Apple, M. Balsamita, is a more slender and graceful plant than the Balsam Pear, M. Charantia, and is not pubescent (hairy). Its fruits are more or less egg-shaped, orange-colored, and less conspicuously warty than those of the Balsam Pear. At maturity the fruits split open, but the seeds lack the splendid coloring that makes those of the Balsam Pear so attractive.

Outdoors in the South. In the South, Momordicas grow readily from seeds sown outdoors, where the plants are to grow, in spring. They are excellent vines for covering porches and trellises. M. Charantia is naturalized in the far South.

Cultivation in the North. In the North the plants should be sown early in spring in a greenhouse with a minimum temperature of 55 degrees; 4- to 5-in. pots are used for seed-growing. These are well drained and a thin layer of rough siftings of compost is placed over the crocks to prevent the soil from washing down into the drainage and blocking it up. A sandy seed soil is suitable. Three seeds are then set in each pot. They are sown half an inch deep and should be set on their sides to prevent rotting. The soil is then moistened with a fine spray, a pane of glass is laid over the pot, and this is placed in the warmest part of the greenhouse. If a propagating case with bottom heat is available, germination will be much quicker.

As soon as the seedlings appear above the soil, the glass is removed and they are exposed to full light, but shaded from the direct rays of the sun. When the first leaf has developed, each plant is potted separately in a 3-in. pot, well watered and shaded. Root action is very rapid and in a week or so the plants will be ready for repotting in 5-in. pots. When well rooted in these, and after the weather is really warm and settled, they may be planted outdoors in a sheltered, sunny spot in rich soil that never suffers from drought.

Details of Management in Pots. When these plants are grown in pots in a greenhouse, the pots are well drained with crocks covered with a thin layer of dried manure. A 2-in. layer of compost is then placed in the pots and made firm. The plants are removed from the small pots, and set in the center of the pot or tub, the compost filled in and made firm; sufficient space must be left at the top for watering. They are then set close to the wall or near the roof and the shoots are trained to wires or a trellis. Alternatively, a tripod of canes can be fixed in the pots, and the shoots trained to these. The best results are obtained by planting them in a

Fruit of the Balsam Pear, Momordica Charantia.

mound of soil on the greenhouse bench. A pailful of the compost is heaped on the bench and the plants are set in the center; as the roots penetrate through the mound, more soil is added until growth ceases in the autumn.

When the plants are in vigorous growth, they require abundance of water, and the compost must not be allowed to become dry or the fruits will drop. When the fruits are forming freely, dilute liquid fertilizer is applied twice a week. The end of each shoot is pinched out just above the leaf beyond each fruit as soon as it has set. A moist atmosphere and shade from bright sunlight are essential.

MONARCH OF THE EAST. Sauromatum guttatum, which see.

MONARDA—*Bee Balm, Bergamot, Horse Mint* (Monar'da). Hardy herbaceous perennial plants which grow wild in North America and belong to the Mint family, Labiatae. The name commemorates Nicolas Monardes, a Spanish botanist.

These plants flourish in ordinary garden soil, and may be planted in autumn or spring. They are easily propagated by lifting the clumps, preferably in early spring, separating them into rooted pieces and replanting the latter at about 18 in. apart. Natural species, but not improved garden varieties, are also easily raised from seeds sown in spring.

The favorite kind is Monarda didyma (Oswego Tea) a plant which has aromatic leaves, and in summer bears heads of red flowers on leafy stems about 2 ft. in height. It is an attractive plant for the herbaceous border and wild garden and spreads quickly, soon forming a good-sized clump.

Other Good Kinds. The Lemon Mint, Monarda pectinata, bears rose-pink blooms on stems about 2 ft. high. The plant called Wild Bergamot, Monarda fistulosa, is more vigorous and will reach a height of 3-4 ft. in good soil; the flowers are of lilac or purplish coloring. Other kinds are sometimes grown in wild gardens. All have aromatic leaves, and flower from July onwards.

In addition to the wild species there are several fine garden varieties of Monarda, notably Cambridge Scarlet, scarlet; Croftway Pink, pink; Mrs. Perry, crimson-red; Adam, red; Mahogany, very deep red; and violacea superba, purplish.

After two or three years the old plants of Monarda often become bare in their centers, and it is a good plan to lift them in early autumn and separate them into pieces for replanting. The weak middle parts of the plants should be discarded, the young outer portions alone being replanted.

MONARDELLA (Monardel'la). Hardy annual or perennial herbaceous plants, with scented leaves, which are closely allied to the Bee Balm or Bergamot, Monarda. They grow wild in western North America and belong to the Mint family, Labiatae. The name is a diminutive of Monarda.

These plants flourish in ordinary garden soil, may be planted in autumn or spring, and are increased by lifting and separating the clumps into rooted pieces for immediate replanting in October.

The chief perennial kind is M. macrantha, a plant which spreads quickly, grows about 9 in. high and bears scarlet flowers in summer. M. villosa, 18 in. tall, with purple, pink or white flowers, is also sometimes cultivated. M. candicans is an annual plant which may be sown out of doors in early spring; it grows about 12 in. high and bears white flowers.

MONDO. Ophiopogon, which see.

MONESES (Mone'ses). A genus of only one

Monarda Croftway Pink has heads of soft pink flowers.

species, M. uniflora. The name is from *monos,* single, and *esis,* delight, and refers to the charm of the solitary flowers. This plant belongs to the Shinleaf family, the Pyrolaceae.

Moneses uniflora is a native of the Northern Hemisphere and an extremely beautiful plant. It is also very difficult to cultivate. It has little rounded, evergreen leaves and large, solitary, saucer-shaped, white, fragrant flowers, borne singly on erect 6-in. stems, in June. The most likely way to succeed with this strange plant is to dig it up in a large, deep sod of its native moss and Pine leaves, transport it whole to a position in the garden as much like that which it inhabited as possible, and then hope for the best. M. uniflora may be dependent on some special condition, such as root association with Pine trees or other vegetation.

MONEYWORT. Lysimachia Nummularia, which see.

MONGOLIAN LINDEN. Tilia mongolica, which see.

MONILARIA (Monilar'ia). Dwarf South African succulent plants allied to Mesembryanthemum and requiring essentially the same cultural care. They belong to the botanical family Aizoaceae. The name is derived from the Latin *monile,* a necklace, and alludes to the fact that the stems are constricted into beadlike joints.

Kinds grown include M. chrysoleuca, about 4 in. tall, white with yellow stamens; M. pisiforme, 2-4 in., yellow, white and pink, stamens red with yellow anthers; M. moniliformis, 4 in., white with yellow stamens.

MONKEY FLOWER. See Mimulus.

MONKEY PUZZLE. See Araucaria araucana.

MONKSHOOD. See Aconitum.

MONOCARPIC. A botanical term meaning fruiting only once, e.g., annuals and biennials.

MONOCHAETUM (Monochae'tum). Tender evergreen flowering shrubs, from tropical America, which belong to the family Melastomaceae. They grow about 2 ft. in height, have ovate, hairy leaves with prominent parallel veins and small purple, red, or rose-colored flowers in early spring. They are little known in cultivation and cannot be expected to thrive where hot summers prevail. The name Monochaetum is from *monos,* one, and *chaite,* bristle, and refers to the connective of the anther of these shrubs.

Flowering Shrubs for a Cool Greenhouse. These shrubs require a minimum winter temperature of 45 degrees, and the best compost consists of equal parts of loam and leaf mold, with a little decayed manure and a free admixture of sand. Repotting is done in March. The shoots are first shortened by two thirds, and frequently syringed to make them break into growth. They are then repotted in pots two sizes larger. These must be well drained with crocks, which are covered with a thin layer of the rough siftings from the compost. After the plants have been transferred to the new pots, the compost is made firm with a potting stick.

Summer and Winter Management. After potting, the shrubs are shaded from sunshine, and the foliage is syringed two or three times daily, to assist root action. When well rooted, they are placed in a light, well-ventilated position in the greenhouse, to ripen the shoots for flower production. During the summer, water must be applied freely to the soil, and liquid fertilizer given twice a week. From September to March the soil is watered only when it becomes fairly dry.

When to Take Cuttings. Propagation is by inserting cuttings in March. Shoots 3 in. in length are taken off the old plants; the leaves from the lower half of the stem are removed, and a cut is made below the bottom node. Pots 3 in. in diameter are used for the cuttings. These are half-filled with crocks, which are covered with a thin layer of moss or leaves, and the pots filled with equal quantities of loam, leaf mold and sand sifted through a fine mesh sieve. The cuttings are inserted around the edges of the pots, and made firm, and the compost is thoroughly moistened. After the surplus water has drained away, the pots of cuttings are plunged in moist peat up to their rims in a propagating case with a bottom heat.

The case is kept closed to maintain a moist atmosphere, which prevents the leaves from wilting. Each morning the top of the frame is raised for a few moments, and the underside of the glass is wiped dry to prevent condensed moisture from falling on the cuttings and setting up decay. When roots have formed, which is indicated by the shoots commencing to grow, more air is given each day, and eventually the pots of cuttings are placed on the greenhouse benches.

The rooted cuttings are then potted separately in 3-in. pots, and subsequently into larger pots. The tops of the main shoots must be pinched off when these are 4 in. in length, and the subsequent side shoots should be treated in a similar manner; the plants will then be well branched.

The chief kinds are M. alpestre, red; M. Humboldtianum, red and purple; and M. Bonplandii (sericeum), mauve.

MONOCOTYLEDON. The Monocotyledons comprise one of the great groups of flowering plants. As the name indicates, they are distinguished by the possession of a single cotyledon or seed leaf. That is to say, the embryo which is contained in the seed possesses only one leaf, in contradistinction to the two seed leaves or cotyledons of the other great group of flowering plants, the Dicotyledons.

As a group, the Monocotyledons are mainly herbaceous, but a few attain the dimensions and character of trees, e.g., the Palms, Dracaenas and Bananas. Contrasting with these forms with upright stems there are many with underground creeping stems or rhizomes (e.g., Iris). The majority of our garden bulbs are Monocotyledons (e.g., Daffodil, Hyacinth and Snowdrop).

All Grasses, both the ornamental types of the garden and those of the meadow and pasture, and including all true cereals, e.g., wheat, oats, barley, etc., are Monocotyledons. The Sugar Cane, which grows to a height of 6-10 ft., and the treelike Bamboos are also included in this group of plants.

MONOECIOUS. A botanical term indicating that the male and female organs are borne in different flowers on the same plant. The word is derived from *monos,* one, and *oikos,* a home.

MONOMERIA (Monome'ria). Evergreen epiphytal orchids which are found wild in North India and Burma. They require a greenhouse in which a warm, moist atmosphere is maintained during summer, and in which the temperature will not fall below 55 degrees in winter. They belong to the family Orchidaceae. The name Monomeria is derived from *monos,* one, and *meris,* a part, and refers to the single-celled anther.

Owing to the straggling habit of growth of the plants, orchid baskets are more suitable than pots for most kinds; provided the compost of three parts of osmunda fiber and one part of sphagnum moss is replenished annually, the plants may remain in the baskets for some years. An increased stock is obtained by cutting off pieces of the rhizomes, each piece having three or four pseudobulbs. Both pseudobulbs and leaves are of hard texture, indicating the need of very infrequent watering during the winter and free exposure to light in the autumn. In summer the plants should be watered liberally, but not too heavily shaded.

The best kind is M. dichroma, from Annam, which bears about nine flowers on a stem, yellow, with dark crimson lip. M. barbata produces a greater number of flowers which are slightly smaller, yellowish, shaded and suffused with reddish-brown.

MONOPHYLLUS. A botanical term meaning having only one leaf.

MONSTERA (Monster'a). Tropical evergreen climbing plants with ornamental fruits and foliage. They are found growing wild in tropical America, Mexico and Costa Rica and belong to the Arum family, Araceae. The derivation of name Monstera is not determined but it probably means monstrous and has reference to the size of the plants or fruits.

The kind chiefly grown in hothouses and as a house plant in North America is M. deliciosa, sometimes called Philodendron pertusum. This plant, known as the Ceriman, in the tropics produces delicious edible fruits, but the fruits are rarely borne outside the tropics. It has woody branches which cling to trees by means of long, cordlike aerial roots developed along the whole length of the stems. It has large, deeply divided leaves, which are leathery in texture and perforated with large holes. The leafstalks are 1-2 ft. long and sheath around the stems at their bases. The flowers, which are surrounded by a spathe, like those of the Calla Lily, are yellow and produce a cylindrical pineapple-like fruit which is edible and has a taste said to be midway between that of the Pineapple and Banana.

A Tropical Climbing Plant. This plant does best in a winter temperature of 60-70 degrees,

Monstera deliciosa, a handsome foliage plant for greenhouse cultivation.

and a compost of three parts of turfy loam, two of peat moss or leaf mold, one of coarse sand and one of well-decayed manure. It is of vigorous growth and therefore only suitable for large hothouses or conservatories and for indoor use in large rooms where a bold foliage effect is required. Planting is done in February or March.

Wires or a trellis should be fixed to the wall and roof, to which the shoots should be trained. During the summer the plants require plenty of water to keep them in vigorous growth. The atmosphere in the greenhouse must be kept moist by frequently damping the floor and benches and syringing daily. Shade is provided during the sunny part of the day. During the winter, water is given to the soil only when it becomes fairly dry, and less atmospheric moisture is required.

Pruning consists of shortening extra vigorous shoots and thinning out weak growths in spring.

Propagation Is by Stem Cuttings. The stems are cut up into lengths, each consisting of 3 or 4 joints. Each piece is inserted in a propagating case heated to 75 degrees. When well rooted, they are potted separately in 4-in. pots and returned to the glass case until established. The next move is into 6- or 7-in. pots.

The chief kind, M. deliciosa, has yellow flowers and pineapple-like fruits. It makes a good house plant in a young state and stands shade well. Other kinds are M. acuminata, M. Friedrichsthalii, and M. dubia.

MONTANA, GARDENING IN. See Regional Gardening.

MONTBRETIA (Montbre'tia). The Montbretias of gardens are hybrids of Crocosmia aurea and C. Pottsii, cormous plants from South Africa. The original hybrid was named Crocosmia (Tritonia) crocosmiiflora. This was raised in France in 1880; since then, a large range of beautiful hybrids has been produced, which have largely

Monstera Friedrichsthaliana has attractive perforated leaves.

Montbretia Lady Wilson, yellow, shaded orange, one of the modern Earlham hybrids.

superseded the older kinds. The latter, however, are the hardier, and will thrive and multiply rapidly in any light garden soil of average fertility, in a well-drained, sunny position.

The modern hybrids are more vigorous than the old type, producing from July onwards spikes up to 3 ft. tall of large, richly colored flowers that are valuable for garden display and cutting. They are not hardy in the North. In milder areas they are perennial or can be overwintered by covering the site with a thick layer of weathered ashes; otherwise it is best to treat them like Gladioli, by lifting the corms in autumn and storing them under dry, frostproof conditions for the winter.

When to Plant. The corms may be planted in early spring, in sunny, well-drained borders, and should be set 3 in. deep and 6 in. apart. In cold districts it is worth while to start the corms in pots in a greenhouse or cold frame, planting them out, without disturbing the roots, in May. They are propagated by offsets.

If desired, these hybrid Montbretias can be raised from seed, sown as soon as ripe, in a greenhouse or frame, but they will not, of course, come true to the color of the variety from which they were saved. In spring the seedlings should be set singly in small pots and grown in these until they die off naturally in the autumn. The following spring they can be planted out in nursery beds.

Earlham Montbretias. Some of the most striking of the Earlham hybrid Montbretias are Aurora, orange; Fiery Cross, orange and red; George Davison, pure yellow; His Majesty, very large, crimson-scarlet, with yellow center; Lady Hamilton, apricot-orange; Lady Wilson, yellow, shaded orange; Lord Nelson, orange-scarlet; R. H. C. Jenkinson, orange-red, yellow center; and Star of the East, large, orange.

MONTEREY CYPRESS. Cupressus macrocarpa, which see.

MONTEREY PINE. See Pinus radiata.

MONTEZUMA CYPRESS. Taxodium mucronatum, which see.

MONTHLY ROSE. A name given to an old pink China Rose, Rosa indica.

MONTICOLA. A name indicating mountain-loving.

MOON DAISY. Chrysanthemum uliginosum, which see.

MOON FERN. Botrychium, which see.

MOON FLOWER. Calonyction, which see.

MOONSEED. Menispermum, which see.

MOONSEED, CAROLINA. Cocculus carolinus, which see.

MOONWORT. A name applied to Botrychium and to Lunaria.

MOOSEWOOD. See Acer Pennsylvanicum.

MORAEA—*Butterfly Iris* (Mora'ea). Corm-forming or rhizomatous plants from South Africa, closely related to Iris and belonging to the family Iridaceae. They are showy plants well adapted for growing outdoors in California and similar mild climates. They require full sun and light, well-drained soil. They are also suitable for growing in sunny greenhouses where, at night, winter temperatures of 40-50 degrees are maintained. The genus is named in honor of R. Moore, an English botanist.

Species in cultivation include M. bicolor, 2 ft., yellow, with purple-brown blotch; M. iridioides, 1-2 ft., white, with yellow or brown spots and lavender shading; M. papilionacea, 6 in., red to pale blue, spotted dark blue and with yellow markings; M. pavonia, 1-2 ft., orange-red, with green-black blotch; M. ramosa, 2-3 ft., golden-yellow; M. spathacea, 1 ft., yellow, fragrant; and M. tristis, 1 ft., brown, with yellow spot. The Moraeas bloom in spring and early summer. They are easily propagated by division in spring and by seeds.

MORAINE or SCREE GARDEN
It Solves the Problem of Growing Many Difficult Alpine Plants

The words Moraine and Scree, as applied to rock gardening, are interchangeable terms for practically the same thing.

A natural moraine in the Alps is a mass of crushed and broken rock, carried down by a glacier, and deposited at its base. There is usually a flow of water percolating through a moraine, supplied by the melting ice of the glacier above. Certain types of alpine plants are found inhabiting active moraines and are specially adapted for life among the loose stony material of which moraines are formed. When transplanted to the close-binding loam soils of the ordinary rock garden, many of these plants are incapable of existing under such entirely different conditions.

A natural scree, on the other hand, is a mass of very similar rock detritus, piled up against the foot of a cliff or mountainside. But a scree is not fed by the same underground percolation of ice water as a moraine. Screes, however, are inhabited by types of plants very like those which are found on moraines, plants which are specially adapted to growing among loose stony material in which there is only a small percentage of loam or humus.

Imitation Moraines. Rock gardeners, having found by experience that such plants were difficult to cultivate under ordinary rock-garden conditions, experimented in the direction of providing small imitation moraines. The early moraine gardens were made by filling a section of the rock garden with a rough imitation of the real moraine material, broken stone or rock with only a very small amount of soil added, and many of them were further provided with arrangements of pipes, etc., by which the underground water flow could be imitated. This water flow could be turned on or off at will.

Some of these arrangements were highly ingenious, and a few of them achieved good results. Practical experiment, however, showed that this artificial underground irrigation was an unnecessary complication, and often a dangerous one. It was found that equally good results could be obtained without such elaborate and costly arrangements, and that all that was necessary to grow the plants of both moraines and screes was to fill a portion of the rock garden with moraine or scree material, broken stone with a minimum of loam added, and leave it at that. Without the underground water supply it was no longer a moraine, and so the name scree is really more appropriate.

The late Reginald Farrer, a noted English

The gray-leaved Artemisia frigida flourishing in a moraine garden.

Androsace villosa, which obviously appreciates its favored location in a moraine.

This moraine is being built with an underground watering system. Its foundation consists of three concrete basins at slightly different levels. The basins are filled with rocks and crushed stone. When they are completed, a constant stream of water will flow through the stones from the highest to the lowest basin and from there to an outlet. The foundation is covered with a scree or moraine mixture to form a gentle slope studded with rocks.

gardener, was one of the earliest experimenters with moraines. It was probably he who coined the term moraine garden, and it was he who first wrote about them and made the system generally known. It was an important advance in rock gardening, and made relatively easy the cultivation of many beautiful but otherwise difficult alpine plants. The modification of the moraine to the simpler scree has now brought the system within the reach of a far wider circle of gardeners than could face the trouble and expense of elaborate underground irrigation.

How to Make a Moraine or Scree. The area used may vary greatly—it may cover many square yards of ground, or it may be not much larger than a sizable table top. The simplest way to explain its making is to assume that the owner of an existing garden wishes to experiment by converting part of the rock garden. He should select a patch of soil with an open sunny exposure. We will suppose that the selected site slopes gently south or southwest, is roughly 6 ft. in length from top to bottom, and 3 ft. wide. It is surrounded and contained by well-laid rocks. The soil must be removed to a depth of 2 ft.

Drainage Is Important. Rough drainage should be put in the bottom—broken bricks, clinkers, or broken stone—to a depth of 6 in. or so. Next, the scree mixture must be prepared. This should consist of broken stone and loam mixture in the proportion of three parts stone to one part loam mixture. Any broken rock will do—limestone, granite, sandstone, millstone grit, or whatever is most easily procured locally. A porous stone is preferable, and although limestone is excellent for the majority of plants, its use will preclude the cultivation of a few lime haters.

Part of the finished moraine with alpine plants thriving in it.

The soil mixture to be added to the broken stone may consist of leaf mold, loam and sand, and this mixture is best made in the proportion of two thirds leaf mold and the other third loam and sand, half and half. In giving these proportions it should be explained that they need not be followed rigidly as though one were dealing with dangerous drugs. The important thing is to keep the scree mixture very poor in soil. The stone chips should really only be made dirty with soil. If too much loam is used, the mixture will consolidate and lose its special virtue of openness and looseness.

As to the size of the stone chips used, they should not be too small and fine—not less than an average of half-inch chips. Road-mending chips are usually graded to a size, and it is not a bad thing to obtain, if possible two grades or sizes and mix them. If naturally broken stone can be obtained from a local quarry, this is, of course, an advantage.

Having prepared the scree mixture, all that remains to be done is to fill up the rest of the excavated site with it. The scree is then ready for planting.

Apart from the free, loose rooting medium it affords to the special plants which enjoy and even require such conditions, the scree has the great virtue of absorbing water quickly, and retaining it for a long time. A can of water soaks in just as fast as it is poured on, and it soaks rapidly down through the stones as it could never soak into ordinary loam; and, having soaked in, it is retained by the scree far longer than it would be by ordinary loamy soil. It is this rapid absorption and long retention of water which makes artificial underground irrigation of the scree unnecessary.

Moraine Plants. Most of the "difficult" high alpine plants can be grown successfully, or at least are worth attempting, in the moraine or scree, especially the rarer Androsaces, Anemones, Campanulas, Dianthus, Drabas, Gentiana verna and others; Geranium Farreri, numerous Saxifragas, Wahlenbergias, etc.

MORELLO CHERRY. See Cherry, English Morello.

MORICANDIA SONCHIFOLIA. See Orychophragmus.

MORINA—*Whorlflower* (Mori′na). Hardy perennial herbaceous plants, with spiny leaves and flowers produced in whorls. They are natives of the Himalayas, and belong to the Teasel family, Dipsaceae. They grow from 12 in. to 3 ft. in height, have thistle-like leaves 6 in. long and 1 in. across, and whorls of red, yellow or purple flowers in summer.

The most popular kind, M. longifolia, grows 3 ft. in height. This is a handsome border plant; the flowers open white, change to a delicate

Morina longifolia, a hardy plant which belongs to the Scabious family, has ornamental leaves, and flowers in summer.

pink and finally to crimson. All three stages are found on the same whorl of bloom, producing a charming effect. Morina is named after Louis Morin, a French botanist.

For a Sheltered Location. In the North these plants require a location which is sheltered from cold winds, and well-drained soil. The site is prepared by deep digging and incorporating liberal quantities of compost. Planting is done in October or spring, and the plants are set from 1-2 ft. apart, according to the kinds.

Raising Seedlings. Propagation is by seeds or division. Seeds are sown in a cold frame in fall or spring. When 2 in. high, the seedlings are set out in seed boxes, 3 in. apart; when large enough, they are planted in their permanent positions.

Division of the roots is best done when flowering is finished, otherwise in spring. The plant is lifted carefully to avoid damaging the roots, and the clump is separated into small portions, with roots attached.

The chief kinds are M. longifolia, 2 ft., white, pink and crimson; M. Coulteriana, 18 in., yellow; and M. persica, 18 in. white.

MORINDA—Indian Mulberry, Royoc (Morin'da). A group of tropical trees and shrubs, some of which produce edible fruits and some of which yield dyes. They belong to the Madder family, Rubiaceae, and are suited for planting outdoors in the warmest sections of the United States only. The name is derived from Morus, Mulberry, and *indica,* Indian.

Morindas are of easy cultivation in a variety of soils. They may be propagated by seeds, air layering, and cuttings.

Two kinds are most commonly seen. One is M. citrifolia, the Indian Mulberry, which is a native of southeastern Asia and Australia and forms a small, smooth-leaved tree. The other is M. Royoc, the Royoc, which is a native of the West Indies and Florida and forms a vinelike or erect shrub to about 4 ft. tall. It is sometimes known as Wild Mulberry and Yawweed.

M. citrifolia yields yellow and red dyes from its roots and flowers. Its fruits are edible; they have an odor somewhat resembling that of aged cheese. A red dye is also obtained from the bark of the roots of the Indian and Malayan species, M. tinctoria.

MORINGA—*Horse-radish Tree, Ben Tree* (Morin'ga). A small group of tropical leaf-losing trees, one of which is sometimes planted in the warmest parts of the United States. Moringa belongs to the Moringa family, Moringaceae. The name is from *Moringo,* the Malabar name for M. oleifera.

Moringa oleifera grows without trouble in southern California, southern Florida and in similar climates. It flowers and fruits freely and continuously. The flowers are fragrant; the foliage may be eaten as greens; the young pods are edible; the root is usable as a substitute for Horse-Radish and the seeds yield a nondrying oil known as ben oil, which is used in the arts.

M. oleifera forms a rather slender tree, about 25 ft. tall, with drooping branches and feathery foliage. It is decidedly ornamental and is propagated by seeds, cuttings and air layering.

MORISIA (Moris'ia). Morisia monantha (hypogaea) is a pretty dwarf rock-garden plant which is found wild only in Corsica and Sardinia. It belongs to the Mustard family, Cruciferae. The name commemorates Professor J. H. Moris.

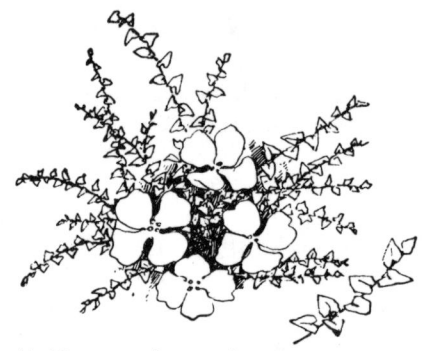

Morisia monantha, a charming little yellow-flowered plant for the rock garden.

The leaves are dark glossy-green, pinnate or feather-shaped, 2-3 in. long, and are arranged in a rosette lying out flat upon the ground. The flowers, which appear in early spring and are extremely showy, resemble small Wallflower blossoms, about ½ in. in diameter. They are of golden color, and each is carried on a ½-in. stem, well down among the leaves. This low, compact mass of gold amid the emerald foliage is most effective, the whole plant having a neat, spruce appearance which makes it suitable for the rock garden, although actually it is not a mountain plant.

A Rock Plant for Lime Soil. Morisia delights in deep, sandy loam containing lime. The plant should be given deep rooting space, good drainage, and a southern or southwestern aspect. Although not difficult to grow, Morisia monantha is choice enough and beautiful enough to deserve some little extra attention; it has a craving for lime that should be satisfied.

Raising Seedlings. After flowering, seed pods are formed, and it is curious to note that the flower stems bend downwards in such a way as to bury the seed capsules at the base of the plant.

In order to propagate Morisia, therefore, the plant must be carefully examined, the seed vessels raised up from their self-burial, collected, and sown in a pot of light, rich loam with plenty of lime in it, in a cold shady frame. Prick out the seedlings when large enough, and, later on, plant them out on the rock garden in well-prepared sites.

Taking Root Cuttings. Morisia monantha may also be increased by means of root cuttings. A plant must be dug up about April and the thonglike roots cut into lengths of 1 in. or 1½ in. These may either be laid flat on a pan of sand and covered with sand to a depth of ¼ in., or they may be dibbled into the sand in an upright position. In either case the pan must be placed in a cold frame, well shaded, and carefully watered.

In a few weeks the root cuttings will send out fresh rootlets at their lower ends, and leaves at their upper ends. They must then be potted and grown for subsequent planting out on the rock garden.

For the Cool Greenhouse. Morisia monantha is a fine plant for growing in the cool greenhouse, but to get the best results it is advisable to procure extra-deep pots to accommodate the very long roots.

As this charming little plant blooms in early spring it responds well to the conditions of the cool greenhouse, there flowering a little earlier than in the open air, and developing its brilliant flowers to greater perfection.

MORMODES—*Goblin Orchid* (Mormo'des). A distinct group of epiphytal Orchids found wild in Central America, Mexico, Brazil and Peru. In general appearance the plants much resemble the allied Orchid, Catasetum. They have stout pseudobulbs and the flowers are remarkable for their curious structure. The name Mormodes is derived from *mormo*, a goblin, from the various shapes of the flowers.

Hothouse Orchids. All are hothouse Orchids and require, during summer, a temperature of 70 degrees at night. In winter the night temperature should be about 60 degrees. During the summer the plants enjoy a moist atmosphere with shading from hot sunshine. In autumn the pseudobulbs must be exposed to full light to harden and ripen them for the winter.

The actual growing season is rather short, and when the plants are in full vigor water may be given freely. In winter very little water is required. The potting compost should consist of cut osmunda fiber or of Fir bark or Redwood bark; small flower pans which can be suspended are preferable to pots. No attempt should be made to excite the plants into growth in early spring, but as soon as signs of growth are observed the old compost should be carefully removed and

A plant of the Goblin Orchid, Mormodes, in bloom.

the plants repotted. The flowers are usually seen in late summer and autumn.

The Chief Kinds. In M. Buccinator, called the Trumpet Orchid, the lip is trumpet-shaped and may be white, yellow or pink; the sepals and petals are usually green. M. pardina is yellow, thickly spotted with red. M. Colossus has flowers 5 in. or more across, red shaded with yellow; the lip is usually bright yellow spotted with red. Several species, M. aromaticum, M. pardina, M. Cartonii and others, are fragrant.

MORNING GLORY. See Ipomoea.

MORNING GLORY, SILVERY. See Argyreia splendens.

MOROCCO TOADFLAX. See Linaria maroccana.

MORUS—*Mulberry* (Mo'rus). Leaf-losing trees of Asia and North America. They are sometimes of considerable size, but, when growing in the open, often develop with a short, stout trunk and a dense, rather wide head of branches. Morus belongs to the family Moraceae, and the name is the old Latin name for the Mulberry. For cultivation, see Mulberry.

Mulberry trees are long-lived, and have a habit of rejuvenating themselves, even though they may have fallen into a state of decay, for a sprout may start from a dormant bud near the base of an old tree and from a strong, young stem. Trees that have been blown down, and have some of the roots exposed, may continue to grow and fruit for many years. The Mulberry withstands impure atmospheric conditions better than many trees, and so thrives well in cities.

The Mulberries can be increased in summer by cuttings of young wood placed in a cold frame kept close, by cuttings of ripened wood placed out of doors in winter, and by seeds. Trees resulting from self-sown seeds are common. The best soil for these trees is well-drained loam.

The Black Mulberry. Morus nigra, the Black Mulberry, grows 25-35 ft. high, with a dense head of heart-shaped leaves. The leaves are usually entire (of even outline), but in young trees and vigorous shoots they may be separated into several lobes. The fruits, like giant Raspberries, ripen in August and September; they are dark red, almost black, when ripe. They stain anything they touch, and so care should be taken when they are falling. To remove the stains from the hands after gathering the fruits, take a few unripe fruits and rub them well into the dark stains on the skin, then wash in the ordinary way, and the stains will disappear.

The Black Mulberry is little known in North America, although it is grown to some extent in the southern United States. An Asiatic species, it is the classical Mulberry of history.

The White Mulberry. M. alba, the White Mulberry, is a very variable Chinese tree, and the kind from which most of the fruiting varieties grown in North America have been derived. It is freely naturalized in many parts of the United States. The leaves vary a good deal in shape on different trees, and the small fruits may be white or pinkish. The leaves are widely used in China for feeding silkworms. M. alba variety Kingan is a fruitless form recommended as a street tree.

The Red Mulberry. M. rubra, the Red or American Mulberry, is native from Massachusetts to Florida and Texas. It is the largest of the Mulberries, in the South attaining heights of 60-70 ft. and girths of 3-4 ft. Its wood is employed for light carpentry and as posts. The fruit is dark red or, when ripe, black, and is pleasant to eat. Some of the named fruit-bearing Mulberries are varieties of this species. The leaves of the Red Mulberry vary greatly in shape on the same tree.

MOSCHOSMA. See Iboza.

MOSES-IN-A-BOAT. See Rhoeo discolor.

MOSS. The gardener finds some kinds of moss very useful for lining the bottom and sides of wire baskets in which various plants of drooping growth are cultivated. The moss prevents the soil from falling out and forms a base on which to set the compost. Moss is often used by exhibitors at flower shows to cover the stands on which the blooms are displayed. It is attractive on shady paths and woodland banks, where it can be encouraged to grow by watering with liquid cow manure. On lawns, however, it can prove a serious menace to the grasses, and must be eliminated. Moss in lawns usually indicates poor subsurface drainage, excessive compaction of the soil, lack of fertility, or soil that is much too acid. See also Mosses and Moss, Sphagnum.

MOSS CAMPION. Silene acaulis, which see.

MOSS, CLUB. Lycopodium, which see.

MOSSES. The Mosses form a large section of plants which differ in many ways from flowering plants. They do not grow to any considerable height and are found on tufts in a variety of situations. The slender stems are soft and fleshy and are covered with minute green or brown leaves. The roots of mosses are like slender filaments, and are known as rhizoids. They serve the same function as roots, by fixing the plants in the soil and absorbing nourishment.

The moss plant does not produce flowers, but bears sexual organs. These are to be found at the tips of the shoots in the center of a crowded rosette of leaves. The rosette is, in appearance, not unlike a flower, especially as the center is frequently of a reddish color. In this cup-shaped rosette the sexual organs are formed. The male and female organs may be both on the same plant or on different plants.

The male cells or sperms reach the female by swimming to them through the drops of water which collect in the cuplike formation of leaves at the tips of the shoots, and fertilization takes place. The fertilized egg cell gives rise to a capsule bearing spores. The spores, when ripe, are dispersed by the wind, and those which alight on moist ground germinate and give rise to a short green thread (protonema). This bears a number of buds, each of which is capable of developing into a moss plant.

MOSS, FLOWERING. Pyxidanthera barbulata, which see.

MOSSING. See Air Layering.

MOSS PINK. Phlox subulata, which see.

MOSS ROSE. See Rosa centifolia muscosa.

MOSS, SPANISH. Tillandsia usneoides, which see.

MOSS, SPHAGNUM. A moss which is used chiefly for mixing with the potting compost for Orchids and such plants as Nepenthes, Anthurium, and Drosera. Chopped or milled Sphagnum is an excellent, sterile medium in which to sow seeds. It can also be used in place of soil as a medium in which to grow pot plants to maturity provided a regular program of fertilizing is followed. The botanical name is Sphagnum, which see.

MOSS VERBENA. Verbena tenuisecta, which see.

MOTHER OF THOUSANDS. See Cymbalaria muralis, the botanical name. This name is also applied to Saxifraga sarmentosa, which see.

MOTHER OF THYME. Thymus Serpyllum, which see.

MOTH MULLEIN. Verbascum Blattaria, which see.

MOUND LAYERING. See Layering.

MOUNTAIN ASH. See Sorbus.

MOUNTAIN AVENS. See Dryas.

MOUNTAIN EBONY. See Bauhinia.

MOUNTAIN FLEECE. Polygonum amplexicaule, which see.

MOUNTAIN FRINGE. Adlumia fungosa, which see.

MOUNTAIN HOLLY. Nemopanthus mucronata and Prunus ilicifolia, which see.

MOUNTAIN LAUREL. Kalmia latifolia, which see.

MOUNTAIN MINT. See Pycnanthemum.

MOUNTAIN SPINACH. See Atriplex.

MOUNT ATLAS CEDAR. See Cedrus atlantica.

MOURNING BRIDE. Scabiosa, which see.

MOURNING CYPRESS. Cupressus funebris, which see.

MOWING. Lawns must be mown regularly to give them a well-kept and attractive appearance, but much depends on the way in which the mowing is done, as explained under the heading of Lawns: The Perfect Setting For Garden Flowers.

MUD FROM PONDS. Mud which is recovered from rivers, streams and ponds contains, as a rule, much organic matter or humus, and it is on that account useful for digging into garden soils to enrich them. It is best scattered on the land in winter and allowed to lie for a few weeks so that the weather may "sweeten" it, then it is dug in. A dusting of lime or gypsum is beneficial. Should the mud be secured in late spring or summer, it should be placed in a heap (with turf walls to retain it, if necessary), and left there until late autumn or winter, when it may be dug into the soil.

MUEHLENBECKIA—*Wire Plants* (Muehlenbeck'ia). Hardy or tender shrubs and trailing plants which are often of climbing growth, sometimes forming dense thickets of wiry branches bearing small dark green or purplish-green leaves. The various kinds are widely distributed in South America, New Zealand, the Solomon Islands, and other countries.

Muehlenbeckia belongs to the Knotweed family, Polygonaceae, and the name was given in commemoration of Dr. Muehlenbeck, a Swiss physician of the early part of the nineteenth century.

The cultivated kinds thrive in light, loamy soil in an open position. Those of vigorous growth may be planted at the foot of a bush, 6-8 ft. high, and allowed to grow at will; eventually, they will cover the bush; dwarfer kinds may be planted on a bank or even on a ledge in the rock garden. They can be increased by cuttings set in sand in a frame, kept shaded and close, in summer, and it is sometimes possible to separate small pieces from the base of older plants in early spring.

M. complexa, Wire Vine, a native of New Zealand, is a suitable plant for outdoor cultivation in mild climates such as that of California. It forms a dense tangled mass of wiry stems 6-8 ft. high, and bears small leaves and yellowish or greenish-white flowers in summer.

M. axillaris is a prostrate plant from New Zealand, Australia and Tasmania, suitable for the rock garden. It is hardy in the North and is often grown under the name of M. nana. Other kinds are M. adpressa, M. chilensis and M. varians. For another plant sometimes called Muehlenbeckia, see Homalocladium.

MULBERRY. The Mulberry, in various species and varieties, is grown for its fruit throughout much of the United States and the milder regions of Canada. Mulberries are not grown commercially, as the fruit is too soft and insipid for market, but a tree or two in a large garden or on a farm is worth while. The fruit ripens over a long period and is useful for the birds, for poultry and pigs, as well as being acceptable for eating out of hand. The fruits are of various colors from white through red to black, and they resemble Blackberries.

In eastern Asia and southern Europe, the Mulberry has long been cultivated for its leaves, which are the food of the silkworm. The development of and rapid increase in the use of synthetic fibers are greatly reducing silk production. Morus alba and M. multicaulis are the silkworm Mulberries.

The White Mulberry, Morus alba, a native of China, is a variable species which has given rise to many forms, among which are pendula, a drooping variety; pyramidalis, a tree of distinct, pyramidal shape; and laciniata, a cut-leaved type.

Improved fruiting varieties have been introduced from time to time, but lack of interest in Mulberries has made it difficult to get them true to name from nurseries. New American is considered the best variety, and it is also sold as Downing, that variety now being rarely grown.

The Russian Mulberry is a race of seedlings of M. alba that is very resistant to cold, drought and neglect, characteristics which have made it popular in the Great Plains region, where it is used for low windbreaks and sheared hedges. It is raised from seeds and is variable, but the fruits are usually inferior and of value only as bird feed.

The native Red Mulberry, M. rubra, grows from Massachusetts to Kansas, and southward to Florida and Texas. In the South it grows on rich soils and reaches 70 feet in height. The varieties Stubbs and Hicks are sometimes planted for hog feed.

The Black Mulberry, M. nigra, from western Asia, is less hardy than the White Mulberry, but it has escaped from cultivation in the South, where it is occasionally cultivated. Black Persian is one variety.

Mulberries are of easy culture, growing on almost any well-drained soil, and apparently without any insect pests or diseases of importance.

Propagation is by seeds and by grafting on seedlings of Russian Mulberry. The ordinary methods are not successful, and flute grafting is done in April. The scion is removed by cutting around it with a two-bladed knife, and is inserted in the stock where a ring of bark has been removed by the same knife. The bud is tied and waxed, except that the bud itself is not covered.

In the South, M. multicaulis is sometimes raised from hardwood cuttings.

MULBERRY, FRENCH. See Callicarpa americana.

MULBERRY, INDIAN. See Morinda citrifolia of southeastern Asia and Australia.

MULBERRY, PAPER. See Broussonetia.

MULBERRY, WILD. See Morinda citrifolia.

MULCHES AND MULCHING

Many Garden Plants Benefit Greatly When the Ground Is Covered with a Mulch

A mulch is any substance, usually an organic material, that is spread on the ground around plants to conserve moisture, prevent erosion and control weeds. A mulch may also be used to cover low-growing plants and provide winter protection. See Protecting Plants.

Mulching, as practiced in gardens, is an adaptation of a natural process. Nature mulches the roots of plants with fallen leaves and with the tops of herbaceous plants and ground covers. There is no repeated cultivation of the surface soil (clean cultivation) where plants grow naturally.

The popularity of mulching as a garden practice has increased greatly in recent years, and its usefulness is generally limited only by the availability of suitable materials at an economical cost. Fruit growers, especially growers of Apples and small fruits, use mulches extensively. Mulching is especially useful to the small commercial growers who do not have the expensive tillage machinery needed for clean cultivation. An advantage to them is that the mulch may be applied during slack periods, whereas cultivation must be done at busy times in spring and summer. Home gardeners more and more are learning to appreciate the value of mulches for flowers, vegetables and shrubbery.

Advantages of Mulching

Mulching has several substantial advantages over clean cultivation as a method of managing the soil in the garden and orchard. These advantages are discussed here for the gardener who may be considering whether to adopt this practice or not.

The greatest advantage of a mulch is the conservation of soil moisture that results from its application. Evaporation from the surface of the soil is greatly reduced by protecting the soil from the direct rays of the sun and moving air. Rain which falls on the mulch is all absorbed and does not pack the soil surface. Erosion, a great destroyer of soil, is eliminated.

A mulch of wood chips around a newly planted tree.

The moisture content of a mulched soil varies much less than that of a clean-cultivated soil in dry seasons, and this uniformity favors root activity and brings other advantages. Uniform growth of Tomatoes, for example, eliminates cracking and blossom end rot, a trouble caused by a fluctuating moisture supply. The size of tree fruits ripening in late summer or fall in a dry year is substantially larger where a mulch is used.

The second important advantage is the control of weeds, particularly annual weeds. Strong-

Tree leaves may be used for mulching.

growing perennial weeds are not controlled by any mulch that it is practicable to maintain in a garden, except an overlapping mulch of special paper or aluminum foil. A mulch greatly reduces the amount of weeding required in the garden. If used in conjunction with a weed killer that kills germinating weed seeds, the benefits in weed control will be greater.

Lower and more uniform soil temperatures in summer follow mulching, and these favor bacterial activity in the soil. High summer temperatures may injure beneficial micro-organisms as well as roots close to the surface and speed the destruction of humus.

Frost penetration under a mulch is much less than where the ground is bare. Where winters are severe and a good snow cover is lacking, the insulating effect of a mulch may prevent serious injury to tender rootstocks and to evergreens that of necessity must absorb moisture from the soil in winter and cannot do so if the soil is frozen to a great depth.

Most mulches improve soil structure and tilth because the decaying organic matter works down into the topsoil. The increased friability (crumbly condition) of the soil favors water penetration, and the better aeration that follows stimulates both biological activity in the soil and growth of the roots. Materials which decay rapidly bring these benefits about more quickly than slowly decomposable materials. Chopped Alfalfa is, for example, much superior to peat moss in achieving a desirable crumbly condition of the soil.

Decaying mulch materials add plant nutrients to the soil. The amount and variety of these vary greatly with the type of mulch used. Some mulches, such as peat moss, Buckwheat hulls and shredded Redwood bark, provide little in the way of actual nutrients; a mulch of partially rotted manure is a rich source of nitrogen as well as other nutrients, and Tobacco stems afford a good supply of potash in addition to some nitrogen and phosphorus. Hay, often favored as an orchard mulch, is an excellent source of plant nutrients and so is good compost, being formed of a variety of vegetable wastes such as leaves, weeds and grass.

A mulch of hay, straw or other organic material has a very beneficial effect on the potash content of the soil and its availability for plant growth. In a clean-cultivated soil, the potash is fixed in an unavailable form in the surface soil and moves downward very slowly because of alternate wetting and drying. In a mulched soil, fixation is very slow under the continuous moisture under the mulch material, and the potash moves downward to the root zone, where the plants can get it. If potash is the limiting nutrient in fruit tree growth and production, or in the growth of other plants, it may be supplied quickly and effectively in conjunction with a mulch.

A mulch prevents the packing of heavy soils either by vehicles or by their being walked upon soon after a rain. This is especially beneficial in the case of clayey soils, which may easily be permanently damaged by such traffic.

Root injury from surface cultivation, which can be much more extensive than is generally thought, is eliminated when a mulch is used. Feeding roots develop in the topsoil just under the mulch. This is normally the best-quality soil, and a mulch makes it possible for the plants to make full use of it. This is especially important with surface-rooting plants such as Rhododendrons, Mountain Laurel, Azaleas and Blueberries.

Some mulches, especially peat moss, Buckwheat hulls, Pine needles, shredded Redwood bark and some others, improve the appearance of the garden, and are especially valuable for covering beds near the house or in other areas where neatness is an important factor.

A mulch prevents the bruising of fruits that drop and land on it rather than on stones, hard ground or stubble. A mulch keeps soil from splashing on Raspberries, Gooseberries, Strawberries, Daffodils and other fruits and flowers that are near the ground.

Mulched orchards can be sprayed earlier in wet weather in the spring, as the spray rigs can get around when they cannot on cultivated ground. The mulch prevents muddy shoes when one is walking among the flowers in the spring or after a heavy rain.

Preventing Winter Injury. Mulches are used to protect low-growing, evergreen plants and somewhat tender plants, including many bulbs, from winter injury from low temperatures when there is no snow cover. Placed around plants newly set out in the fall, a suitable mulch will prevent them from being heaved out of the ground by alternate freezing and thawing during the winter.

Disadvantages of Mulching

The cost and lack of availability of some mulches are a drawback to large-scale mulching, especially on farms. In small gardens, the costs are not generally excessive for the benefits and the area involved. With straw, hay and some other mulches, however, there is a fire hazard. A lighted cigarette carelessly dropped among pine needles, salt hay or dry leaves used as a mulch about shrubs can easily result in the loss of valuable plantings.

Mice are often more serious among mulched plants than others, but they may be controlled by poisoning and trapping. Nitrogen starvation sometimes occurs when sawdust and straw are used as mulches, but this is easily corrected by using additional nitrogen as a fertilizer. If mulches are applied too early in the year to crops that need a warm soil, such as Tomatoes and Corn, growth may be delayed.

These disadvantages, however, are minor compared to the benefits derived from mulching.

Mulching Materials

A suitable mulch for extensive use, to be worth while economically, must be available in quantity from nearby sources. Mulches are grown or purchased, or sometimes may be had for the hauling. Many materials are suitable, but only a few are generally available at reasonable cost. Some of those listed are available only from processors in certain areas. The user of mulches should search out cheap, local sources. Something that may be had free from a nearby source at the user's convenience is probably the most economical material to use if it is suitable for the plant and area to which it is to be applied.

Hays of various types are available wherever grasses are grown. They are suitable for orchards and for use around newly planted trees. Because of their appearance, they are less suitable for many garden purposes than other neater-appearing mulches. Rain-spoiled hay from a dairy farm and roadside hay from the highway department are often available. Orchardists often grow hay between the trees in a young orchard, fertilize it heavily, mow it and rake it around the trees. Land not suitable for fruit because of poor drainage or frost hazard is sometimes used to grow hay for mulching.

Orchard grass will grow on a wide range of soils and, if heavily fertilized with nitrogen, will furnish a nearly complete supply of nutrients for fruit trees, in addition to its mulching effect. Timothy is a high-yielding grass for good soils, and Reed Canary Grass will produce heavily on wet soils not suitable for other crops.

Millets, Sudan Grass and wild grasses from marshlands are all good mulches. Siberian and German Millets sown about June 1st, cut September 1st, and followed by Rye which is cut in the spring, will produce a lot of mulch if fertilized heavily.

An acre of land is needed to produce the mulch for an acre of fruit. Hay is excellent for fruit and the larger vegetables, but not for the flower garden.

Legume hays, Alfalfa, Clovers and Soybeans

are high in nitrogen and are valuable sources of plant nutrients, besides being good mulches. Pea vines are high in nitrogen, and are suitable orchard mulches. With hay, particularly well-fertilized hay or legume hay, the mulch can provide most, if not all, of the nutrients needed in addition to those available to the plant from the soil. Heavy mulching with hay builds up a reserve of available nutrients which lasts for several years. In fact, with fruit plants the money spent on fertilizers and tillage might even be expended to better advantage for mulching materials.

In one experiment, mulched Apple trees substantially outyielded cultivated trees, even when the mulched trees were not fertilized and the cultivated trees were fertilized. The profitableness of this practice will depend on local circumstances, the availability of mulching material at a reasonable cost, the labor situation, moisture relations and soil fertility in the fields to be mulched. Straw is lower in nutrients than hay, but furnishes considerable potassium. The other mulches are mostly low in nutrients.

Wheat, Rye, Oat and Buckwheat straws are good mulches but furnish less nutrients than hay. They constitute a fire hazard and may bring in weed seeds, especially Bindweed. The insulating value of straw is good, which makes it excellent for preventing deep freezing of the soil and providing protection for low-growing plants. The application of supplementary nitrogen in the form of fertilizer may be needed during the first three or four years of a straw mulch. Shredded cornstalks are good when available.

Tree leaves are available almost everywhere and are excellent for fruit trees, shrubbery and evergreens, but they mat down too much for perennials and bulbs unless used thinly. Leaves that have rotted down to leaf mold are excellent wherever a mulch is needed. Leaves rot rapidly, and a covering 8 or 10 in. of fresh leaves will be nearly all gone in twelve months.

Because of their value as mulch material, the burning of leaves is a wasteful practice. They are a valuable source of humus, and gardens are much in need of the organic matter they can supply. Leaves contain as much plant nutrients per pound as does manure of the same moisture content. For these reasons every gardener should collect all leaves possible and either compost them or use them as mulches.

Oak leaves mat down less than the others and are especially recommended for Rhododendrons and Azaleas. Pine needles are often collected in Pine forests for mulching Strawberries, and they are equally good for the flower garden. They do not mat down and are fairly durable. In the southern states, Spanish Moss is sometimes used as a mulch, and it may be had for the gathering.

Peat moss is generally available from garden supply stores, and is a good mulch, but is generally too expensive, except for the flower garden and ornamental plantings. It is attractive to look at and durable; however, when dried, it intercepts most of the rain from light showers. When wet and frozen, it loses its insulating value, but it is a good insulator when dry.

Sawdust is being used in increasing amounts as a mulch material as it becomes known that it is not toxic to plants and does not make the soil acid. It does cause nitrogen starvation, because the bacteria which rot the sawdust draw heavily on the soil nitrogen for their life processes. Supplementary nitrogen should be added to the soil at the rate of 110 lb. of ammonium nitrate, or its equivalent in some other nitrogen fertilizer, to a ton of dry sawdust. The need for supplementary nitrogen is indicated by the development of a yellowish color in foliage which should be dark-green.

Sawdust is very low in plant nutrients, decomposes slowly, and tends to pack down, so that light rains penetrate it with difficulty. For mulching purposes it matters little whether the sawdust is fresh, or well-rotted, or from hardwood or softwood trees.

Sawdust is excellent for Blueberries, Rhododendrons, Azaleas, Heathers, and other members of the botanical family Ericaceae, as well as for bulbs and small plants which push through it more readily in the spring than they do through the coarser mulches.

Wood shavings are similar in most of their properties to sawdust, but mat down less and tend to blow away in exposed situations. Wood chips from chipping machines are a new product available in some places. Other wood materials are shredded Redwood bark, excelsior and Balsam wool.

Spent hops from a brewery are one of the best mulches. They ignite with difficulty and are durable; moreover, the beery odor, which may at first be unpleasant, is soon dissipated. Grape growers use the pomace (Grape refuse) from wineries and grape-juice processing plants in their vineyards.

Ground corn cobs are an excellent mulch. On Roses, they have proved more effective than peat moss in conserving soil moisture and in increasing the organic matter of the soil. They have a pronounced beneficial effect on soil structure.

Peanut shells, cocoa bean shells, coconut fiber refuse, shredded sugar cane fiber, shredded tobacco stems, shredded banana stalks and cotton screenings are other possibilities as mulch materials.

Manure is sometimes used for mulching purposes, but often contains weed seeds and may cause the soil to become too fertile for some plants. It should be used on crops responding to high fertility, such as Rhubarb, and on trees and shrubs that need fertilizing as well as the other benefits that a mulch supplies.

Special mulch paper was tried extensively as a mulch for vegetables in the 1920's, but it was expensive and did not stand traffic well. It did increase the yield of hot-weather crops such as Peppers and Tomatoes, but soon passed out of fashion. Aluminum foil is also effective, but is not likely to be used widely because of its comparatively high cost. Special plastic films are also available for mulching.

Glass wool is a good winter mulch for small plants which remain green through the winter; light passes through it and it gives good protection without matting down. Vermiculite is also suitable for small-scale mulching. Newspapers and flattened cartons have a smothering effect on weeds and conserve moisture. If used, they should be covered with something that is better-looking than themselves and will keep them from blowing around.

Stone chips or gravel is used around rock-garden plants and is very satisfactory. As a mulching material, flat stones have their advocates. They are certainly durable, and no weeds or moisture can get through them, but obviously their usefulness is very limited. These nonorganic materials do not, of course, supply plant nutrients or humus.

Ground-cover plants provide the shading effect of a mulch for bulbs and shrubbery and also some cover for winter. Evergreen boughs laid on the ground provide some protection and hold the snow; this is important because the snow itself is one of the best of all winter mulches, although it unfortunately does not form a dependable, lasting cover in most areas.

Managing the Mulch

A mulch may be applied whenever convenient for fruit trees and shrubbery. If there is a fire hazard, late fall application is safer, as the mulch will soon be wet from rain and snow, and partly rotted by the time dry weather arrives in the spring.

Perennials and annuals should be mulched after they are nicely started in the spring. Fall-planted bulbs should be mulched any time after they are planted, but before deep freezing occurs. Tomatoes and vine crops should be mulched before they spread out, but not until the soil has warmed. No warm-weather crops should be mulched until the soil is warm and the plants are nicely started.

Mature Apple trees need 200 to 300 lb. for the first mulching and 100 lb. a year thereafter. A depth of 6 in. of mulch is necessary to keep down weed growth.

Sawdust, peat moss and similar materials are applied to a depth of one to several inches, depending on the crop or plants to which they are applied and the amount of mulch available. An inch is sufficient for moisture conservation, but two or three inches or more will give better weed control. If the mulch is in short supply, it should be used on dry areas and on slopes subject to erosion.

Fruit trees and other trees and shrubs should be mulched as far outwards from their trunks as the limbs spread. With old trees the bulk of the mulch should be under the outer portions of the more far-reaching limbs, as the shade will keep down weed and grass growth near the trunk and the main feeding roots are out towards the limit of the branch spread.

Nitrogen. With sawdust and straw, supplementary nitrogen may be needed for three or four years to prevent nitrogen starvation. With hay, especially legume hays, the nitrogen content of the soil may increase to the point where Apples color poorly and drop excessively, and tree growth is overvegetative. The mulch should then be reduced and some grass allowed to grow up through it to use the excess nitrogen. Straw and hay, especially near highways and public areas, are likely to be fire hazards. Cultivated strips should be left between the trees to serve as fire breaks.

Mice are often a problem in a mulched orchard and among mulched trees and shrubs. The trees may be protected with mounds of coarse gravel, crushed stone or cinders 5-6 in. high and 3-4 ft. in diameter. Wire guards around the trunk furnish good protection. Poison baits should also be used in mulched orchards. These may be obtained from local farm bureaus in fruit-growing regions.

Special Hints on Mulching. Planting sites for trees may be mulched to good advantage a year before planting the trees. The mulching kills out the grass and weeds and may have other benefits: the trees grow very well when planted on a mulched site.

A mulched vegetable garden on heavy soil should be plowed in the fall or the mulch removed early to permit the ground to dry out for spring plowing. Turning the mulch under adds organic matter to the soil.

Fall-bearing Raspberries respond well to a mulch, as the fall crop ripens during the driest part of the year.

Strawberries are mulched to protect the crowns from low winter temperatures, to keep the berries clean, to conserve moisture and keep down weeds. Wheat, Rye and Oat straws and marsh hay (salt hay) are the best materials, but others may be used. The mulch is spread on the bed to a depth of 3 or 4 in. in late fall after the plants have experienced 2 or 3 hard frosts, but before temperatures have dropped below 20 degrees F.

Everbearing Strawberries are best grown in hills and mulched with an inch of sawdust, which is applied a few weeks after planting. No runners are allowed to set, and weeds are removed by pulling. Yields are much heavier than with the clean-cultivated matted row.

MULE. A term applied to hybrids which are sterile and cannot be propagated by seeds.

MULGEDIUM. Another name for the ornamental Lettuces, now included in the genus Lactuca, which see.

MULLEIN. See Verbascum.

MULLEIN, CRETAN. See Celsia cretica.

MULLEIN, MOTH. Verbascum Blattaria, which see.

MULTIFLORUS. A botanical term meaning many-flowered. It is used as a species or second scientific name of plants.

MUMMY PEA. A variety of Pisum sativum, a Pea of the Mediterranean region, which may develop with normal stems or with stems that show a good deal of fasciation (which see) and are sometimes an inch in diameter. The name originated through seeds having been brought from Egypt which were said to have been taken from ancient Egyptian tombs; the story goes that the seeds had been sealed up in the tombs for many hundreds of years and were still in a condition to germinate. This story, like that of wheat germinating after being closed up in tombs for 2,000 or 3,000 years, has long been proved false.

The Mummy Pea bears purple and white flowers, the standard petal being white, the wings reddish-purple and the keel greenish-white. It can be grown in gardens in the same way as culinary Peas. A similar Pea with fasciated stems was known and described as long ago as 1580, for it was figured by Tabernaemontanus in his Herbal published in that year.

MURIATE OF POTASH. Muriate of potash is the commercial name for potassium chloride, an important potash salt which is frequently used in horticulture and agriculture. See Fertilizers.

MURRAEA EXOTICA—*Orange Jessamine* (Murrae′a). A tall, evergreen shrub or small tree that is a native of India and adjacent regions and is popular as an ornamental plant in southern California, southern Florida and similar warm climates. It belongs to the Rue family, Rutaceae, and is quite closely related botanically to the Orange. Its name, sometimes spelled Murraya, honors the Swedish botanist Johan Andreas Murray, who was a pupil of Linnaeus and edited some of his publications.

Murraea exotica is an easy plant to grow. It thrives without difficulty in any moderately good soil and is easily propagated by means of seeds and cuttings. It makes a good hedge subject.

This shrub is of dense growth, has handsome, dark-green, glossy foliage and clusters of white, very fragrant flowers which are succeeded by berry-like fruits; these are at first green but become bright red at maturity. M. exotica bears several crops of bloom each year and is always attractive. This shrub would be well worth trying as a house plant. It flourishes when planted in ground beds or in tubs in greenhouses.

MUSA: BANANAS AND PLANTAINS
Tropical Fruiting and Ornamental Plants of Distinction

(Mu'sa). Vigorous, treelike herbaceous plants, natives of warm countries, which are suitable for outdoor cultivation in the United States in only the warmer parts of Florida and other essentially frost-free places, although if fruit is not the objective they may be cultivated somewhat further north. In colder areas they are suitable for growing in a hothouse, or for planting out of doors in the summer months for the decorative value of the large and handsome leaves. They belong to the family Musaceae. The name honors Antonius Musa, physician to Augustus Caesar, the first emperor of Rome.

Cultivation. Musas need rich soil that is kept always fairly moist throughout the season of active growth and is never permitted to dry entirely. For the best results the soil should contain liberal amounts of humus—preferably rich compost or rotted manure.

Specimens grown in pots or tubs should be repotted, or if the plants are already in containers as large as can conveniently be handled, they should be top-dressed each spring. The greenhouse temperature for most should be a night minimum of 60 degrees in winter and at least 10 degrees higher from spring through fall. M. Ensete and M. Basjoo will stand lower temperatures.

If they are kept indoors, light shade from strong summer sunshine should be provided, but plants set outdoors for the summer will stand full sun. Well-rooted specimens grown in containers benefit immensely from weekly applications of dilute liquid fertilizer. Keep the atmosphere in the greenhouse humid at all times by frequently wetting benches, walks and other surfaces and by spraying the plants themselves

Bananas have large paddle-shaped leaves. These are growing in a greenhouse at The New York Botanical Garden.

on all clear days with generous amounts of water.

In frost-free or nearly frost-free warm climates, Musas planted for ornament are seen to best advantage when planted where they are somewhat sheltered from sweeping winds, which are likely to tear the huge leaves to shreds. Rich soil and sufficient moisture at the roots are requirements for real success.

The Common Banana. The well-known Common Banana is botanically M. paradisiaca subspecies sapientum. It grows 15-20 ft. tall and bears agreeably flavored, nourishing, seedless fruits that are edible without cooking. It exists in many distinct varieties; most have yellow skins but some are colored red. Among better-known varieties are Gros Michel, Red Jamaica, Apple, Orinoco and Champa (Lady-Finger Banana). Variety vittatum has its foliage beautifully variegated with white and pink. For the cultivation of these, see Banana. The Common Banana is derived from an Asiatic species.

The Dwarf Banana, M. nana, or M. Cavendishii as it was at one time called, is a native of southern China that bears most excellently flavored Bananas that are eaten without cooking. This species grows only about 6 ft. tall and is readily propagated by offsets. It does not produce seeds. This is one of the most popular kinds for outdoor cultivation in the deep South, and it is a most excellent kind for growing in large tubs in warm greenhouses, where, with a little attention, it fruits freely. See Banana.

The Plantain is a species of Musa that grows about 30 ft. tall and produces green or greenish-yellow seedless fruits that are edible after cooking. It is not much grown in the continental United States but in most tropical countries it forms a staple article of diet.

The Plantain is M. paradisiaca and is most probably a native of India.

Manila Hemp or Abaca is a valuable fiber, the product of M. textilis. It is produced commercially in the Philippines, of which islands M. textilis is native. M. textilis grows to a height of about 20 ft., and its inedible fruits contain many black seeds. Except as a specimen in a botanical garden or other educational plantings, M. textilis is rarely cultivated in America.

In southern Japan yet another species, M.

A young bunch of Bananas developing among the leaves.

Basjoo, is cultivated as a source of fiber which is used for making coarse fabrics, and in Africa M. Ensete is similarly employed. Both of these are described in detail below.

Ornamental Kinds. All of the Musas are noble plants and are of great value for creating tropical effects in gardens. Some are grown particularly for such purposes.

One of the commonest of these is the Abyssinian Banana, M. Ensete, a species which, at maturity, reaches a height of 40 ft. and has leaves 20 ft. long. The fruits are inedible but the large black seeds they contain afford an easy means of raising a stock of plants. Decorative small specimens can be raised from seeds sown in a tropical greenhouse in January, and may be set outdoors in the summer garden by June. This kind is a native of Abyssinia (Ethiopia).

M. rosacea, from India, is a dwarf kind that usually grows about 6 ft. tall and has prettily colored bracts as an attraction when the plants are in bloom. M. sumatrana attains a height of about 8 ft. Its leaves are glaucous beneath.

M. zebrina is distinguished by the beautiful markings of bronze-purple or chocolate-red that occur as irregularly scattered stripes and bands on the leaves. This plant may be a variety of M. sumatrana or of M. malaccensis. It grows about 10 ft. tall and is easily propagated by means of suckers.

M. Basjoo is a native of the islands just south of Japan, the Ryukyu Islands. It grows about 10 ft. tall and, like M. Ensete, is somewhat more resistant to cold than most kinds. It forms offsets freely and in Japan is a source of fiber.

M. coccinea, native of Vietnam, has fiery crimson bracts and yellow flowers. It is very attractive in bloom.

MUSCARI—*Grape Hyacinth* (Muscar'i). Hardy spring-flowering bulbs which grow wild in southern Europe and Asia Minor; they belong to the Lily family, Liliaceae. The name is derived from *muscus*, musk, and refers to the smell of the flowers of some kinds.

Spring-flowering Bulbs. The Grape Hyacinths are very attractive little bulbs which are in full beauty in March and April; they grow 6-12 in. high, and bear grapelike clusters of flowers on erect stems; the flowers are chiefly of blue coloring. They thrive in ordinary, well-tilled garden soil, and are of easy cultivation. Before planting the bulbs in heavy, clayey land, it is an advantage to mix in sand freely; the addition of leaf mold or compost also renders the ground more porous and more suitable for these bulbs.

Splendid for Naturalizing. The Muscari are not so suitable for planting in formal flower beds as many other bulbs, for they form large, leafy masses which become untidy; they are seen at their best in the less formal parts of the garden, as, for instance, in open spaces among shrubs, on the outskirts of the rock garden, on grassy banks, and in half-wild places. There they will flourish and spread, by means of self-sown seeds as well as by offsets, and annually furnish a feast of bloom.

Color Schemes with Grape Hyacinths and Flowering Shrubs. The Grape Hyacinths provide an admirable ground covering beneath some of the spring-flowering shrubs, particularly the Golden Bell or Forsythia, and the Star Magnolia, M. stellata: the former has yellow, and the latter, white flowers, and the blue of the Grape Hyacinth associates perfectly with both of them. Grape Hyacinths are delightful also when massed beneath one of the pink-flowered ornamental Cherries.

Bulbs Must Be Planted Early. To ensure a satisfactory display of bloom during the first spring, it is necessary to plant the bulbs as early as possible in the autumn, for they start into growth far sooner than most other spring-flowering bulbs. They should be set in the ground in August or early September, preferably; their

Muscari comosum monstrosum, the Feather Hyacinth. Its flowers are sterile, and consist of narrow bluish-violet filaments, carried in a large inflorescence.

Muscari armeniacum (Heavenly Blue), the Grape Hyacinth, ranks among the most valuable of the spring-flowering bulbous plants. It is excellent for naturalizing among shrubs and for planting as edgings to spring flower beds.

Grape Hyacinths or Muscari bloom freely and are very attractive when planted close together in pots or pans and forced into early growth in a cool greenhouse or sunny window in a cool room.

leaves will then appear above ground in a few weeks. If planting is delayed until late autumn or early winter, the bulbs will have little chance to become well rooted before the cold weather sets in, and their chances of providing a first-rate show of bloom during the first year will be jeopardized.

How Deep to Plant. The bulbs should be set about 3 in. apart and at such a depth that the tops are covered by 2 in. of soil. They may be left undisturbed for many years—until they become so crowded that they fail to bloom freely.

When it becomes necessary to lift and separate the bulbs, the work should be done as soon as the leaves have turned yellow. The clumps should then be taken up and separated into single bulbs. The latter should be graded in sizes before they are replanted; the smaller ones could then be grown for a year in a nursery border and the larger ones set out in their permanent places.

The Chief Kinds. The most brilliantly colored of all the Grape Hyacinths is Muscari armeniacum (Heavenly Blue); the flower stems reach a height of 8-9 in., and the grapelike clusters of bright blue flowers, on erect stems, provide glorious groups of color in the spring months. This is one of the best bulbs for naturalizing and for association with spring-flowering shrubs. Another fine kind is the blue-flowered M. botryoides. There are also white and pink forms of M. botryoides.

The Tassel Hyacinth, M. comosum, bears a large spike of urn-shaped fertile flowers, above which are nonseeding flowers in a terminal cluster, the color being a mixture of blue and green. Even more striking is the Feather Hyacinth (M. comosum monstrosum), with all the flowers sterile and the inflorescence consisting of a mass of bluish-violet filaments carried in a dense, branched tuft 12 in. or more tall, in May.

The Musk Hyacinth, M. moschatum, 6-8 in., is worth growing for the sake of its fragrant, purplish-blue flowers; the variety named flavum, which bears yellow flowers flushed with purple, is also fragrant and is recommended.

Other cultivated kinds include M. latifolium, producing a solitary leaf and spike, 9 in. tall,

Planting Grape Hyacinths or Muscari amidst a low ground cover in a rock garden. The bulbs are set with their tops 2 in. beneath the soil surface.

of deep blue flowers; M. paradoxum, 6 in., flowers a combination of blue-black and green; M. racemosum, the Starch Hyacinth, 6 in., dark purple, plum-scented; and M. Tubergenianum, 8 in., rich blue.

For the Cool Greenhouse. The Grape Hyacinths are suitable for cultivation in pots in cool greenhouses, where they will be in full beauty in March. The bulbs should be set in pots of sandy, loamy soil in September and kept in a cold, shady frame for 5-6 weeks until the pots are full of roots, or they may be placed out of doors on a paved or asphalt path and covered with old, sifted ashes, sand or peat moss. When well rooted, the plants should be placed in the greenhouse or brought into a sunny, cool sunroom. When indoors they need watering freely.

After they are through blooming the pots may be stood outdoors and kept watered until the foliage dies naturally, then the bulbs may be taken up and stored until fall when they may be planted in the outdoor garden.

For Bowl Cultivation. Muscari may also be grown in bowls of fiber in the home. Care must be taken to keep them as cool as possible and to set them in the lightest position. In fact, when growth has started, the bowls of bulbs should be placed out of doors whenever the weather is mild; otherwise the leaves will become unduly long and untidy, and spoil the appearance of the display when the blooms are out. A location where the night temperature is 40-50 degrees and the day temperature 50-60 degrees is best.

Increasing Your Stock. As Grape Hyacinths produce seeds freely, these may be used to increase the stock of any particular kind. They should be gathered as soon as they are ripe in summer and sown at once, in drills half an inch or so deep, on a border in fine soil; or scattered broadcast where they are wanted to grow.

MUSHROOM: A FUNGUS DELICACY
How to Grow It Successfully Outdoors and Indoors

The cultivated Mushroom (Agaricus campestris) may be grown indoors in sheds, cellars, or properly designed Mushroom houses, almost all the year round, and outdoors in beds or in lawns or meadows during summer.

Indoors, the chief essentials are: scrupulous cleanliness, excellent ventilation, 80 per cent humidity, a temperature of 50-65 degrees F., but never below 40 degrees or above 70 degrees at any time. Darkness is not vital, but it is desirable. A bed begins to yield 6-8 weeks after spawning and casing (see below), and will crop 3-4 months, giving 8 to 12 oz. per sq. ft.

Mushroom House. The properly designed Mushroom house or cellar is dark, well ventilated and insulated to give even temperatures, with a central pathway and space for the beds on each side. A site sheltered from cold winds is desirable. A level floor of earth, dusted with lime, is best. Adapted buildings should be rain-, draft- and vermin-proof. Some artificial heat is necessary in the colder parts of North America for winter crops.

Propagation is effected by spawning or impregnating beds of fermenting manure or organic compost with a pure culture containing the spores of the fungus. Pure culture spawn has superseded the old-fashioned brick spawn

A good crop of Mushrooms.

and is supplied in the forms of small blocks or cylinders or powdery particles, with the maker's instructions.

Materials for a Mushroom Bed. The best material is fresh stable manure from horses fed on corn or oats, and bedded on straw, preferably wheat. Manure from sick, medically treated horses is not desirable, and that of horses fed on grass, hay or roots will not give the best results. Ideally, the manure should be half droppings, half short straw. Long straw should be shaken out.

To prepare, stack the manure on a clean disinfected site in a heap 4-5 ft. square and 5 ft. high, watering each foot layer with a fine spray, adding 1 teaspoonful of Lysol to each 2 gallons of water. The heap will heat up. When it begins to sink after 7-8 days, turn top to bottom and sides to middle and remake, shaking and breaking any caked lumps with a fork. The heap should be moist, but not wet. Any burnt or dry portions should be watered. Turn again after 3-4 days, and repeat turning up to 4-5 times until the whole heap is free from obnoxious smell, is rich-brown in color, and yields hardly any moisture when squeezed.

Mushroom Bed Compost. When stable manure cannot be obtained, mushroom-bed compost may be made from organic materials such as straw decomposed by a special chemical activator. The manufacturer's instructions should be strictly followed.

Making the Beds. When ready, the compost may be made into beds, either flat or of ridge type, or on shelves. Flat beds are most suitable for indoors. They should be 4 ft. wide, 9-10 in. deep in summer, 12-15 in. deep in winter; on shelves, they may be 8 in. deep. The shelves are arranged in tiers, and are made of hardwood, treated with wood preservative. They usually consist of 1-1½-in.-thick planks on suitable supports and 4 in. by 2 in. uprights, readily dismantled for cleaning purposes.

Ridge beds are essential outdoors, and may be used indoors, being 30 in. wide at the base, tapering to 6 in. at a height of 24 in., and as long as necessary. If desired, smaller ridge beds can be used indoors.

The compost is shaken and stacked evenly when the bed is made, and firmed evenly and smoothly by treading on a board and pounding down with a block of wood to the finished depth. A ton of compost gives 50-60 sq. ft. of bed. The bed will heat up, and the temperature should be checked with a hotbed thermometer. Ventilate well to counteract sweating. When, in a few days, the temperature falls to 70 to 75 degrees F., the bed is ready for spawning.

Spawning consists of inserting pieces of spawn, about walnut size, 1 in. deep, 10 in. apart, in the prepared bed with a trowel, and firming the compost around the spawn afterwards. The bed may then be covered with straw, especially if the weather is cold.

Soiling or Casing. In 7-9 days, when the spawn is sending tiny threads of mycelium out, the bed must be cased with soil. A sandy soil is best, and it should be pure subsoil. If topsoil is used, it should be sterilized, and free from chemical fertilizers or vegetable matter. The soil, whatever its source, is mixed with an equal bulk of moist sifted peat. It is applied 1 in. thick to indoor beds, 1½-2 in. thick to outdoor ridge beds, and finished smooth but not beaten hard to form a crust.

After casing, cover with straw, 4 to 12 in. thick, according to the weather. Out-of-doors, the straw needs to be 9 to 18 in. thick, and covered with burlap.

Management. At first, it is wise to keep the beds rather dry. In watering, the aim must be to damp the soil without wetting the manure compost. The beds need watering every 7 to 10 days, using a salt solution (2 teaspoonfuls per gallon of water), and a fine spray. Paths and walls should be damped down in warm weather.

The first Mushrooms may be expected in 6 to 8 weeks, appearing first in groups at the point of spawning, and later over the whole bed. The crop should be gathered frequently, the Mushrooms being twisted and then pulled free. They should not be cut to leave remains that would decay in the soil.

When a bed ceases to yield profitably, the old compost should be cleared out, the station disinfected or sterilized, and a fresh bed made up. The old compost is excellent for enriching the garden or for use in potting soil compost.

When to Start. The most favorable time to make up Mushroom beds is in June–July for late summer or autumn cropping. For a succession, beds can be made monthly until the spring.

The Outdoor Mushroom Bed. This should be made on a sheltered, well-drained site, preferably in June–July. If necessary, the bed may be made on a plank base, raised above the ground. The ridge type of bed is made, spawned, cased and strawed as for an indoor bed. The straw may be thicker, especially in the cooler weather months, and a tarpaulin cover or semicircular sheets of corrugated iron may be used to give increased shelter from wind and rain. One ton of manure gives a ridge bed three yards long. After cropping, the site should not be used again for mushrooms for two years.

Mushrooms in Turf. Growing Mushrooms in a lawn or meadow is a gamble, as so much depends on weather conditions. The simplest method is to take out small squares of turf, 1½ in. thick; then remove 3 in. of soil and replace it with tightly packed lawn mowings or freshly made Mushroom manure compost. Water and insert pieces of spawn, then replace the turf. Late May, June and July are the times to do this, and Mushrooms may appear 8-12 weeks later. In a meadow, it is often sufficient to lift the turf in late May, insert spawn 1½ to 2 in. deep, and replace the turf. A few pieces of spawn may always be inserted in old hotbeds or beds used for Melons or Cucumbers, or any soil or bed which has been kept liberally mulched with organic material.

MUSK. See Mimulus.

MUSK HYACINTH. Muscari moschatum, which see.

MUSK MALLOW. Malva moschata, which see.

MUSK MELON. See Melon.

MUSK ROSE. Rosa moschata, which see.

MUSSAENDA (Mussaen'da). Evergreen shrubs with attractive flowers for the greenhouse. They are native of tropical Africa, China and India, and belong to the family Rubiaceae. These shrubs grow up to 8 ft. in height, have oblong-ovate leaves with pointed tips, and produce terminal clusters of white, yellow or red flowers at various periods of the year. These flowers have long, slender tubes at the base, and spread out horizontally at the tops into five petals; they bear some resemblance to the Bouvardia of the same family. Mussaenda is the native name of the plant in Ceylon.

Evergreen Flowering Shrubs for a Warm Greenhouse. These plants require a minimum winter temperature of 55 degrees and a soil compost of two parts of loam, one part of peat, one of leaf mold, and a scattering of sand. Repotting is done as soon as growth commences in the spring. The plants are knocked out of their pots, and all crocks and loose soil removed; they are then repotted in larger pots which have been thoroughly cleaned inside and out and half-filled with crocks, and the soil is made firm.

After potting, the plants are shaded from sunshine, and syringed daily to induce rapid root action. When established, they are given more light but shaded from the strongest rays of the sun. The atmosphere of the greenhouse should be kept moist by frequently damping the floor and benches.

Summer Management and Pruning. During the summer the soil must be kept moist, and well-rooted plants require a biweekly application of liquid fertilizer. Pruning, which consists of slightly shortening the shoots, is done as soon as the flowers have faded.

When to Take Cuttings. Young plants are raised from cuttings in April. Side shoots 3 in. in length are removed, the lower leaves are cut off, and a cut is made close beneath the lowest node. The cuttings are then inserted in either sand, sand and peat moss, or vermiculite in a propagating case with a bottom heat of 65-70 degrees. The frame is kept close, except for a daily airing for a few minutes each morning to allow excessive moisture to escape. Shade from bright sunlight must be provided.

When roots have formed, more and more air is admitted to the propagating case each day. Finally the cuttings are potted separately in 3-in. pots, and shaded and lightly syringed daily until the roots have penetrated the new soil. They are then moved to the greenhouse benches; later they are potted in 5-in. pots and treated as advised earlier for older plants.

The chief kinds are M. erythrophylla, 12 in.,

yellow flowers, crimson bracts, winter; M. frondosa, 2-3 ft., yellow, bracts white, August; M. luteola, 5-6 ft., yellow, bracts white and M. macrophylla, 4 ft., orange, summer.

MUSTARD. This is a name applied to several members of the genus Brassica. The White Mustard, B. alba, is a common weed. The Black Mustard, B. nigra, is a tall annual of no garden importance; it is grown commercially for its seeds, which are the chief source of the condiment mustard. The Leaf Mustard is B. juncea, an Old World annual that is grown in gardens to some extent, particularly in the South, for its leaves, which are the vegetable "mustard greens." Most usually the varieties grown are those with crisped leaves, such as Southern Curled and Ostrich Plume.

When grown for greens, Mustard is sown from early spring to August for summer and fall picking; in warm regions it is sown in fall to provide an early spring crop. The seeds are sown in rows 1-1½ ft. apart, and the plants in the rows are thinned out so that they will be spaced 5-6 in. apart. Mustard thrives in any ordinary garden soil. Like its relatives Cabbage, Kale and Turnips, it appreciates earth that is not acid.

MUTATION. A mutation is the sudden appearance, in a single generation, of a new type of plant not the result of cross-breeding or of hybridization. Such "breaks" are fairly common in some plants but comparatively rare in others. One of the most spectacular mutations was the production of the modern "Spencer" or waved variety of Sweet Pea, which appeared suddenly in 1901, and constituted a great advance on the older grandiflora type. Mutations such as this afford valuable material on which the plant breeder can work with the aim of selecting new and purebreeding strains.

Vegetative mutations or "sports" are common in some plants—Chrysanthemums, for example. Here new types are produced spontaneously from buds and shoots rather than as seedlings. The cut-leaved Beech is a well-known example of a vegetative mutation which appeared in the first case on a few branches only of an ordinary Beech tree. The cause of mutations is not clear.

MUTISIA (Mutis'ia). Tender evergreen flowering shrubs, of climbing or bushy growth. They

A flower of Mutisia retusa, the ray florets of which are pink. It is a lovely climber from Chile.

are natives of Peru and Chile, and belong to the Daisy family, Compositae. They grow 10 ft. in height, have pinnate or lanceolate leaves, and bear large heads of scarlet, purple or orange flowers in summer. Each head of bloom is made up of a number of small flowers (this is characteristic of the members of the Daisy family) and is surrounded by a large number of overlapping bracts.

The name Mutisia commemorates José C. Mutis, a South American botanist.

Climbing Plants for a Cool Greenhouse. These plants require a minimum greenhouse winter temperature of 40 degrees, and a soil compost of two parts of loam, one part of leaf mold and a scattering of sand. They are grown in large pots or tubs, or planted in a prepared bed in the greenhouse. The shoots are trained to wires or a trellis fixed to the greenhouse roof. The pots or tubs should have several inches of crocks in the bottom for drainage, these being covered with pieces of fibrous turf. A bed on the greenhouse floor is prepared by taking out a 2-ft. depth of soil; a layer of rough stones or broken bricks, 6 in. in depth, is placed in the bottom and covered with pieces of turf, and the remainder of the space is filled with the prepared compost. Potting or planting is done in February or March.

After planting, shade from bright sunlight is necessary, and the plants must be frequently syringed to assist root action. During the summer months, the soil must be kept moist, and a humid atmosphere maintained by frequently damping the floor. After flowering, the shoots should be slightly shortened. Plants in large pots or tubs can be kept growing vigorously for many years by being top-dressed annually in spring with the prepared compost.

When to Take Cuttings. Young plants are raised from cuttings taken in June; the lower leaves are cut off, and a cut is made close beneath the lowest node. They are then inserted around the edge of 3-in. pots; the pots must be well drained and filled with sandy soil. After the cuttings are inserted, the soil is thoroughly moistened and the pots of cuttings are covered with a bell jar. This is shaded from strong sunlight, and the moisture is wiped from the inside each morning.

When roots have formed, more and more air is admitted, and finally the bell jar is removed. The cuttings are potted separately in 3-in. pots, and when the roots have reached the sides of these pots the plants are repotted in 5-in. pots. When well rooted in these, they are potted in large pots or tubs or planted in a bed of soil.

For Planting Out of Doors. In mild climates, such as that of California, Mutisias may be grown out of doors. The one most commonly grown in California gardens is M. Clematis; it should be planted in spring in light, well-drained soil. The shoots are trained to wires or a trellis. In dry weather the soil must be kept moist by watering.

The chief kinds are M. Clematis, orange-scarlet; M. illicifolia, pale pink or mauve; M. retusa, pink, and its variety alba, white; M. oligodon, pink; and M. decurrens, orange.

MYCELIUM. This term describes the vegetative "body" of a fungus. The familiar Mushroom, for instance, is only the spore-bearing part of a fungus; the vegetative body from which it develops consists of a mass of fine white threads which permeate the soil and the organic material where these plants grow. Such fungal threads are termed the mycelium of the plant.

MYOPORUM (Myop'orum). Tender evergreen trees and shrubs of eastern Asia, Australia, New Zealand, Hawaii and other Pacific islands. They belong in the Myoporum family, Myoporaceae. The name, derived from *myo*, to shut and *poros*, pore, refers to the translucent spots on the leaves.

Myoporums are grown outdoors in mild climates and in greenhouses in sandy, peaty soil. Propagation is by seeds and cuttings. Kinds include M. acuminatum, a white-flowered shrub, M. insulare, 30 ft., white spotted purple, M. laetum, 15 ft., white spotted purple, M. sandwicense (Bastard Sandalwood), 60 ft., white or pink.

MYOSOTIDIUM HORTENSIA (NOBILE) —*Chatham Islands Forget-Me-Not* (Myosotid'ium). This remarkable plant grows wild in the Chatham Islands, and, although introduced to cultivation nearly 80 years ago, it has remained uncommon. It belongs to the Borage family, Boraginaceae. The name Myosotidium is derived from Myosotis, the Forget-Me-Not—its flowers resemble those of the Forget-Me-Not.

This handsome herbaceous plant has not become common in gardens for two reasons: it is not easily managed, and it is not very hardy. It is suitable for planting out of doors only in those mild parts of North America where fairly cool summers prevail, as in parts of the Pacific Northwest. It is sometimes seen in a flourishing condition out of doors in mild, sheltered places on the West Coast, but rarely in other districts.

A Striking Plant. When well developed, Myosotidium is a striking plant, about 18 in. high, with large leaves, and in spring it bears a raceme of small blue flowers like those of the Forget-Me-Not. It likes cool and moist conditions, and is happiest in maritime gardens or in those not far from the coast. But it is a capricious plant, and it may fail without apparent reason, even when provided with the same soil and position in which it flourishes in other gardens in the neighborhood.

This plant must have a sheltered position, not open to the sunshine during the hottest part of the day, and the soil most likely to suit it is deep moist loam. It should be planted in early autumn.

Although the Chatham Islands Forget-Me-Not can be increased by division, it is unwise to disturb flourishing plants. If you wish to increase the stock, you should do this by sowing seeds in late summer in loam and leaf mold in a frame.

MYOSOTIS: THE FORGET-ME-NOT
Perennials and Biennials for Spring and Summer Gardens

(Myoso′tis). This group of hardy biennial and perennial plants is invaluable in spring and early summer. Some of them are suitable for the rock garden, others for providing masses of color in spring flower beds and borders, and for planting by the waterside or in the bog garden. They grow wild chiefly in North America, Europe and New Zealand. Forget-Me-Not belongs to the Borage family, Boraginaceae. The name Myosotis was that used by Dioscorides.

For Spring Flower Beds. The Forget-Me-Nots which are so popular in gardens for their profusion of bloom in April and May are varieties of Myosotis sylvatica, a plant which grows wild in Europe and Asia. They are very easy to grow and, in fact, when Forget-Me-Nots are established in a garden, self-sown seedlings often spring up in large numbers. This, however, is not altogether an advantage if the variety which has established itself is a poor one, for the Forget-Me-Not seeds so freely that it is sometimes difficult to get rid of it.

There are several fine varieties of the common Forget-Me-Not which bear flowers of rich blue coloring, and they are greatly to be preferred to those which are of poor pale-blue shades of color. Yet in some gardens the Forget-Me-Nots are of this type. They should be destroyed before they go to seed, or else it may be impossible to exterminate them; a fresh stock should be raised by purchasing seeds of one of the named varieties.

Sowing the Seeds. Although it is not necessary to sow the seeds in drills, this method is to be preferred to sowing broadcast, for the care of the seedlings is so much more convenient when they are in drills or lines. The seeds should be sown thinly in drills half an inch or so deep in a nursery border or in a cold frame in June–July. They germinate very freely and the seedlings make quick progress. The young plants need shade from summer sun.

Before they become overcrowded, the seedlings should be transplanted to nursery beds or cold frames, where they are set 6-8 in. apart. Here they will form fine plants suitable for setting out in the garden in fall or the following spring. The best varieties are listed in seedsmen's catalogues.

Forget-Me-Nots provide a charming groundwork in beds of May-flowering Cottage and Darwin Tulips, and it is possible to create many beautiful color schemes.

Self-sown Seedlings. When the garden contains a stock of plants of a good variety, the simplest way to raise a fresh supply is to lift the Forget-Me-Nots when the flowers have faded and set them in a nursery border in partial shade or in a shaded cold frame. There the seeds will fall and seedlings will spring up in large numbers. When well developed, they should be transplanted 6 in. apart in rows, there to remain until they are set in the positions in which they will bloom the following year.

Forget-Me-Nots for Naturalizing. Myosotis sylvatica and its varieties are delightful flowering plants for naturalizing in informal parts of the garden, in the shrubbery or by the side of walks in open spaces among trees. To begin with, it is worth while raising seedlings in a border in the way explained previously, and setting out the

Myosotis Royal Blue, a compact, free-flowering variety, ideal for spring bedding.

[7—8]
Ceriman
(Monstera deliciosa)

[7—8a]
Banana (Musa)

[7—8b]
Pitcher Plant
(Nepenthes)

[7—8c]
Nidularium Innocentii

[7—9]

Narcissi naturalized

The Water Forget-Me-Not, Myosotis scorpioides, is a perennial kind that thrives in moist soils and blooms profusely in spring and summer.

plants when they are well developed. They will then usually increase by means of self-sown seedlings.

There are varieties of Myosotis sylvatica having blue, white, and pale rose-colored flowers. These charming Forget-Me-Nots are seen at their best in semishady places in soil which does not dry out in hot weather.

For the Rock Garden. Myosotis alpestris, a Swiss mountain plant which grows about 6 in. high and bears blue flowers, is suitable for planting in the rock garden; it needs a partially shady place and well-drained loamy soil with which sand or grit has been mixed freely. The variety Victoria is of dwarf compact growth, and variety Ruth Fischer has larger flowers.

Another blue Forget-Me-Not suitable for the rock garden is Myosotis azorica, which grows wild in the Azores; it is less hardy than others and needs well-drained gritty soil. There is a white form of this, variety alba.

The Water Forget-Me-Not, Myosotis scorpioides (palustris), which reaches a height of 9 in. and blooms throughout a long period in spring and summer, is suitable for planting by the waterside, in the bog garden, and in other places where the soil is moist. It self-sows freely.

Forget-Me-Nots make excellent pot plants for the slightly heated greenhouse. Plants may be lifted from the open ground in October, and potted in 5-in. pots in a compost of loam and leaf mold with a little sand added. If watered and placed in a cold frame, which is then kept closed for a few days, the plants will soon become established and may be brought into the greenhouse. They need rather careful watering during dull wet weather in winter or the leaves will damp off. The soil should not be watered until it is moderately dry.

Midwinter Blooms. Instead of relying on ordinary spring bedding Forget-Me-Nots lifted from the garden, it is better to choose a variety that is especially suited to cultivation in pots. Such varieties are offered in seed catalogues. These plants begin to bloom in midwinter and continue gay for many weeks in a greenhouse from which frost is excluded. They are raised from seeds shown in a flat of sifted soil in June or July; the flat is placed in a frame, and, when the seedlings are large enough, they are potted singly first in 3-in. and later in 5-in. pots. Until autumn, they are kept out of doors or in a frame that is ventilated very freely; then they are placed in the greenhouse.

Owners of greenhouses would do well to make greater use of Forget-Me-Nots to provide flowers in the early spring months. The chief trouble in the greenhouse, an excessively damp atmosphere, will be prevented if care is taken to ventilate the greenhouse very freely in mild weather. Watering must be done with great care; the soil ought not to be moistened until it is dry.

MYRICA—*Wax Myrtle, Bayberry, Sweet Gale* (Myric'a). Tender and hardy evergreen shrubs and small trees grown for their decorative value; one, M. rubra, is cultivated for its edible fruits. These plants belong to the Sweet Gale family, Myricaceae, and occur throughout most of the Northern Hemisphere. The name is an adaption of the Greek *Myrike,* which probably referred to the shrub Tamarisk.

The Bayberry of eastern North America is M. pensylvanica, sometimes known as M. carolinensis. It is an extremely hardy shrub that occurs naturally from Nova Scotia to Florida and Alabama, and is well adapted for growing on poor, dryish soils in exposed locations, especially near the coast.

Although leaf-losing, this Bayberry holds its foliage well into the fall or early winter. The leaves are pleasingly aromatic. The fruits (berries) are densely covered with grayish wax and are very attractive. The wax is used for making Bayberry candles.

The Wax Myrtle, M. cerifera, occurs wild in damp or wet sandy or peaty soils from southern New Jersey to Florida and to Texas and Arkansas, and is hardy north of its natural range. It is evergreen and attains a height of 35 ft. The fruits are covered with grayish white wax. This shrub is also sometimes called Bayberry or Tallow Shrub.

The Sweet Gale, M. Gale, occurs in swamps and along moist shores from Newfoundland north to Alaska and south to southern New York, Michigan and Washington. It also occurs in North Carolina and in northern Europe and Asia.

The Sweet Gale has the sexes on separate plants. It is leaf-losing, grows about 4 ft. tall and is of no great garden value except as an object of interest to grow in acid bogs. Its foliage is fragrant.

The California Bayberry, M. californica, grows to 35 ft. tall and occurs naturally on poor, sandy soils from Washington to California; in other parts of the country it is not hardy in the North. It is evergreen, and its foliage is very decorative. Unfortunately, this handsome shrub is somewhat difficult to transplant and propagate.

M. rubra, a native of China and Japan, is hardy in mild climates only. It is evergreen, grows about 15 ft. high and bears subacid, edible fruits that may be eaten or used in making a beverage.

The native Bayberry of eastern North America, Myrica pensylvanica.

Culture. The Myricas are all acid-soil plants that thrive in soils of a peaty character. They are propagated chiefly by seeds. Layering and air layering may also be employed as a means of propagation, and M. Gale can also be increased by suckers. Cuttings taken in late summer or early fall and inserted in a firmly packed bed of peat moss and sand offer yet another method of securing increase.

MYRICARIA GERMANICA — *False Tamarisk* (Myrica'ria). A leaf-losing shrub which is widely distributed in a natural state in central and southern Europe and western Asia. It grows 3-6 ft. high and forms a rather loose bush with long, slender, plumelike branches covered with small, tamarix-like leaves. From the ends of the branches small pinkish flowers are produced during summer.

This shrub thrives in moist, loamy soil, and is increased by cuttings of ripened wood, 9-12 in. long, inserted in a sheltered border out of doors or in a frame in autumn. In spring the previous year's shoots should be cut down to within a few buds of the base. Myricaria is closely allied to Tamarix and belongs to the same family, Tamaricaceae. It is hardy in the North.

This is not a very ornamental shrub—it is less so than several kinds of Tamarix—and cannot be recommended for gardens of limited space. One other kind is known, M. dahurica from northern China and Siberia. It is not very different from M. germanica. The name Myricaria is said to be derived from *myrike,* which may have been an ancient name for Tamarix.

MYRIOPHYLLUM—*Water Milfoil* (Myriophyll'um). Dainty aquatic plants with finely cut, bright green foliage; they are suitable as oxygenating plants for shallow pools or indoor aquariums. The name is derived from *myrios,* a myriad, and *phyllon,* a leaf, and the plants belong to the family Haloragidaceae.

Hardy species include M. alterniflorum, with delicate hairlike foliage; M. heterophyllum, often bronze-tinted; M. japonicum, M. spicatum and M. verticillatum. These plants thrive in loamy soil under water.

Myriophyllum proserpinacoides, from Brazil, is the most desirable kind; it is known by the common names of Parrot's-Feather and Water Feather. This kind is not reliably hardy in the North but is suitable for planting in outdoor pools in the summer. In climates where little frost is experienced, it may be grown permanently outdoors. It is also suitable for growing in indoor pools and aquariums.

Myriophyllum proserpinacoides produces long stems that are clothed with bright green feathery foliage. The stems spread on the water surface and form pleasing patterns. Propagation is easily effected by means of cuttings. The plants thrive in any good soil. The soil surface should be 2-8 in. under water.

MYRMECOPHILA (Myrmecoph'ila). This name has been given to a number of orchids which formerly were included with Schomburgkia. The Myrmecophilas have tall, conical, hollow pseudobulbs which terminate in a long, arching spike carrying several flowers in summer and autumn. Myrmecophila belongs to the family Orchidaceae. The name is from *myrmex,* ant, and *philos,* loving—the hollow pseudobulbs provide homes for ants.

Though hollow, the pseudobulbs are of very hard texture, indicative of the need for a decided rest in winter and full exposure to light in autumn. A tropical atmosphere is required, and during winter the temperature should not fall below 60 degrees. Growth is very rapid; hence the plants should be kept dormant as long as possible. When growth is vigorous it should be encouraged by liberal waterings; when growth is complete for the year the bulbs should be ripened by being kept in the lightest possible position during autumn. A potting compost of osmunda fiber or of Fir bark, Redwood bark or Tree Fern fiber should be used. Repotting should be done as growth commences.

The kind most frequently seen is M. tibicinus, a native of Honduras. The pseudobulbs may reach a height of 2 ft. The spikes, 4-5 ft. long, bear several flowers with reddish sepals and petals, the side lobes of the lip being rose and yellow streaked with purple, and the front lobe whitish, shaded with purple. It is known as the Cow's Horn orchid of Honduras. M. Sanderiana has rosy-purple flowers. M. Thomsoniana, from the West Indies, has creamy white sepals and petals, the mid-lobe of the lip being deep purple.

Others are M. chionodoxa, M. lepidissima, and M. Humboldtii.

MYROBALAN. See Terminalia.

MYROBALAN PLUM. Prunus cerasifera, which see.

MYRRH. A fragrant gum resin obtained from several kinds of Commiphora, stunted shrubs found in northeastern Africa and Arabia. The official Myrrh of the United States Pharmacopoeia is obtained from natural exudations and from exudations following incisions of the stems of Commiphora Molmol and other species. The name Myrrh is also applied to Myrrhis odorata.

MYRRHIS ODORATA—*Sweet Cicely* (Myrr'his). A fragrant plant of herbaceous growth found wild in many parts of Europe and cultivated for a very long period as a potherb (any herb used as a food or seasoning) and for its fragrant and medicinal properties. The plant grows 2-3 ft. high and produces many aromatic leaves and many-flowered, flattened heads of white flowers in summer. The fruits are large, dark brown, and fragrant. Myrrhis belongs to the Carrot family, Umbelliferae, and the name refers to the myrrhlike odor of the plant.

For the Herb Garden. Myrrhis odorata was at one time a popular plant in herb gardens, where it was grown under a variety of names, such as Sweet Cicely and Sweet Chervil. At one period or another, all parts of the plant were used—roots, stems and leaves—sometimes as a potherb, at others as a salad or in medicine. Roots, stems and leaves have a stomachic, carminative and expectorant action, and have been used in preparations for coughs and colds, and also as a stimulant in some kinds of stomach trouble. At one period, a decoction of the plant was also used as an ointment for application to ulcers, etc. Sweet Cicely is also sometimes planted in gardens for bees, as they appear to be very attentive to the flowers.

This is an easily grown plant, for it can be raised by sowing seeds out of doors in early spring in any good garden soil. There are other kinds of Myrrhis in Europe and North America, but this is the only one found in cultivation, and even it is much less prominent now than in the past.

MYRTILLOCACTUS (Myrtillocac'tus). Tree-like Cacti with short trunks that grow wild from Mexico to Guatemala. The name is derived from *myrtillus,* the diminutive of Myrtle, and refers to the appearance of the fruits; the plants belong to the Cactus family, Cactaceae.

Kinds include M. Cochal, 10 ft., flowers light green tinged with purple, fruit red, edible; M. geometrizans, 15 ft., much branched, stems bluish, flowers white, fruit (called Garrambulla) bluish or purplish, edible; M. Schenckii, flowers cream to pale yellow. For cultivation, see Cacti.

MYRTLE. See Myrtus.

MYRTLE, BOG. Myrica, which see.

MYRTLE, CRAPE. Lagerstroemia, which see.

MYRTLE, RUNNING. Vinca minor, which see.

MYRTLE, SAND. See Leiophyllum.

MYRTLE, WAX. Myrica cerifera, which see.

MYRTUS—*Myrtle* (Myr'tus). Evergreen trees or large shrubs that are natives of Chile, Peru, Australia, New Zealand and the Mediterranean region; some, like the Common Myrtle, Myrtus communis, have attractive flowers and fragrant leaves. Although not hardy in the North, they are cultivated there in pots and tubs; they are hardy in the lower South and in California. Myrtus belongs to the Myrtle family, Myrtaceae;

The Common Myrtle, Myrtus communis, bears white flowers in summer.

A New Zealand Myrtle, Myrtus bullata.

the name is taken from the original Greek name of the tree, *myrtos*.

Propagation. Roots are formed in the course of a few weeks if cuttings of half-ripe or partly woody shoots, about 4 in. long, are taken in July with a slight heel of old wood, and inserted in a sand bed in a glass case in a frame or greenhouse. The young plants should be potted in sandy, peaty soil.

Established Myrtles require well-drained loamy soil with a little peat or leaf mold placed about the roots at planting time. Planting is best done in spring. The more attractive kinds are sometimes grown in pots and tubs. These should be set in a compost of two parts fibrous loam and one part peat with a sprinkling of sand. When overgrown plants are to be pruned, the work should be done in early spring immediately before new growth appears on the plant.

Myrtles grown in tubs or pots in the North must be kept in a frostproof greenhouse or other light but cool place during winter and spring. They may be grown outdoors during the summer months.

The Common Myrtle. Myrtus communis is the common or true Myrtle of the Mediterranean region. A large bush 8-10 ft. or more in height, it has dark green, glossy leaves an inch or so long; these are delightfully fragrant. The white flowers, borne during summer, are very attractive. Sprigs of Myrtle are very popular for floral decorations and, in Europe, are frequently used in bridal bouquets—more particularly the neat, small-leaved variety tarentina, which appears to be hardier than the typical kind. There is also a variety variegata with variegated leaves; the several other distinct varieties include minima and nana, which are dwarf plants.

A handsome kind from Chile is M. Ugni; in early summer this bears white flowers, followed by fragrant and edible red or black fruits. Other notable Myrtles are M. bullata, a native of New Zealand, with curiously wrinkled leaves; M. obcordata and M. Ralphii, from New Zealand; and M. tenuifolia, from Australia. The plant known in gardens as Myrtus Luma is Eugenia apiculata, which see.

N

NAEGELIA (Naege'lia). Tender herbaceous flowering plants, found wild in Mexico and South America. They have rhizomes (underground stems) with fleshy scale leaves, and grow 18-24 in. in height. The stems are cylindrical and fleshy, the leaves roundish, 3-4 in. in diameter, heart-shaped at the base and crenate (toothed) at the edges. The leaves are mostly green, suffused with crimson, and the whole plant is covered with fine silky hairs.

The inflorescence is at the tip of the shoot and in the form of a long panicle. The tubular, pendent flowers are 1½ in. in length. They are red, scarlet or yellow, and are produced in summer or autumn. The name Naegelia commemorates K. von Naegeli, a German botanist. Some botanists use the name Smithiantha instead of Naegelia for these plants; they are closely allied to Achimenes and belong to the Gesneria family, Gesneriaceae. Naegelias are sometimes called Gesnerias. Hybrids between N. zebrina and various Achimenes are named Eucodonopsis.

Flowering Plants for a Warm Greenhouse. They require a minimum winter temperature of 55 degrees and a soil compost of two parts of peat, one part of loam, one of leaf mold, and a free admixture of sand. The rhizomes are started into growth in March, April or May. If a few are started in each of these months the flowering period is extended into late autumn or winter.

Starting the Roots into Growth. The rhizomes, or root stocks, which have been resting in the pots during winter, are shaken out of the soil and placed in shallow flats or pans containing a layer of leaf mold or peat moss. They are then lightly covered with either of these materials and are set in the hothouse. When young shoots appear, potting is begun. Pots 5-6 in. in diameter are well crocked and filled to within 1 in. of the top with the prepared compost. Three pieces of rhizome, each having a strong shoot, are placed in a 5-in. pot, or more in larger pots. They are covered with half an inch of compost, and the pots are set in a shaded part of the greenhouse.

Details of Management. Water is applied very moderately until the plants are 3-4 in. high; when the pots are well filled with roots, the soil must be kept moist until the flowers have faded. The plants should be shaded from strong sunlight, and the atmosphere of the house kept moist by frequent damping of the floor and benches, but the leaves must not be syringed.

When in flower, the plants are rather top-heavy, and the stems need supporting.

After the flowers have faded, the water supply is gradually lessened, and when the foliage has withered, no more water is given. The pots containing the rhizomes are stored on their sides under the greenhouse benches during the winter.

Propagation by Leaf Cuttings. The chief method of propagation is by division of the rhizomes at potting time. Young plants can also be raised from leaves. The leaves are taken off in summer and inserted as cuttings, the leafstalk ends being set in peat moss and sand or in vermiculite in a propagating case with a bottom heat of 65-70 degrees.

Young shoots eventually form at the bases of the leafstalks; when 1½ in. in length, they are potted and treated in the same way as the mature plants.

Raising Seedlings. Seeds may be sown in well-drained pots of sandy peat in spring. The seeds are scattered thinly on the surface of the soil, and covered only with a thin layer of sand. The compost needs moistening, and so the pot should be immersed to its rim in a pail of water and then placed aside for half an hour for the surplus water to drain away. A pane of glass is laid over the pot, which is plunged in a propagating case with a bottom heat of 65-70 degrees.

The glass is wiped on the underside each morning to prevent condensed moisture from

Naegelia cinnabarina is a handsome relative of the African Violet that is suitable for growing in warm greenhouses.

dripping on the soil and setting up decay. When the seeds have germinated, the glass is removed and the propagating case is ventilated freely. As soon as the seedlings are large enough to handle, they are pricked out, 1½ in. apart, in seed flats or pans filled with the compost advised for potting, but this is first sifted through a half-inch sieve. The seedlings are watered and given the same treatment as the mature plants.

The chief kinds are N. cinnabarina, scarlet; N. fulgida, scarlet; N. multiflora, white; and N. zebrina, yellow and scarlet.

NAMES OF PLANTS
How Plants Get Both Their Common and Scientific Names

The better-known plants, wild and cultivated, have at least two names each. One of these we call the common or vernacular name, and the other the scientific, botanical or "Latin" name. Some plants have more than one common name; on the other hand, sometimes one common name is used for different kinds of plants by people in different places.

The common name of a plant is one by which it is generally known among lay people who have no special knowledge of botanical nomenclature or scientific names. Often common names have been in use from generation to generation by people acquainted with the plant as it grows wild in meadow, hedgerow, or woodland, or by people who have grown it through the centuries in their gardens.

Some "common" names have been invented and applied by nurserymen, advertisers, writers and promoters during recent years; some of these names have "caught on" and are now commonly accepted. Examples of these are Pick-a-back Plant (Tolmiea Menziesii) and African Violet (Saintpaulia). Other attempts to invent common names have proved much less successful.

The history of plant names forms quite a romantic story, going back to ancient times. For the better understanding of present-day rules of botanical nomenclature, we must therefore have some idea of the history of the subject and a knowledge of the ways in which the names of plants have arisen.

The First Known Book on Plants. The sage who wrote the first known book on plants was Theophrastus, a Greek, who lived about three centuries before the time of Christ. Theophrastus called plants by the common names that were current in Greece in his day, and it is interesting to note that many of these names have survived as the scientific names of genera right down to modern times. A few of these are mentioned below.

We cannot pass over the ancient Greek writers without mentioning the famous Dioscorides, A.D. 64, a celebrated physician, whose writings on plants were standard down to the fifteenth century. Indeed, after the time of Dioscorides, botanical history can boast of very little until the days of the herbalists, or early botanists. The history of herbals (early books describing plants and their uses in medicine) is intensely interesting, but beyond the scope of this article. Reference, however, is made below to certain herbalists under derivation of plant names. As far as plant names are concerned, there was no definite order and most botanists used the names that they liked best.

Consequently, many plants were known by many different names, and as the number of recognized species increased, so the names became increasingly difficult to remember: the species were named by "diagnostic phrases," which occasionally meant a fairly long Latin sentence.

The Linnaean System of Naming Plants. This system of naming continued along more or less the same lines until the time of Linnaeus, the great Swedish botanist, who published a work, known as the *Species Plantarum,* in which he gave to each species a name consisting of two words of Latin form, these being the generic name and the specific epithet—e.g., Ranunculus arvensis—the Cornfield Buttercup. This "binary nomenclature" was so convenient that very soon it was universally adopted; it is from Linnaeus *Species Plantarum*, 1753, that we derive our modern system of naming plants.

Rules Which Govern Plant Names. Nowadays, plants must not be named in the haphazard way that was customary in olden times. Many rules exist, known as the International Rules of Botanical Nomenclature, and the naming of plants must be in conformity with these rules. These rules have been carefully constructed and revised at various International Botanical Congresses, from the first which was held in Paris in 1867, to the eighth, held in Paris in 1954.

At present, there are about seventy Articles or Rules and a fair number of Recommendations. It is quite impossible in this short article to go into all these Rules, but probably the most far-reaching is the Rule of Priority.

The Rule of Priority. If, for a moment, we turn to the "Index Kewensis," which is a monumental work containing the name, place of publication and country of origin of all known flowering plants from 1753 down to our own time, we shall see that for many species there is more than one name. Now, according to the Rule of Priority, the earliest name, since 1753, which is published in accordance with the rules, is retained, or "kept up," and the other names "fall," or become "synonyms."

For example, Geranium tuberosum Linn. (1753) is "kept up" and Geranium radicatum, M. Bieb. (1808), another name for the same species, becomes a synonym.

The Earliest Name Is Used. It very often happens that a greater knowledge of plants means that a particular species has to be transferred from one genus to another to which the plant is found to belong, and a "new combination" has to be made. According to the international rule of priority the earliest specific epithet, published in accordance with the rules, must be retained, unless by so doing the author is duplicating an existing name under the new genus. Geranium zonale Linn. (1753), on transference to the genus Pelargonium, becomes Pelargonium zonale (Linn) Ait. (1789). The original author's name is retained in brackets before that of the author of the new combination. The abbreviations Linn. and Ait. denote Linnaeus and Aiton respectively, who are the authors of the above names.

It is often urged that common plant names be used in preference to botanical ones, but most of them are useless for identification. Some plants have several common names, and in some cases, e.g. the summer bedding Geranium, the botanical name of one plant has been used as the popular name of another.

The Rule of Valid Publication. No name is accepted unless it is "validly published." This entails two important factors: the name must be published in a work accessible to botanists either by being placed on sale to the general public or by general distribution among representative botanical institutions; the name must be accompanied by a description or a reference to a former description.

Perhaps mention should be made of one more rule—that concerning the language in which the plants may be described. At Cambridge in 1930 it was decided that no name is validly published unless accompanied by a Latin diagnosis—the main description of the plant may be given in any language, but Latin must be employed for the diagnosis. This rule took effect on January 1st, 1932.

It happens occasionally that the same name is given independently to two different plants. Such identical names are known as homonyms, and the International Rules declare that later homonyms can never be maintained. For example, two different species of Astragalus were described under the name Astragalus rhizanthus, namely, A. rhizanthus Royle (1835), a native of the Himalayas, and A. rhizanthus Boiss. (1843) from Asia Minor. The latter was therefore renamed Astragalus cariensis.

Of course, it is very obvious that to adhere strictly to rules, with no exceptions, would mean continued changes in nomenclature the more thoroughly the various groups were worked out. When, therefore, it is found that a very well-known generic name must be changed because of the existence of a little-known earlier name, the rules provide that the well-known name may be conserved by being placed on a list of "Nomina Conservanda" ("Names to be conserved").

Before a name can be placed on this list it has to be submitted to an international congress and passed by a special committee appointed by the congress to inquire into such cases. Some well-known generic names that are on the list of Nomina Conservanda are Taraxacum (Dandelion), conserved against the earlier name Hedypnois; and Sequoia, conserved against Steinhauera. Conserved names must be used regardless of the existence of one or more earlier names for the genus.

The Spelling of Plant Names. Some readers may have experienced difficulty with regard to the spelling of scientific names, for often different forms of spellings are employed. To meet this the rules provide that the original spelling must be retained, unless it can be proved to be a typographical or orthographical error. Therefore, if the adjective "sylvestris" is spelt in the medieval way with the "y," it must be retained and not be transcribed "silvestris." The older botanists usually adopted the medieval spelling.

Origin of Plant Names. Many names of common garden plants are very ancient, dating from several centuries before Christ. Among those found in Theophrastus (370-285 B.C.) are Adiantum, Anemone, Arum, Daphne, Erica, Heliotropium, Iris, Narcissus and Orchis. Most of these are still used for the same genera, but the "Daphne" of the ancient Greeks was the common European Laurel, now known as Laurus nobilis, and the name Daphne is now given to the Mezereon and the Spurge-Laurel, which do not belong to the true Laurel family.

Through the ages new names have been coined and old names given to new plants, so that the history of plant names is almost the story of plant discovery and cultivation. The Ilex of the ancient Romans was the Holm Oak, but the name Ilex is now given to the Hollies. So many names have been transferred to other plants that it is quite out of the question to go back to the earliest one for each plant, and botanists therefore agreed, as stated above, to make a fresh start from the year 1753 and ignore all the names used before that date.

Plants Named after Gods and Goddesses. The Carnations and Pinks were the divine flower of Dianthus; the Walnut was Juglans, the nut of Jove; and Artemisia the flower of Artemis or Diana. In later times, when chocolate was discovered and brought from tropical America to Europe, the tree was christened Theobroma, the food of the gods. The yellow-flowered weed called Barbarea commemorates St. Barbara. Our garden Fuchsias and Lobelias remind us of the celebrated German and Flemish herbalists of the sixteenth century, Fuchs and Lobel, who gave pictures of medicinal herbs with directions on how to use them.

Plants were classified by their uses in those days, and quite unrelated plants were put together if they served the same purpose or even tasted alike. Those with a pungent taste were dubbed nasturtium or "nose-twister." The original Nasturtium seems to have been the Common Cress, but the name Nasturtium is now given by botanists to the Water Cress. The Indian Cress, when first brought from America, was naturally called Nasturtium indicum, America being then taken for part of India, and it is still commonly called "Nasturtium" in gardens, though its correct name is now Tropaeolum.

Syringa. Lilac and Mock Orange were both originally called Syringa and, unfortunately, botanists kept the name Syringa for the Lilac, while gardeners kept it for the Mock Orange, which is the Philadelphus of botanists.

Rosemary has no connection with Roses, but was named ros marinus (sea dew) because the grayish leaves looked as if salt spray had condensed on them. The rough leaf of the land Forget Me Nots suggested a mouse's ear and was therefore called Myosotis. The Greek name for Snowdrop was Galanthus, meaning milk-white flower, which is hardly as appropriate as the English one. Calceolaria refers to the slipper-like front petal, and Campanula to the bell-shaped flower, while Helianthus (Sunflower) and Helianthemum (Rock Rose) both mean sunflower.

Useful hints for cultivation are sometimes given by plant names: thus Gypsophila, to the person who knows the derivation of plant names, is obviously a lime or chalk-loving plant, and Arenaria might be expected to thrive on sandy, well-drained soils.

The Naming of Garden Varieties. During the past hundred years the continued increase in the number of garden varieties of vegetables, flowers and fruits has raised many problems of nomenclature. Such plants, which have usually arisen as the result of deliberate crossing and selection, are properly termed "cultivars" to distinguish them from natural or wild varieties; and it has long been thought desirable that the names they bear should be of a different form from the botanical names of wild species and varieties. A system of nomenclature drawn up by an international committee of experts was adopted by the Thirteenth International Horticultural Congress held in London in 1952 and published by the Royal Horticultural Society under the title *International Code of Nomenclature for Cultivated Plants*. A few of the more important points of the Code are outlined below.

The aim of the Code is to promote uniformity, accuracy and fixity in the use of **names**. To assist in this it is proposed to publish and periodically revise international registers of cultivar names for the larger groups of garden plants such as Rose, Daffodil and Rhododendron. The Code insists that Latin names ought to be reserved for wild species and varieties and that cultivars should be given names of a popular or fancy form, consisting of not more than two words, written with capital letters and enclosed in quotation marks; for example "Yellow Queen" or "Fortune."

It is recommended that in naming new cultivars the following should be avoided: titles such as "Mr.," "Mrs.," or "Miss," the articles "a" and "the," and abbreviations for personal and geographical names, for example, "Wm." for "William" or "Mt." for "Mount."

The names of hybrids originating in cultivation, in addition to receiving a cultivar name of the form described, may also include a parentage formula enclosed in parentheses and put before the cultivar name, for example, Rhododendron (repens x didymum) "Carmen." In this example the cultivar named "Carmen" is shown to have been raised from a cross between two species of Rhododendron, R. repens and R. didymum.

Under the terms of the Code a plant name will have no standing unless validly published with a description of the plant concerned in a dated horticultural book, periodical or catalogue.

It is further recommended that when a cultivar is introduced from one country to another its name should remain unchanged, thus avoiding the use of two different names for a single plant.

Some time must necessarily elapse before the requirements of this Code become widely known, but it is plain that its universal acceptance will greatly help to minimize the confusion which can so easily arise from haphazard naming and can cause so much irritation and inconvenience to gardeners and botanists alike.

NANANTHUS (Nan'an'thus). A group of small, stemless, succulent plants from South Africa that at one time were included in the genus Mesembryanthemum and that are suitable for growing under the same general conditions as Cacti. They have slightly warty leaves which appear in tufts of 3-6 pairs together. The name is presumably derived from *nannos*, dwarf, and *anthos*, a flower, and refers to the dwarf character of these plants. For their cultivation, see Mesembryanthemum.

Among kinds likely to be grown by succulent fanciers are N. aloides, yellow-flowered; N. Jamesii, flowers yellow with red lines; N. Pole-Evansii, flowers light yellow with central red lines on each petal; N. rubrolineatus, flowers yellow with red line down center of each petal; N. vittatus, bright yellow with a central red line on each petal.

NANDINA DOMESTICA—Heavenly Bamboo, Japanese Bamboo (Nandi'na). A tender, evergreen flowering shrub from Japan, which belongs to the Berberis family, Berberidaceae. In the colder parts of North America it requires the protection of a greenhouse in winter, but in the South and even as far north as Philadelphia (and even further north in sheltered positions) it can be grown out of doors. It is a favorite garden plant in the southern United States. Nandina is derived from *nandin*, the Japanese name for the shrub.

This shrub has unbranched stems 6-8 ft. in height, and large, deeply divided leaves, 12 in. to 2 ft. in length. The numerous leaflets are 3 in. long, lanceolate (lance-shaped), pointed, smooth, tinged with red when young, and

Flowering spray of Nandina domestica, a beautiful summer-flowering evergreen shrub. The flowers are followed by showy red berries.

purplish in the autumn. The flowers, which are produced in summer, are in the form of an erect panicle at the tip of the stem. They are white, with yellow anthers, and measure ¼-½ in. across. In the autumn they are succeeded by small red berries.

Suitable for a Large Conservatory. When grown indoors, Nandina requires a minimum winter temperature of 40 degrees, and a soil compost of equal parts of peat and loam. Planting is done in April, the shrub being set in a large tub or in a specially prepared bed. The tub is well drained with crocks, and these are covered with rough siftings from the compost. Rich potting soil is then placed in the tub; the plants are set in position, and the remainder of the soil is added.

When Nandina is to be planted in a bed in a conservatory, a hole is dug to a depth of 2 ft., and a few inches of broken bricks are placed at the bottom for drainage. These are covered with rough leaves or grass sod and the remainder of the space filled with the prepared compost described previously. After this has settled, planting is begun, the roots being well spread out. The plants are shaded from bright sunlight and the atmosphere kept moist by frequent damping of the floor and other surfaces. During the summer the soil is regularly moistened; throughout the winter, however, water is given only when the soil becomes fairly dry.

Treatment Out of Doors. This shrub requires a position sheltered from cold winds, and prefers a peaty soil that is not excessively dry. It thrives in shade or sun. Planting should be done in spring and the soil kept moist in dry weather by watering.

Propagation Is by Cuttings. Shoots 3 in. long are taken off in summer, inserted in sandy peat, and covered with a bell jar until roots are formed; then the shoots are potted separately in small pots and subsequently in larger ones. Plants can also be raised from seeds.

NANKEEN LILY. See Lilium testaceum.

NANKING CHERRY. The Nanking Cherry, Prunus tomentosa, is a wide-spreading, compact small tree growing to 8 ft. in height. The white flowers appear with the earliest shrubs of spring and are followed in late June by a heavy crop of small, pleasantly flavored cherry-red fruits. In flower and in fruit the plant is attractive and well worth a place in the garden. It is a native of Japan, northern China and Manchuria.

Selections of superior types have been made at the Minnesota Agricultural Experiment Station. One of these, Drilea, and some numbered selections are being sold by nurseries. The plants are very hardy and are easily grown on any good well-drained soil. Propagation is by seeds, which should be stratified (stored in slightly moist peat moss and sand in a cool place for several weeks) before sowing. The improved varieties are budded on seedlings of the species.

NANNYBERRY. See Viburnum Lentago.

NANUS. A botanical term used in the naming of plants which are of low or dwarf growth.

NARCISSI or DAFFODILS
Universal Spring Favorites

A large group of mostly hardy bulbs, Narcissi bloom chiefly in March and April out of doors, and in greenhouses from December to March. There are many species or wild types and innumerable named varieties; the latter increase in number every year. Most of the species or wild types are natives of southern Europe. Narcissus belongs to the Amaryllis family, Amaryllidaceae. The name Narcissus is taken from that of a youth in Greek mythology who is said to have changed into the flower. The word Daffodil is from the Dutch *de affodil,* and ultimately from the Greek *asphodelos.* The name Daffodil is most commonly applied to those Narcissi which have large trumpets but may be used for all types. The name Jonquil most properly belongs to the rush-leaved Narcissus Jonquilla and its hybrids, but in some parts of North America it is used as a common name for all types of Narcissi.

The Narcissus, with its wealth of species and varieties, is one of the loveliest of all early spring flowers and is suitable for cultivation in many

Daffodils naturalized beside an open woodland walk.

Daffodils naturalized at The New York Botanical Garden.

ways. It can be naturalized in open spaces in woodland or shrubbery or at the edge of the lawn; some kinds are suitable for the rock garden or for growing in pots in the alpine greenhouse; in a heated greenhouse it is possible to maintain a long succession of bloom from December onwards by cultivating Narcissi in pots and flats. Many kinds are superb as cut flowers.

In recent years an immense amount of crossbreeding has been practiced, and innumerable beautiful new varieties have been raised. As a result of this intensive crossbreeding the old lines of demarcation between the various groups no longer exist. The Royal Horticultural Society of Great Britain has drawn up a set of regulations defining the different types, and separating them into divisions. This classification is generally followed in North America, Europe and elsewhere where Narcissi are cultivated. It is the standard generally used by exhibitors at flower shows, and is usually called for in flower show schedules and demanded by judges at flower shows.

White Lion is a handsome double-flowered variety.

The large, golden-yellow Trumpet Daffodil named Magnificence.

The richly colored Narcissus Damson, with yellow perianth and orange-scarlet cup.

Firetail, white perianth and scarlet-orange cup, is one of the loveliest of the small-cupped Narcissi.

The R.H.S. Classification

"Colored" means yellow or some color other than white. "White" means white or whitish.

The length of a perianth segment is the extreme length measured on the inside from its junction with the corona (central cup or trumpet of the flower) along the midrib to the extreme tip, and the length of the corona is the extreme length measured from its junction with the perianth to the end of its furtherest extension when the edge is flattened out.

Except in Division X the Narcissi that properly belong in the following classification are all varieties of garden origin.

Division I. Trumpet Narcissi. Distinguishing characters: One flower to a stem; trumpet or

The white Trumpet Daffodil Beersheba.

The popular golden Daffodil King Alfred.

Narcissus Geranium is a Tazetta variety with white perianth segments and a brilliant orange-scarlet cup.

One of the loveliest of the small Daffodils, Narcissus moschatus, bears drooping, fragrant sulphur-white flowers. It is good for the rock garden.

corona as long or longer than the perianth segments.

(a) Perianth colored; corona colored, not paler than the perianth.

(b) Perianth white; corona colored.

(c) Perianth white; corona white, not paler than the perianth.

(d) Any color combination not falling into (a), (b) or (c).

Division II. Large-cupped Narcissi. Distinguishing characters: One flower to a stem; cup or corona more than one third, but less than equal to the length of the perianth segments.

(a) Perianth colored; corona colored, not paler than the perianth.

(b) Perianth white; corona colored.

(c) Perianth white; corona white, not paler than the perianth.

(d) Any color combination not falling into (a), (b) or (c).

Division III. Small-cupped Narcissi. Distinguishing characters: One flower to a stem; cup or corona not more than one third the length of the perianth segments.

(a) Perianth colored; corona colored, not paler than the perianth.

A very charming miniature Narcissus, the Cyclamen-flowered N. cyclamineus.

One of the smallest of the yellow-flowered Daffodils, Narcissus minor.

A naturalized group of the fascinating Hoop Petticoat Narcissus, N. Bulbocodium. There are several varieties of it.

A container of the golden yellow-flowered Tazetta type Narcissus Grand Soleil d'Or.

(b) Perianth white; corona colored.

(c) Perianth white; corona white, not paler than the perianth.

(d) Any color combination not falling into (a), (b) or (c).

Division IV. Double Narcissi. Distinguishing character: Double flowers.

Division V. Triandrus Narcissi. Distinguishing characters: Characteristics of Narcissus triandrus clearly evident.

(a) Cup or corona not less than two thirds the length of the perianth segments.

(b) Cup or corona less than two thirds the length of the perianth segments.

Division VI. Cyclamineus Narcissi. Distinguishing characters: Characteristics of Narcissus cyclamineus clearly evident.

(a) Cup or corona not less than two thirds the length of the perianth segments.

(b) Cup or corona less than two thirds the length of the perianth segments.

The dainty little Rush-leaved Narcissus, N. juncifolius. It is a charming little bulb for growing in pots in the cool greenhouse.

Narcissus Paper White, the most popular of all for winter flowering in the home and greenhouse.

Division VII. Jonquilla Narcissi. Distinguishing characters: Characteristics of any of the Narcissus Jonquilla group clearly evident.

[7—10]
Small-cupped Narcissus
Asta Nielson

[7—10a]
Tazetta Narcissus La Fiancee

[7—10c]
Double Narcissus Texas

[7—10b]
Trumpet Narcissus Music Hall

[7–11]
Lotus
(Nelumbium Nelumbo)

[7–11a]
Hardy Water Lily Rose Arey

[7–11b]
Hardy Water Lily Sunrise

[7–11c]
Tropical Water Lily
Mrs. George C. Hitchcock

Narcissus Fortune has beautiful large golden flowers.

(a) Cup or corona not less than two thirds the length of the perianth segments.

(b) Cup or corona less than two thirds the length of the perianth segments.

Division VIII. Tazetta Narcissi. Distinguishing characters: Characteristics of any of the Narcissus Tazetta group clearly evident.

Division IX. Poeticus Narcissi. Distinguishing characters: Characteristics of the Narcissus poeticus group without admixture of any other.

Division X. Species and Wild Forms and Hybrids. All species and wild, or reputedly wild, forms and hybrids.

Division XI. Miscellaneous Narcissi. All Narcissi not falling into any of the foregoing Divisions.

The exquisite white-flowered Angel's Tears, Narcissus triandrus albus.

Narcissi in Beds and Borders

Narcissus bulbs are invaluable for filling flower beds and borders, either alone or in association with other spring-flowering plants. They thrive in ordinary well-tilled garden soil, but are at their best in well-drained loamy ground. On light land the flowers are not usually so fine or so long-lived as those from bulbs planted on loamy soil. Before bulbs are planted on clayey ground, sand should be added freely and compost or other organic matter may be dug in with advantage.

It is a mistake to apply fresh manure to land in which Narcissi are to be planted. On poor light ground, however, well-decayed manure is beneficial; it should be dug in to a depth of 9-12 in. There is no better fertilizer for Narcissi than bone meal: this should be scattered on the soil at the rate of 2 oz. per square yard and forked in before the bulbs are planted.

The best time to plant Narcissus bulbs, so far as their cultivation in an average garden is concerned, is in September and early October. Those who grow flowers for exhibition should plant as soon as possible after the leaves have died down, in July–August. The bulbs may, however, be planted at any time during the autumn months, even as late as December, but the later the bulbs are put in the more disappointing will be the results the first year.

How Deep to Plant. The depth at which the bulbs are set must depend on their size, for some are very much larger than others. Large bulbs of the Trumpet Narcissi should have a soil covering of not less than 4-5 in. Those of medium size should be covered with 3-4 in. of soil, and smaller ones with 2-3 in. One of the commonest mistakes made by amateur gardeners is to put the bulbs too near the surface.

Narcissi can be left undisturbed for many years—in fact, until they become so crowded that they fail to bloom freely. But generally it will be found that bulbs planted in flower borders need to be lifted at the end of three or four years. When Narcissi are planted in grassland or woodland, it is usual to set the bulbs farther apart than when they are set in flower borders, so that they can be left undisturbed for a longer period.

The very finest flowers are obtained by lifting and replanting the bulbs annually, or in alternate years, as soon as the leaves have died down; that is the practice followed by exhibitors.

Groups of Narcissi planted in the perennial border provide a gay show of color in the spring. The bulbs should be planted in early fall.

It is important not to remove the foliage of Narcissi until it has completely died down. To keep them from appearing untidy in the process of dying down, the leaves of Narcissi in perennial borders may be tied together in bundles after flowering is through.

When planting Narcissi for naturalistic effects, scatter the bulbs informally and plant them where they fall.

A special bulb-planting tool may be used to remove plugs of sod to make holes for the bulbs.

Propagation of Narcissi

The propagation of Narcissi is a fairly simple matter. When they are lifted, the old bulbs, more particularly when they have been planted for two or three years, will be found to be surrounded by several offsets or small bulbs, either detached or lightly joined, and easily separated at the base. These offsets, when replanted, will form flowering bulbs within one or two seasons, according to their size. They should be taken

A bulb is placed in the bottom of each hole and the plug of sod fitted back on top of it.

The plug of sod is pressed into position by stepping upon it.

off as soon as the leaves have died down, and may be replanted at once or stored until autumn.

Yet another method by which Narcissi may be increased is that of bulb cuttings (see Propagation) but this is worthwhile only in the case of a rare kind.

Raising Narcissi from Seeds. The propagation of Narcissus by seeds is practiced only for the purpose of raising new varieties, or species, as the seedlings will not grow into flowering bulbs until five years or even more from the time of sowing. The seeds should be sown as soon as they are ripe in late summer or early autumn, in a cold frame. The seeds should be set about 1 in. apart; the seedlings may then be left undisturbed until the leaves have died down the following July. In September the small bulbs should be set in a bed of sandy soil made up in a frame or on a prepared border out of doors.

Cultivation in Pots, Flats and Other Containers

The Narcissus is one of the easiest of all bulbs to grow in pots for the decoration of the greenhouse, conservatory and house in winter and early spring. By potting bulbs at intervals of a few weeks, from August until the end of September, it is possible to have plants in bloom from December until the middle of March. The way to achieve success is to use a compost of loam (old turf) with which a little leaf mold and decayed manure and a good sprinkling of sand have been mixed. The bulbs will do far better in such a mixture than if soil from the garden is used.

If, however, loam is not available, good soil taken from the garden will serve; leaf mold and decayed manure should be added, together with sand, unless the soil is naturally light.

The bulbs should be set at such a depth that the greater part of each one is covered with soil; the smaller bulbs may be wholly buried. The number of bulbs that can be set in a pot must, of course, depend on their size; four bulbs of moderate size or three large bulbs can be placed in a 6-in. pot.

When potting is finished, the pots of bulbs should be placed outdoors on a bed of cinders or a hard base and watered thoroughly; the grower

When Narcissi are lifted, the small bulblets that form around the bases of the large bulbs may be removed and used for propagation.

must make sure that the soil is moistened right through. They are then covered with old sifted ashes, sand or peat moss to a depth of 6 or 7 in. It is most necessary that old ashes—those which have been exposed to the air for some time—be used; if ashes fresh from the fire are put on the bed, it is probable that the bulbs will be seriously damaged. No further watering is needed.

After six weeks the bulbs should be examined. Most of them will have become well rooted and top growth of the earliest varieties will have started. The pots containing bulbs which have begun to grow should be taken from beneath the ashes and placed in a cold frame or in a greenhouse where the bulbs may grow under cool conditions yet not be subjected to frost. It is necessary to shade them for a few days; if this is not done, the sudden change from darkness to full light, and possible strong sunlight, may cause the leaf tips to turn yellow.

By placing the pots of bulbs, a few at a time, in a higher temperature, a succession of flowers will be assured. A temperature of 50 degrees is high enough at first, though this may be increased to 55 or even 60 degrees when the flower buds show, if flowers are wanted quickly.

In early summer the bulbs that have been

forced in this way may be planted in the garden, in a place where they are unlikely to be disturbed; there they will recover, become established, and bloom in future years. Except in mild climates, the Paper White Narcissus and other tender kinds are not worth keeping. It is usual to purchase fresh bulbs annually for cultivation in pots, for they are much more reliable than bulbs dug up from the garden; the latter, however, often give good results if they are not forced too rapidly.

Cultivation in Flats. When Narcissi are forced into early bloom to provide cut flowers it is usual to grow them in flats. The bulbs are planted, almost touching each other, in flats that are about 4 in. deep (containers shallower than this are scarcely practicable). The type of soil required, time of planting and after care of the planted flats are the same as are detailed above for the cultivation of Narcissi in pots.

In Other Containers. In houses Narcissi are sometimes grown in other types of containers and in media other than soil. Varieties of the Tazetta section particularly, especially the varieties Paper White, Soleil d'Or and orientalis

After potting, the bulbs may be buried under 6 or 8 in. of ashes or cinders outdoors.

Alternatively, the pots containing the newly planted Narcissi may be placed in a root cellar or other cool frost-free building and covered with a few inches of peat moss.

When Narcissi are to be forced in pots, the bulbs should be planted close together with good soil beneath them.

After the bulbs are set in position, soil is filled in between them and is pressed firm with the fingers.

After several weeks the bulbs will have rooted and produced short shoots. The pots may then be removed to a protected cold frame or may be brought into a cool greenhouse and kept out of direct sun until the shoots turn green.

As soon as the shoots turn green the pots of Narcissi must be placed in full sun in a window where the night temperature is 50 to 55 degrees. They make rapid progress.

The flowers of Narcissi grown in pots remain in good condition longest if the pots are kept in a cool place out of direct sun.

(Chinese Sacred Lily), are often cultivated in undrained containers in pebbles and water or in bulb fiber or vermiculite. See In Homes and Greenhouses under the Encyclopedia entry Bulbs For The Garden And Home. See also, House Plants.

Naturalizing Narcissi

The practice of naturalizing Narcissi—planting the bulbs in groups in grassy places in the less formal parts of the garden—ensures delightful results. They look well among trees and shrubs, on grass banks, on the edge of the lawn, in the orchard, and in those odd corners which are often neglected and allowed to run wild.

Care should be taken to plant the bulbs in informal masses; this can be assured by scattering them by hand and planting them where they fall, though this method is not wholly suitable for planting in grass.

The best time to plant the bulbs is in early autumn, when the ground is fairly moist. It is useless to attempt planting while the ground is hard and dry. A special tool made for the purpose of planting bulbs in grassland is very convenient for use and saves time and trouble.

An alternative method is to cut and roll back the turf, fork over the soil, set the bulbs, and replace the turf.

Bulbs which are naturalized should not be planted closely together; there should be 6-8 in. between them; otherwise they will become

Narcissi of the Paper White type may be forced in pebbles and water. Here, bulbs of Narcissus Paper White are stood on a bed of pearl chips or pebbles in the bottom of a waterproof container.

Between the bulbs, which are placed close together, more chips or pebbles are poured.

When planting is completed, the container is filled with water and put in a fairly cool place.

After the shoots are 3 or 4 in. high, the container of bulbs must be removed to a sunny location. Flowers develop in a few weeks.

In their early stages the bulbs may be kept either in darkness or light. They soon develop roots and shoots.

overcrowded in a few years and will cease to bloom freely. The bulbs should be covered with about 3 in. of soil. The most charming flower pictures result when each group consists of one variety; if mixed bulbs are planted—say, Trumpet Daffodils and small-cupped Narcissi together—the effect is not nearly so pleasing.

Miniature Narcissi For Planting Outdoors

These are charming bulbs for the rock garden, or a sheltered border at the foot of a wall or fence. The chief kinds are N. Bulbocodium (Hoop Petticoat Daffodil), in several varieties; N. cyclamineus (Cyclamen-flowered Daffodil), yellow; N. gracilis, fragrant, yellow; N. juncifolius (Rush-leaved Daffodil); N. triandrus (Angel's Tears) and its hybrids and varieties.

The bulbs should be planted in September in well-drained, sandy, loamy soil in sheltered places.

Miniatures for the Greenhouse. The bulbs of miniature kinds should be potted in September in 5-in. pots, the bulbs being set about an inch apart and covered with an inch or less of soil. The pots of bulbs should be placed in a cold,

Narcissi grown in pots and forced into early bloom are welcome indoor decorative plants in late winter.

shaded frame for six weeks to ensure the development of roots before top growth begins; if then placed in a cool greenhouse where night temperatures of 40-50 degrees are maintained they will prove very beautiful in winter or early spring.

Selections for General Planting

Of the numerous varieties in all sections, the following Daffodils and Narcissi are recommended for general planting:

Trumpet Narcissi. *Yellow:* Apotheose, Dawson City, Godolphin, Golden Harvest, King Alfred, Magnificence, Rembrandt, Unsurpassable, Wintergold. *Bicolors:* Bonython, Glory of Sassenheim, President Lebrun, Queen of the Bicolors, Spring Glory, Trocadero. *White:* Beersheba, Gloria, Imperator, Mrs. E. H. Krelage.

To obtain early cut flowers, bulbs of Narcissi are planted close together in flats that are about 4 in. deep.

Large-cupped Narcissi. *Yellow, with colored cup:* Aranjuez, Carbineer, Carlton, Croesus, Damson, Fortune, Havelock, Helios, Killigrew, Marian Cran, Rustom Pasha, Scarlet Leader. *White, with colored cup:* Bodilly, Brunswick, Daisy Schaffer, Dick Wellband, Hades, John Evelyn, Mata Hari, Mrs. Barclay, Mrs. R. O. Backhouse (the Pink Daffodil), Orange Flag, Penvose, Semper Avanti, Tunis. *White:* Tenedos, White Nile.

Small-cupped Narcissi. *Perianth and corona colored:* Bath's Flame, Gulliver, Margosteen, Seraglio, Tridore. *White perianth, colored cup:* Firetail, Lady Diana Manners, Lady Moore, La Riante, Sunrise. *White:* Mitylene, Mystic, White Queen.

Double Daffodils. Double White Poeticus (albus plenus odoratus), Inglescombe, Mary Copeland, Texas, Van Sion (Telamonius plenus).

Jonquilla Narcissi. Golden Perfection, Golden Scepter, Lanarth, odorus rugulosus, Trevithian.

Tazetta (Poetaz or Bunch-flowered) Narcissi: Admiration, Elvira, Red Guard, Scarlet Gem, St. Agnes. In the South the varieties Paper White, Soleil d'Or and orientalis (Chinese Sacred Lily) may be grown outdoors.

Poeticus (Poet's) Narcissi. Actaea, Horace, poeticus recurvus (Old Pheasant's Eye), Red Rim, Sarchedon.

Good Varieties for Forcing. *Trumpet Narcissi:* Apotheose, Dawson City, Golden Harvest, Golden Spur, King Alfred, Magnificence, Rembrandt, Spring Glory, Winter Gold. *Narcissi, Large-cupped:* Carlton, Damson, Fortune, Helios, Marion Cran, Scarlet Elegance, Scarlet Leader, Yellow Poppy, Hades, Monique. *Small-cupped:* Bath's Flame, Lady Moore, La Riante, Verger, White Queen. *Double Narcissi:* Insulinde, Irene Copeland, Texas, Van Sion. *Tazetta Narcissi:* Soleil d'Or, Paper White, Admiration, Cheerfulness, Geranium, Halvose, Primrose Beauty, Scarlet Gem, St. Agnes—in fact, all members of this section. A popular variety for growing in homes is N. Tazetta orientalis which is called the Chinese Sacred Lily.

NARTHECIUM — *Bog Asphodel* (Narthe'cium). Rushlike bog plants, natives of the Northern Hemisphere and belonging to the Lily

When Narcissi are grown in flats, large numbers of flowers are produced from a limited area. The bulbs require the same treatment as those planted in pots.

family, Liliaceae. They have slender, creeping, underground rootstocks which give rise to linear (long and narrow) leaves 6-12 in. long, and are formed in tufts similar to the Iris. In midsummer, slender spikes of small yellow flowers are produced on stems 6-20 in. long, and are formed in tufts similar to the Iris. The derivation of the name Narthecium is apparently from *Narthex*, giant Fennel.

For a Sunny Bog Garden. Bog Asphodels are planted in fall or spring in the bog garden or some other moist, sunny position. Ordinary garden soil is suitable. Once they have been planted, very little attention is required, except to restrict the size of the plants when they exceed their allotted space.

Propagation is by division of the plants at planting time or by seeds. The seeds are sown direct in the moist soil of the bog garden in April, or in a flower pan of ordinary garden soil. When sown in a flower pan, they should be set ½ in. deep; the pan is covered with a pane of glass and set in a cold frame. The compost must be kept perpetually moist. The seedlings are planted in their permanent positions in autumn or spring.

N. americanum is a rare native of Pine bogs in eastern North America. N. californicum occurs in marshes from California to Oregon.

NASTURTIUM—*Water Cress* (Nastur'tium). The plants grown in gardens for their showy flowers as Nasturtiums are botanically called Tropaeolum (which see), and belong to the Geranium family, Geraniaceae, whereas the true Nasturtiums, of which the Water Cress is the best-known, belong to the Mustard family, Cruciferae. Some modern botanists now refer these to the genus Roripa and regard the name Nasturtium as invalid.

The Nasturtiums are found wild in Europe and Asia and are naturalized in North America. N. officinale, the edible Water Cress, has divided leaves and terminal tufts of white, four-petaled flowers. The other kinds are found on marshy ground and waste places, and have yellow flowers. The name Nasturtium is derived from *nasus*, the nose and *tortus*, twisted, and refers to the pungent odor of Nasturtium officinale.

Water Cress is grown for the market in specially prepared beds. The small plants are set in the soil at the bottom of the bed and the surface is covered with fine gravel to keep it clean. A stream of fresh water to a depth of 3 or 4 in. is kept constantly running through them. The beds are cleaned out and replanted twice a year, in May and October.

Growing Water Cress in the Garden. Water Cress may be cultivated in the garden, but it is inferior in quality unless running water is available. One method is to take out the soil to a depth of 1 ft. in a shady part of the garden. Well-decayed manure is then dug into the bottom and the surface of the soil is covered with a thick layer of sand. Tips of shoots, 2 in. in length, are inserted 3 in. apart in the soil. The soil is kept moist by frequent waterings.

Water Cress in a Tank or Tub. Water Cress is also grown in large tanks or tubs. A few inches of rich soil is placed in the bottom and the shoots are dibbled in; water is then poured in until it reaches to the tip of the shoots. The success of this method relies on the frequent draining off and replenishing of the water, the ideal being a constant flow. When the produce begins to deteriorate, the plants and soil must be cleared out and replenished.

Water Cress can be raised from seeds which are sown in April or August in large pans of ordinary light garden soil. A pane of glass is laid over the pan and the soil is kept constantly moist. When the seedlings are 1 in. in height they are pricked out into the beds in the way described for the cuttings.

There are three kinds of Water Cress: the green-leaved, small brown-leaved, and large brown-leaved. The latter is the easiest to cultivate without running water.

NATAL PLUM. Carissa grandiflora, which see.

NATURALIZED. In botanical usage, plants that are not original natives of a region but which have established themselves so successfully that they persist and reproduce themselves are said to be naturalized. Examples of well-known kinds that have naturalized themselves in North America are the Ox-eye Daisy (Chrysanthemum Leucanthemum), from Europe and Asia; the Common Dandelion (Taraxacum officinale), from Europe and western Asia; and the Tree of Heaven (Ailanthus glandulosa), from eastern Asia.

Gardeners speak of naturalizing plants when they plant them (usually in informal arrangements that give the illusion that the plants have not been set by man but have sprung up naturally) among grass, in woodlands, along stream banks and in other informal areas with the expectation that they will make themselves at home and persist, and perhaps increase, with minimum care. Narcissi, Scillas, Grape Hyacinths, Snowdrops and other bulbs are frequently naturalized; so are such favorite plants as Primroses, Japanese Irises, Siberian Irises and shrub Roses.

NAUTILOCALYX (Nautiloca'lyx). Tropical, mostly erect but sometimes trailing, herbaceous plants of the Gesneria family, Gesneriaceae. Natives of South America. The name is derived from *nautilos* and *calyx* and refers to the nautilus-shaped calyx.

Three erect kinds are cultivated chiefly for their attractive foliage. They thrive best in a humid atmosphere where the temperature is 60-65 degrees at night and 10-15 degrees higher in the daytime. Shade from strong sun is necessary.

Daffodils naturalized in an open meadow.

The soil should be coarse, porous and rich with decayed organic matter, such as leaf mold, peat moss or compost and should be kept always evenly moist. Propagation is by cuttings, leaf cuttings and seeds.

Kinds. N. bullatus (sometimes misnamed Episcia tesellata), olive-green or bronzy green creped foliage, flowers pale yellow; N. Forgetii, bright green leaves with darker veins, flowers with reddish calyx lobes spotted with green; N. Lynchii (Alloplectus Lynchii), leaves shining dark green or red-purple, flowers pale yellow with red hairs.

NAVELWORT. See Omphalodes and Umbilicus.

NAVELWORT, VENUS'S. Omphalodes linifolia, which see.

NEAPOLITAN CYCLAMEN. Cyclamen neapolitanum, which see.

NEBRASKA, GARDENING IN. See Regional Gardening.

NECK. This term is used by gardeners to denote the extreme base of a plant just above the roots; it is also used in referring to the upper part of a bulb.

NECKLACE PLANT. See Abrus.

NECTARINE. The Nectarine is a smooth-skinned or fuzzless Peach. The fruit is usually smaller than a Peach and is considered by some to be sweeter, to have a more vinous flavor, a distinctive aroma, and flesh that is a little less melting. There are yellow-fleshed, white-fleshed, clingstone, and freestone varieties, as with Peaches. The tree is identical with the Peach tree.

Nectarines may originate from Peach pits, or as bud variations on Peach trees, and Peaches may arise from Nectarines in the same manner.

Nectarines are a choice and distinctive fruit for the home garden. In the East they are not grown commercially, but a small commercial Nectarine industry exists in California, and some of the crop is shipped to eastern markets.

Varieties for the East are Surecrop, white-fleshed; and Rivers Orange and Garden State, both yellow-fleshed. Nectacrest, Nectaheart and Nectarose are new eastern varieties.

In California, there are a number of varieties now being grown. Yellow-fleshed varieties are John Rivers, Flaming Gold, Kim, Le Grand, Freedom, Mabel, and Pioneer. Among the white-fleshed varieties are Gower, Stanwick, Quetta, Gold Mine, Dixie and Silver Lode, as well as some of the eastern varieties.

Avoiding Damage. Nectarines have the same climatic, soil and cultural requirements as Peaches. Because of the smooth skin, they are more subject to damage by Plum curculio and Oriental fruit moth than Peaches. In California the grass thrips finds the fuzzless pistil to its liking, and the insect may cause serious injury where it is abundant. Nectarines are also rather susceptible to brown rot. Sprays do not stick as well to the smooth skin as to the fuzzy skin of the Peach; hence the spray program must be more thorough but is otherwise the same as for Peaches.

NEEDLE. A name given to the acicular or needle-like leaves of Pines and certain other plants.

NEEM TREE. Melia Azadirachta, which see.

NEILLIA (Neil'lia). Deciduous shrubs from China and the Himalayas, which are allied to the Spiraeas and belong to the Rose family, Rosaceae. The name commemorates Dr. Patrick Neill of Edinburgh, a Scottish botanist.

These shrubs grow 3-6 ft. high, have gracefully arching or spreading branches and bright green leaves, and bear white or pink flowers in May–June. They thrive in sun or partial shade in ordinary garden soil which contains plenty of humus, so that it remains moist in dry weather. Planting may be done in autumn or spring.

Ripe Fruits of Nectarines.

Propagation is by division of the clumps or by the removal of offsets, the best time to do this being in fall or early spring. Neillias are also propagated by cuttings in June or July. These should be made of the ends of the side shoots, 3-4 in. long, and inserted in sand in a frame or greenhouse. They may also be raised from seeds.

Pruning should be done after flowering, as the blooms are borne on the previous year's growths. When the branches of stems become crowded, cut old, worn-out growths and very weak shoots to the ground in June, after the flowers fade.

The North American species previously included in this genus are now called Physocarpus, which see.

The principal species are Neillia longiracemosa, 3-6 ft., rose-pink terminal racemes; N. sinensis, 5-6 ft., white; N. thyrsiflora, white; and N. thibetica, 5 ft., flowers pink.

NELUMBIUM—*Lotus* (Nelum'bium). Aquatic plants with ornamental flowers and foliage, which belong to the Water Lily family, Nymphaeaceae. There are two kinds. One, N. Nelumbo (speciosum), is found wild in tropical Asia; the other, N. pentapetalum (luteum), is a native of North America. Nelumbium is derived from the Cingalese name of N. Nelumbo.

The Hindu and Chinese Lotus, N. Nelumbo, has for ages been regarded as sacred in India and China. (The sacred Egyptian Lotus is generally considered to be Nymphaea Lotus.) N. Nelumbo has rhizomes (underground stems) which grow in the mud at the bottom of the water. From these arise large, glaucous (blue-gray), peltate (umbrella-like) leaves which stand several feet above the water when fully grown. The water-lilylike flowers are white, tipped with rose, 6-12 in. across, and fragrant; they are borne singly on long stems, equalling or in some cases exceeding the height of the leaves.

There are many color forms of the Hindu Lotus, including album, white, the Magnolia Lotus; album plenum, double; roseum plenum, rose-pink, double; pekinense rubrum, amaranth; and Shiroman, cream-white with greenish tinge.

The American Lotus, N. pentapetalum, is similar in habit to N. Nelumbo but has smaller leaves and fragrant yellow flowers somewhat resembling those of Tulips.

Aquatic Plants. These plants require a minimum winter temperature above freezing and a soil compost of two parts of loam and one part of well-decayed manure. Large tubs or pools, indoors or outdoors, are required for their cultivation. From 12-18 in. of the compost is placed

Both the flowers and leaves of Nelumbiums are carried well above the water. They are handsome aquatic plants for pools and water gardens. These are growing at The New York Botanical Garden.

in the vessel, and the rhizomes are planted 4 in. below the surface in spring. The vessel is then filled with water, which is replenished as it evaporates or is used up, during the summer. Or the tubs containing the plants may be filled with soil and then be submerged so that the soil surface is 8-12 in. below the water.

Yet a third plan is to plant the tubers, in rather late spring, just before they start into new growth, in rich soil in the bottom of a pond in water that is 1-3 ft. deep.

If the roots are covered with sufficient water to prevent them from freezing, they will winter over satisfactorily. However, if the water is not deep enough for this, the pool should be drained in the fall and the tubs containing the plants should be moved to a cellar or some other place where a temperature between 35-45 degrees is maintained; or the plants should be covered with 3 ft. or so of leaves, salt hay, or straw and left outdoors over winter.

Propagation is effected by division of the tubers in spring at planting time and by seeds.

Seeds are sown in pans of sandy soil, which are immersed in a tank or vessel of water heated to 60 degrees. The seedlings are allowed to grow in the seed pans until large enough to plant out in tubs or tanks as advised.

NEMASTYLIS (Nemas'tylis). Tender bulbous plants from the southern United States and Mexico, which belong to the family Iridaceae. They have linear (long and narrow) leaves and bear small clusters of six-petaled blue or purple flowers, half an inch in diameter, on stems 6 in. to 2 ft. in height in summer.

Nemastylis is suitable for planting out of doors for the summer or for cultivation in pots in a cool greenhouse. The name Nemastylis is derived from *nema,* a thread, and *stylus,* a style, and refers to the threadlike styles.

Cultivation in Pots. The bulbs are potted in November. The pots are well-drained and filled with a soil compost of two parts of sandy loam, one part of leaf mold, and a small quantity of well-decayed manure and sand. Five bulbs are then set in a 5-in. pot, or more bulbs in larger pots, and they are covered with an inch of compost. The potted bulbs are set on a bed of ashes in a cold frame, and covered to the depth of 3 in. with peat moss, sand or fine ashes.

When growth commences, the plants are taken into a greenhouse with a minimum temperature of 40 degrees. They are watered carefully at all times during their growing period. Extremes of wetness or dryness are to be avoided; the soil must be kept uniformly moist.

When the flowers have faded, less water is given; after the foliage has died down, the soil is kept quite dry until the bulbs are repotted.

Treatment Out of Doors. In the South, where they are hardy, the bulbs may be planted in the fall and left to grow out of doors permanently; where not winter-hardy, the bulbs are planted out in March. Light, well-drained soil and a sunny position are required. The site is prepared by digging in a moderate amount of well-decayed manure; heavy soils need lightening with sand or leaf mold. The bulbs are planted 4 in. deep and 4 in. or more apart, according to the vigor of the kind.

In early summer the surface of the bed is mulched with well-decayed manure or compost, and during the growing and flowering periods the soil is kept moist by watering. In fall the bulbs are lifted and stored in a frostproof place for the winter.

Propagation is chiefly by offsets. The smaller bulbs are separated from those of flowering size, and are potted or planted in a nursery bed out of doors in spring, where they will attain flowering size in a year or two. They must be lifted in autumn, stored during the winter months and replanted out of doors in April, or they may be grown in pots in greenhouse or frame.

The chief kinds are N. acuta (geminiflora), 2 ft., and N. floridana, to 4 ft. All bear blue or violet flowers in summer.

NEMATANTHUS (Nematan'thus). A small group of native Brazilian plants of the Gesnera family, the Gesneriaceae. The name is derived from *nema,* thread and *anthos,* flower, and refers to the slender pedicels of one kind.

The only species cultivated in North America is N. longipes which has brilliant scarlet flowers hanging on long pedicels. Nematanthus require the same cultural conditions as Columnea, which see.

NEMATODE. See Pests and Diseases.

NEMESIA (Nemes'ia). Annual and tender perennial plants which grow wild in South Africa;

A bed of half-hardy annual Nemesias, in various brilliant shades, in full summer beauty.

where cool summers prevail they are of great value for summer flower beds. They are also grand for cultivation in pots in the greenhouse for spring blooming. They are part of the Snapdragon family, Scrophulariaceae. Nemesia is from an old Greek name.

Few of the wild kinds or species are in cultivation, but there are numerous varieties having flowers of brilliant coloring. The plant from which the modern strains of Nemesia have been chiefly raised is Nemesia strumosa, which bears orange-yellow flowers.

When to Sow Seeds. To provide plants which will be ready for planting out of doors in May, seeds should be sown in a temperature of 55 degrees, towards the end of March. As the seeds often germinate somewhat irregularly, they should be sown thinly; as the seedlings become large enough, they should be transplanted, the smaller ones being left undisturbed until they, too, are large enough to be moved.

If the seeds are sown thickly, it will be impossible, or difficult, to transplant the most advanced seedlings without damaging the smaller and later ones. The seeds must not be covered deeply; a sprinkling of fine soil is sufficient. The seed flats are covered with paper and the soil is kept moist. As soon as most of the seedlings show through the soil, the paper covering should be removed, though shade from bright sunshine is required.

Managing the Seedlings. When the small plants are well developed and large enough to be handled conveniently, they should be transplanted, about 3 in. apart, in other boxes filled with a well-drained, fertile, rather sandy soil. For a few days after transplantation, the Nemesias should be kept in a warm greenhouse to enable them to become established quickly in the new soil, but subsequently they must have perfectly cool treatment; they will then develop into strong, sturdy plants.

Planting Out. The Nemesias will be large enough to be planted out of doors as soon as danger of severe frost is over. They should be set about 6 in. apart in soil which has been dug and enriched with decayed manure or compost.

Nemesias are plants that react favorably to sun.

Packets of mixed seeds of the large-flowered Nemesia will provide blooms in many delightful colors—orange, yellow, crimson, buff, rose, blue, and so forth.

Most beautiful of all the named varieties of Nemesia is Blue Gem. The plants form compact little bushes which bear a profusion of bloom and are most attractive. Distinct colors of which seeds can be purchased are orange, crimson, scarlet, blue, salmon and yellow.

Those who do not possess a greenhouse may sow the seeds in a frame in early spring in the way explained. If the seedlings are treated as advised, they will be large enough to be planted out of doors towards the end of May.

Sowing Nemesias Out of Doors. Nemesias may be sown out of doors in early spring where the plants are to bloom in summer. To ensure successful results from this sowing, the ground must be cultivated deeply and enriched thoroughly; it is useless to sow out of doors on poor or light land that will dry out rapidly in hot weather or in regions where hot summers prevail.

The seeds must be sown moderately thickly to allow for the nongermination of some of them, but the seedlings should be thinned out until they are not less than 6 in. apart. This method of cultivation is not so reliable as raising seedlings indoors and later planting them out.

For Winter Bloom. In common with certain other annuals—for example, Stocks and Mignonette—Nemesias will bloom in winter if raised from seeds sown in late August. At this time it is better to sow the seeds in the pots of soil in which the plants are to bloom, than to transplant the seedlings.

Five-in. or 6-in. pots are drained by placing a few crocks in the bottom, and are filled to within half an inch of the rims with a mixture of loam and leaf mold with which sand and a little decayed manure have been mixed. The compost is made moderately firm and then watered through a fine spray nozzle on the watering can. Several seeds should be sown on the surface and covered very lightly with soil. The pots must be placed in a cold frame, covered with paper and shaded.

When the seedlings are well grown, they should be thinned out to one in each pot. If given perfectly cool treatment during the early autumn months, they will develop into sturdy plants. Careful watering is necessary until the pots are full of roots; the soil should not be moistened until it is moderately dry.

If placed in a greenhouse having a minimum temperature of 50 degrees, in October, the plants will come into bloom in winter.

To Provide Flowers in Spring. If a further sowing of seeds is made in September, Nemesias will bloom in the greenhouse in March and April, and the plants will be finer than those which flower in winter. The seeds should be sown in a pot of soil and later transplanted individually to small pots. As the plants grow they are repotted. They finally occupy 6-in. pots. They are kept in a greenhouse or frame having a minimum temperature of 50 degrees during the winter months, but need cool, airy conditions, which are assured by ventilating freely in mild weather. The plants should be pinched two or three times to ensure bushiness and should be staked neatly.

In addition to the large-flowered strain of Nemesia, which is chiefly grown, there are dwarf varieties; these may be grown in pots or planted as an edging to flower beds.

NEMOPANTHUS—*Mountain Holly* (Nemopan'thus). A hardy, leaf-losing shrub that is closely related to Holly and occurs natively in cool, moist situations in North America, chiefly in swamps and bogs. It ranges from Newfoundland and Quebec to Minnesota and southward to West Virginia and Indiana. It belongs to the Holly family, Aquifoliaceae. Its name derives from the Greek *nema,* a thread, *pous,* a foot, and *anthos,* a flower, and has reference to the slender pedicels on which the blooms are borne.

Nemopanthus mucronata is a branching shrub up to 8 ft. tall. Its foliage turns a handsome yellow in fall and its bright red berries are exceedingly decorative. It has no beauty of flower.

This shrub may be grown in moist or wet peaty soils and is well adapted for partially shaded locations. It is propagated by two basic methods. The first is to sow seeds either out of doors or in a cold frame, as soon as they are ripe.

The second is to make cuttings of leafy growths in June or July and insert them in a propagating case in a greenhouse or under a bell jar or in a close cold frame.

NEMOPHILA (Nemoph'ila). North American annuals, mostly found wild in California. They belong to the Waterleaf family, the Hydrophyllaceae. The name is derived from *nemos,* a grove, and *phileo,* to love, and alludes to the preferred natural habitat of some kinds.

Nemophilas are easy to grow but they do not thrive where summers are very hot. The seeds may be sown outdoors, directly where the plants are to bloom, in early spring for summer flowering or, in mild winter climates, in fall to produce spring bloom. The seedlings should be thinned out so that they stand 9-12 in. apart.

A light, well-drained soil is preferred and, when the plants are grown outdoors, a sunny or very slightly shaded location. These are good plants for the fronts of flower borders and may be used effectively in rock gardens.

In cool greenhouses Nemophilas may be had in bloom in late winter and early spring from seeds sown in September and October. They make attractive plants in 4-in. or 5-in. pots and are decorative for a long period. A night temperature of 45-50 degrees suits them, with a daytime temperature a few degrees higher.

They need full sun and a rich and well-drained soil which should be maintained in an always evenly moist, but not constantly saturated, condition. After the pots are well filled with healthy roots, weekly or semiweekly applications of dilute liquid fertilizers are distinctly beneficial.

Kinds worth cultivating include N. maculata, Five-Spot, a spreading or partially erect Nemophila that grows 6-12 in. tall and has white, saucer-shaped flowers that have a prominent

Nemophila Menziesii, the native California Baby Blue-Eyes, is a showy blue-flowered hardy annual.

dark purple spot at the tip of each corolla lobe. In the variety N. maculata purpurea the flowers are purple; in variety grandiflora they are larger than in the typical species.

N. Menziesii, Baby Blue-Eyes, has prostrate or partially erect stems 10-20 in. long, and saucer-shaped clear blue flowers that measure 1½ in. across. A variety of this species named grandiflora has even larger flowers; variety alba has white flowers, and variety marginata has flowers that are blue with white margins; a number of other color forms exist.

N. phacelioides attains a height of 2 ft. and has bell-shaped blue flowers that have white centers. N. rotata resembles N. Menziesii, except that its foliage is less divided and its flowers are smaller.

NEOBENTHAMIA GRACILIS (Neobentham'ia). An epiphytal Orchid which grows wild in tropical Africa, near Zanzibar. It has slender, branching stems which attain a height of several feet; the leaves are about 6 in. long, narrow, and arranged at short intervals on the stems. The flowers are borne in terminal spikes in clusters and, though small, are very attractive; the sepals and petals are white or blush and the lip is white, spotted with rose-purple. Large plants bear a number of inflorescences, usually in summer, and are then very attractive. The prefix *neo*, new, was given to distinguish the genus from Benthamia, a name previously applied to a totally different family. Neobenthamia belongs to the family Orchidaceae.

A Hothouse Orchid. This Orchid must be grown in a greenhouse with a tropical atmosphere; even in winter the temperature should not fall below 65 degrees, and the plants must be kept moist at the roots throughout the year. The straggling stems are insufficient to carry their own weight and must be supported by stout sticks. Overpotting should be avoided.

The plant requires shading in the summer, but should have as much light as possible in the winter. The potting compost should be cut osmunda fiber, Fir bark, Redwood bark or Tree Fern fiber; drainage must be free.

Propagation is easily effected by taking off pieces of the stem, with aerial roots attached, at any time from April to August, and potting them, taking care to support each one with a stick.

NEOBESSEYA (Neobes'sya). A small genus of Cacti (family Cactaceae), previously included in Mammillaria, which see for details of cultivation. The name is in honor of Dr. Charles Bessey, of the University of Nebraska.

The best-known kind is N. missouriensis, of rounded growth, with spiraled tubercles, furnished with slender, gray spines, and bearing comparatively large greenish yellow flowers. It is a native of the southern United States and Mexico.

NEOLLOYDIA (Neolloyd'ia). Small Cacti of cylindrical form, close to Mammillaria and requiring similar cultural treatment. The plants are furnished with tubercles in spiral rows, heavily furnished with spines, and the flowers are comparatively large. This genus, of the family Cactaceae, is named after Professor T. C. Lloyd, an authority on Cacti.

The principal kinds are N. Beguinii, flowers pink; N. ceratites, purple; N. clavata, cream-white; N. conoidea, purple; and N. horripila, purple. All are natives of Mexico.

NEOMAMMILLARIA. The Cacti sometimes named Neomammillaria are by many botanists considered to be Mammillarias. They are treated under Mammillaria in this Encyclopedia.

NEOMARICA—*Apostle Plant, Twelve Apostles* (Neoma'rica). Tender herbaceous perennial flowering plants which closely resemble the Iris, to whose family, Iridaceae, they belong. They are found wild in tropical America and are often cultivated under the name Marica. Like the Iris, they have a thick, fleshy rhizome (underground stem) from which arise the sword-shaped leaves, 1-2 ft. in length and 1½-2 in. in width.

The summer flowers, which are either blue, white or yellow, are very short-lived. They are produced in clusters on the ends of flat leaflike stalks nearly as long as the leaves. The three outer petals spread out almost horizontally and are obovate (broader at the tip than the base) and are 1-2 in. in length. The three inner petals are shorter and fiddle-shaped.

For the Greenhouse and Window Garden. These plants may be grown in pots in a

The Apostle Plant, Neomarica, is so called because it is popularly supposed to have 12 leaves. This number, however, is an approximation rather than constant. Neomarica is an interesting house plant. In summer it bears short-lived Iris-like flowers.

greenhouse having a minimum temperature of 60 degrees, or in a sunny window. The best compost consists of equal parts of loam and leaf mold with sand added. Planting is done in February or March. Plants in pots are taken out of the pots and all compost is removed from the roots. The plants are then divided into several portions; the strong pieces are retained for repotting and the remainder discarded or used for propagation.

The strong, healthy pieces are potted in well-drained pots, three being sufficient for a 7-in. or 8-in. pot. After repotting, water is carefully applied to the soil until new roots have formed.

For the remainder of the summer the compost is kept moist, and occasional applications of liquid fertilizer are given to well-rooted plants.

In early autumn the water supply is gradually reduced, and from November to February the soil is kept somewhat dry, sufficient water only being given to prevent the rhizomes from shriveling.

Propagation is by division at potting or planting time.

The chief kinds are N. caerulea, light blue; N. gracilis, white and blue; N. luctea, bright yellow; N. Northiana, white and violet; and N. vittata, white, yellow and orange-red.

NEOMOOREA IRRORATA (Neomoor'ea). An epiphytal Orchid which grows wild in tropical South America; it has ovoid pseudobulbs, 2-6 in. high, and large, broad, evergreen leaves, sometimes nearly 3 ft. long. The bulbs are almost hidden by masses of adventitious aerial roots, which develop from the true roots. The flower stems from the base of the bulbs are as tall as the leaves and usually arched, and bear many flowers, each about 2 in. across. Sepals and petals are a curious shade of red, almost white at their bases; the lip is bright yellow marked with dark purplish-red. This Orchid flowers chiefly in the spring.

The name was originally Moorea, but as this had been given previously to other Orchids, the prefix *neo,* new, was attached.

An Orchid for a Warm Greenhouse. This Orchid is by no means difficult to grow, but requires a warm greenhouse. In winter the temperature should not fall below 60 degrees. At that season the plants must be watered often enough to prevent the pseudobulbs from shriveling, but the compost must never be in a sodden state. In summer the atmosphere should be moist, and drafts are very injurious.

To the usual compost of two parts osmunda fiber and one part sphagnum moss, a little loam fiber may be added. Repotting should be done when young growths are seen early in the year; however, while the compost remains good and the plants have sufficient room to develop, repotting is better deferred.

NEOPORTERIA (Neoporter'ia). A group of Chilean Cacti, family Cactaceae, of rounded or cylindrical body form. The name honors Charles Porter, a Chilean entomologist. For their cultural needs, consult Cacti.

Kinds include N. fusca, globular, 4 in. in diameter, flowers yellow; N. Nidus, rounded to nearly cylindrical, nearly 4 in. across, flowers reddish; N. nigricans, short-cylindrical, flowers white or yellowish-green; N. Reichii, globose, 3 in. in diameter, flowers yellow.

NEOREGELIA. See Aregelia.

NEPENTHES—*Pitcher Plant* (Nepenth'es). Hothouse, evergreen plants which are grown for

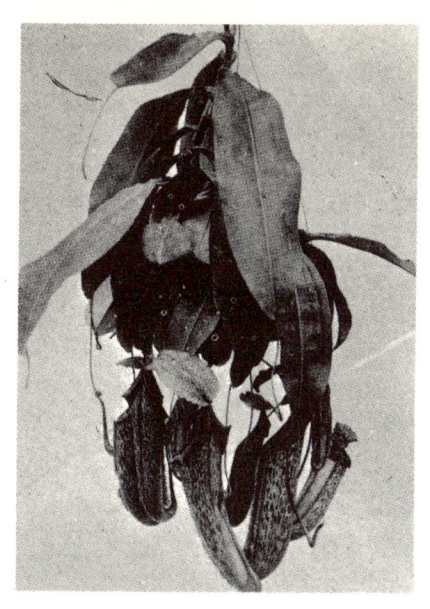

One of the most attractive hybrid Pitcher Plants, Nepenthes mixta.

the beauty of the pitcher-like appendages at the ends of the leaves. They are natives of Malaya, Borneo, India and China and belong to the family Nepenthaceae.

In their native habitats these plants grow 60 ft. in length, climbing upwards among the branches of other trees, or creeping horizontally along the ground. The stem is woody, measuring up to 1 in. in diameter, and the leaves are lance-shaped, smooth, green, or tinged with red, and mostly sessile (joined to the stem without a leafstalk). The midrib is very rigid and grows out beyond the tip of the leaf into a pitcher-shaped appendage. These appendages vary in shape and size, some being as small as thimbles and others large enough to hold a pint or more.

With Colored Pitchers. The pitchers are striped and blotched with various colors, including green and brown, red, purple, crimson, and bright red. When young, they are covered at the top with a lidlike structure which is hinged at the highest point and eventually lifts up and stands erect. This is also brightly colored. The rim, or mouth, of the pitcher is folded outwards. The inner part of the rim is armed with small teeth projecting downwards into the cavity.

Insectivorous Plants. These pitchers are used by the plants for attracting and trapping insects. (See Insectivorous Plants.) The insects are attracted by the glistening drops of honey-like substance secreted by glands inside the pitchers near the top. In attempting to reach the nectar, the insects slip on the smooth rim and are precipitated into the fluid collected in the bottom of the pitcher. The inside walls of the pitchers are smooth and offer no foothold, so that they are unable to escape, and their dead bodies are eventually converted into a solution which is absorbed into the plant's system.

Flowers are freely produced but they are unattractive. They are dioecious (male and female on separate plants), on slender spikes, each flower being about $\frac{1}{4}$ in. in diameter and colored either yellowish-green or reddish-green. Unless they are required for cross-fertilization, they are removed as soon as seen.

How to Grow Pitcher Plants. These plants require a minimum winter temperature of 60 degrees. They may be grown in ordinary flowerpots or orchid pots, but do best in baskets. The best compost consists of equal parts of peat and osmunda fiber and half a part of sphagnum moss. Repotting is done in January or February. The shoots are shortened to two or three nodes (joints) and syringed frequently. When new shoots commence to form, the plants are taken out of the pots or baskets and the old soil is removed from the roots. This is best done by washing the roots in warm water, as they are very brittle.

If pots are used, they are half-filled with crocks, and these are covered with a layer of osmunda fiber or fibrous material from the peat. The baskets do not require draining, but are lined with either of the materials used to cover the crocks.

Potting and General Management. The plants are then set in position and the compost is worked between the roots with a pointed stick. After potting, the plants are watered carefully until new roots have formed, after which the compost is kept moist throughout the summer. They must be shaded from sunlight until the pitchers are fully formed; thereafter, they are exposed to all but the hottest rays of the sun, to color the pitchers. They require a moist, tropical atmosphere, and therefore the floor and benches, as well as the interior walls of the greenhouses, are frequently damped, and the foliage is sprayed several times daily during the summer.

During winter less moisture is required, but the compost is not allowed to become very dry, and syringing and damping are still necessary. If allowed to grow unstopped, the stems will become several feet in length, and a large number of pitchers will be produced.

Larger and better-formed pitchers are produced by stopping each shoot when it has formed five or six leaves.

Propagation. One-year-old shoots are taken off when they are 3-6 in. long, at any time during spring or summer. The best method is to insert the base of each cutting through the drainage hole at the base of a small flowerpot which has been inverted. The inverted pots are then set on a bed of peat moss in a propagating case with a bottom heat of 75-80 degrees. The case is kept closed until roots are formed, except for a few minutes each morning, when the sash is lifted and the underside of the glass is wiped to remove the condensed moisture.

When rooted, the plants are potted separately in 3-in. pots, which are half-filled with crocks. The same soil compost as advised for older plants is used, but it is chopped more finely. After potting, the plants are returned to the propagating case and kept close and moist until established, whereupon they are removed to the open greenhouse. When these pots become filled with roots, the plants are repotted in larger pots or teak baskets.

The chief kinds include N. albomarginata, green and red; N. Curtisii, crimson-purple; N. Northiana, green and purple; N. Rafflesiana, green and red; N. ventricosa, red and brown.

The following are some of the best hybrids: N. Chelsonii, crimson-purple; N. Balfouriana, green and crimson; N. Curtisii superba, blood-red and yellowish-green; N. Mastersiana, blood-red; N. mixta, cream, flushed green, blotched red; and N. Tiveyii, green and brown. The color descriptions refer to the pitchers.

The gray-leaved, mauve-flowered Catmint, Nepeta Mussinii, is excellent for planting at the front of perennial borders.

NEPETA—*Catmint* (Nep′eta). A large group of hardy herbaceous plants, of which few are in cultivation; they are found wild in parts of Europe and Asia and some are naturalized in North America. These plants belong to the Mint family, Labiatae. The name is an old Latin one; it is thought to be derived from Nepi, an Italian town.

The Mauve Catmint. The favorite kind is the Mauve Catmint, Nepeta Mussinii (now called N. Faassenii by some authorities), a hardy herbaceous plant of free and somewhat spreading growth, which has slender leafy stems covered with gray leaves; it bears small lavender-blue or pale-mauve flowers in profusion, chiefly in June. It is thought to be of hybrid origin as it rarely sets seeds.

The Mauve Catmint may be planted in groups towards the front of the perennial border, or on top of a dry wall, or it may be used as an edging. When in full bloom, the plants reach a height of about 18 in., and more across, and the pale mauve flowers on slender, graceful shoots associate charmingly with the gray leaves and produce a delightful display.

Hints on Cultivation. During June there are few more attractive plants than the Mauve Catmint, and it continues flowering intermittently throughout summer. It flourishes in ordinary well-drained garden soil, but in clayey ground that becomes very wet in winter it is liable to perish after the first summer. Such land, however, can be made suitable by adding compost and grit or sand freely. This Catmint is particularly happy on rather light land and should always be planted in a sunny place.

Some charming color schemes can be arranged by associating it with other flowers, for instance, the white Madonna Lily (Lilium candidum), the Orange Lily (Lily croceum), Iceland Poppy, the yellow and orange-colored Geums and others, but its gray leaves and mauve flowers are a perfect color scheme in themselves. Planting is best done in April.

The old plants may be left undisturbed for three years or even longer if they remain in good condition, but young plants are more vigorous and bloom more freely than old worn-out ones, and are so easily raised from cuttings that it is worth renewing the stock of plants before they begin to deteriorate.

Nepeta nervosa, a native of the Himalayas, is a good perennial kind that bears light blue flowers in June.

When to Take Cuttings. The cuttings form roots quickly at any time during June and July, and these are the best months in which to take them. Small flowerless side shoots, about 3 in. in length, are taken off the old plants. The lowest leaves are removed and the shoots are cut beneath a joint, to form the base. They should be inserted in pots or flats of sandy soil or sand, watered, and placed in a cold frame, which is kept closed and shaded from hot sunshine. They must be moistened occasionally with a fine spray.

In four weeks the shoots will be well rooted, and will then need watering more frequently. The frame must be ventilated gradually; a little more air should be admitted each day as soon as the cuttings have formed roots, and finally the sash or top of the frame is taken off.

Before the roots are so numerous as to become matted together, the plants should be separated and replanted out of doors in a nursery border or, preferably, in the positions where they are to remain. They will grow into good plants, and flower the following year.

Another way of treating the cuttings is to make up a bed of sandy soil on a shady border out of doors, about 3 in. deep, and insert the cuttings in this an inch apart. If covered with a bell jar, they will soon form roots. Every day the glass covering ought to be removed for a few minutes and wiped dry inside to get rid of excessive moisture, which might cause the cuttings to damp off.

Increase by Division. Mauve Catmint is easily increased by division of the plants in April. The large clumps are split into tufts of half a dozen shoots or so, the woody roots being trimmed off. If planted where required to grow, these shoots will have made large clumps by the autumn.

When the flowers have faded the plants should be trimmed into shape so that they will be neat and compact. If desired, many of the clippings can be inserted as cuttings. Six Hills Giant is a vigorous variety, 3 ft. tall.

Other perennial-border kinds are N. nervosa, 18 in., light blue, June; N. spicata, 12-18 in. lavender-blue flowers, in June; N. Souvenir d'André Chaudron, 2 ft., lavender-blue, summer.

Catnip or Catnep. The plant known by these names is N. Cataria, a kind which has a particular attraction for cats. It is an erect perennial, about 3 ft. high, that grows in full sun.

A Trailing Kind. Nepeta hederacea (Glechoma hederacea), which is commonly known as Gill-over-the-Ground or Ground Ivy, is a hardy plant which is widely naturalized in North America, on banks and shady roadsides where it creeps along the ground, forming a carpet with its small, heart-shaped leaves. Short spikes of blue flowers are produced during the summer. The plant is rarely cultivated, except in woodland gardens, where it is used for carpeting the soil. There is, however, a kind with variegated leaves which is used for edging beds of shrubs or for covering dry banks. It is also used for growing in hanging baskets on porch or veranda and as a window-garden plant.

NEPHELAPHYLLUM (Nephelaphyl'lum). Terrestrial Orchids of creeping growth which are natives of tropical Eastern countries. The flowers are not showy, but the evergreen leaves are ornamental. These plants belong to the family Orchidaceae. The name is derived from *nephela,* a cloud, and *phyllon,* a leaf. The markings on the leaves are clouded and not distinct.

These Orchids must be grown in a greenhouse with a warm, moist atmosphere, and the temperature should never fall below 65 degrees. A compost of two parts of cut osmunda fiber, two parts of sphagnum moss, with a little leaf mold and sand added, suits them. Flower pans are preferable to pots.

Care must be taken to avoid drafts, hence the plants are often grown under a bell jar. In winter, when they are resting, less watering is needed. N. pulchrum, the kind most frequently grown, has silvery green leaves.

NEPHRODIUM. A name previously used for ferns now included in the genus Dryopteris.

NEPHROLEPIS—*Ladder Fern, Sword Fern* (Nephrole'pis). Tender Ferns which are found wild in many tropical areas, including Africa, America, Malaya and the West Indies. They belong to the family Polypodiaceae. The name is derived from *nephros,* a kidney, and *lepis,* a scale, and refers to the kidney-shaped, scalelike spore-case covering.

Beautiful Kinds. Nephrolepis is a small genus or group, but contains many beautiful kinds well adapted for growing in pots in greenhouses and as house plants. The most popular are the varieties of N. exaltata, a plant occurring wild from Florida southward into Brazil, and in Africa and eastern Asia. This Fern produces fronds 3-5 ft. long and 2-6 in. wide. They have rigid midribs, covered with fine brown hairs, and the leaflets (pinnae), which are about $\frac{1}{2}$ in. wide and have crenate edges, are set closely along each side of the midrib.

There are many beautiful varieties of N. exaltata. A most notable one is N. exaltata bostoniensis, the Boston Fern, which is well known and has long, graceful, drooping fronds.

Other varieties of Nephrolepis exaltata are N. exaltata bostoniensis compacta, the Dwarf Boston Fern, which is similar to the Boston Fern but has shorter fronds and is of more compact growth. The fronds of N. exaltata Piersoni, N. exaltata Piersoni improved, and N. exaltata Massii are bipinnate—that is, each of the leaflets is divided into segments, so that the fronds have a distinctly feathery or plumelike appearance. In some other kinds the divisions of the leaflets are again divided into segments, so that the fronds are tripinnate and are very finely plumelike or feathery in appearance. Of the kinds with tripinnate fronds, popular varieties are N. exaltata

Nephrolepis are propagated by division. The roots of old specimens are partly cut through and then the ball is pulled into pieces with the hands.

To form young plants small divisions, each consisting of a vigorous crown with roots attached, are selected.

The divisions are potted individually in small pots, or three or more may be planted together in larger containers.

elegantissima, N. exaltata elegantissima Trevillian, N. exaltata Whitmanii and N. exaltata Whitmanii compacta. Two of the most satisfactory for growing as house plants are the Boston Fern and the Dwarf Boston Fern.

Nephrolepis cordifolia, a native of the tropics and subtropics, is an excellent species, with rather erect fronds which are 1½-2 ft. long and 2½ in. wide. The sharp-toothed leaflets (pinnae) are 1-1¼ in. long and bright green. The rootstocks of this species produce small tubers. There are several varieties of N. cordifolia, including compacta, gigantea, plumosa, tesselata and variegata.

Nephrolepis Duffi, a species that is native to Malaya and northern Australia, has upright-growing fronds 1-2 ft. long which are branched near their tips. The leaflets (pinnae) are rounded or fan-shaped and are in overlapping pairs. This kind does not produce spores.

Culture. These Ferns require a minimum temperature of 55-60 degrees and a moderately humid atmosphere. The best soil for them consists of three parts of loam and one part of leaf mold or peat moss with a free admixture of sand and crushed charcoal.

Repotting should be done in February or March as soon as new growth commences. The plants are taken out of their pots, the crocks and all loose soil are removed from the roots, and the plants are repotted into slightly larger pots.

After the potting, the soil should be thoroughly watered to settle it but for some time afterwards (until the new soil is permeated with roots) care must be taken not to overwater. Once the plants are well rooted, they may be watered freely, and weekly or biweekly applications of weak liquid fertilizers are given. The plants are shaded from sunlight until established, and then exposed to full light, but protected from strong sunshine. In greenhouses a moist atmosphere is maintained by frequently damping the floors and benches.

Young specimens of Nephrolepis may need potting more than once in a year; in addition to receiving this attention in late winter, they are likely to benefit from being moved into larger containers about midsummer. The summer potting should be carried out without disturbing

Varieties of Nephrolepis exaltata are splendid for growing in hanging baskets in greenhouses.

the soil or roots any more than is absolutely necessary. Treatment after potting is the same as is advised above for after potting in late winter.

Ferns for Hanging Baskets. These Ferns are suitable for growing in hanging baskets, especially N. exaltata and its varieties, the fronds of which become pendent as they mature, and hang downwards over the sides of the baskets, to form balls of delicate greenery. The baskets, after being lined with moss, are half-filled with soil, and well-rooted plants are set in the center. The remainder of the space is now filled with soil, which is pressed moderately firm. The baskets are then thoroughly watered and hung up in a warm, moist greenhouse. When the Ferns are established, the baskets are used for decorating greenhouses or suspended under a porch out of doors during the summer.

Propagation. These plants are easily propagated by means of runners, which are formed plentifully by most kinds, and by division. Spores also form a means of propagation, but are rarely used because the other methods are reliable and easier.

Division is best carried out at repotting time in late winter or spring. The more vigorous, outer portions of the plants should be chosen for replanting, rather than the worn-out central parts. Young rooted plants formed on runners may be taken from old plants in spring and be potted individually in a sandy, peaty soil mixture in small pots. They should be kept in a humid atmosphere and a temperature of 60-70 degrees until they are well established.

Basket plants need frequent attention, as the soil must not be allowed to become very dry or the fronds will turn yellow and wither. The best method is to immerse them in a pail of water for a few minutes, and hang them up in a convenient spot to drip before suspending them in the accustomed position.

The most popular kinds for hanging baskets are N. exaltata and its varieties, but other kinds are also used. N. pectinata is suitable for small baskets, and N. ensifolia, with fronds 4-5 ft. in length, is only suitable for a large basket in a lofty greenhouse or conservatory.

Propagation by Layering. Most of the Nephrolepis with crested and plumose fronds are propagated by runners, as they do not produce fertile spores, and vegetative reproduction is necessary to perpetuate their special features.

There are several methods of obtaining rooted layers. The simplest is to fill a number of 3-in. pots with compost, and arrange them around the old plant. The tips of the runners are then pressed down into the small pots; when sufficient roots have formed, they are detached and treated as separate plants.

Propagation by Division. Those kinds which produce neither spores nor runners are propagated by division in spring. The plants are taken out of their pots, and the compost is removed with a pointed stick. They are divided with a sharp knife, and each division, consisting of a portion of the rootstock, with roots and fronds attached, is potted separately in a small pot.

Those kinds which produce fertile spores are propagated by sowing the spores as soon as they are ripe in summer, or, if desired, the spores can be stored in seed packets and sown at a later date (see Ferns).

The chief kind is N. exaltata, 2 ft., of which there are several varieties, with plumose fronds and other characteristics. The best of these are todeoides, elegantissima, Whitmanii and superba.

Other kinds are N. cordifolia, 2 ft.; N. acuminata, 2 ft., and its variety, plumosa, 4 ft.; N. rivularis, 2 ft.; and N. biserrata (acuta), 4 ft. The measurements refer to the length of the fronds.

NEPHTHYTIS (Nephthy′tis). Evergreen foliage plants belonging to the Arum family, Araceae, and found wild in tropical Africa. The name is from the mythological Nephthys, mother of Anubis, wife of Typhon or Set.

Nephthytis Afzelii (N. liberica) has a thick, horizontal, creeping rhizome and leaves that have blades up to a foot long and stalks (petioles) two times or more as long. The leaves are arrow-shaped and slender-pointed. The plant bears orange-colored berries.

Nephthytis needs the same culture as Aglaonema and Dieffenbachia, which see.

Plants grown in North America under the name Nephthytis are often wrongly identified. Most often they are kinds of Syngonium (which see).

NERINE—*Guernsey Lily* (Neri′ne). Greenhouse bulbous plants which are found wild in South Africa and belong to the Amaryllis family, Amaryllidaceae. They have ovoid bulbs, about 2 in. in diameter; long, narrow, green or glaucous (blue-gray) leaves; and umbels (clusters on the end of a stalk) of six-petaled flowers, averaging ½ in. in diameter. The flowers are white, or of various colors—scarlet, pink, crimson or salmon, and open in late summer and autumn. In some kinds the flowers appear before the leaves. Many have a glistening luster which in sunlight gives them the appearance of being dusted with silver or gold. The blooms last for several weeks. Nerine is named after the water nymph, daughter of Nereus.

N. sarniensis, having rosy red flowers in the autumn, is the most popular kind. It is commonly called the Guernsey Lily, because it is a popular belief that bulbs were washed ashore on the island of Guernsey in the English Channel from a wrecked ship and became established in gardens on the island.

For Window or Greenhouse. These bulbs can be cultivated in a really cool, sunny window or greenhouse where the winter temperature does not fall below 40 degrees. The best soil compost

Nerines thrive best when pot-bound. At the end of their dormant season the pot of dry soil containing the bulbs should be soaked in water *(lower left).* When the soil has drained, its surface should be scratched off and new rich compost added *(lower right).* The pots of bulbs grown in a cool greenhouse or sunny window soon develop very handsome heads of flowers *(top).*

consists of four parts of loam, one part of well-decayed manure or leaf mold, and a scattering of sand and crushed charcoal.

The bulbs should be set in well-drained pots in August. Small pots, which allow about 1 in. of compost around the bulbs, are used, and the latter are buried to one quarter their depth in the compost. They are placed in a cool greenhouse, but no water is given until the flower spikes show. The soil is then moistened and they are watered regularly until the following April or when growth ceases; then they are dried off by gradually lengthening the periods between waterings and finally withholding water altogether. When the leaves have withered, the pots are stored on their sides on a shelf or window ledge. When the flower spikes show, in early autumn, the soil is moistened and they are treated as advised above.

Flower Best When Pot-bound. Nerines flower

A choice Nerine variety of garden origin.

best only when in a pot-bound condition. They are therefore kept in the same pots for many years; the bulblets which develop around the plants eventually reach flowering size and a mass of bloom is produced. Pot-bound plants are kept growing vigorously by annual top-dressing. When growth commences, a little of the surface soil is replaced with fresh compost.

When repotting becomes necessary, it should be done just before the bulbs start into growth; a slightly larger pot is used and this is well drained with crocks. The plant is then removed from its pot, the crocks are extracted and the ball of soil is placed intact in the new pot.

Propagation. The principal method of propagation is by detaching the offsets (young bulbs that grow from the bases of older bulbs); these are potted in small pots in August and treated as newly potted plants.

For a Sunny Border. In mild parts of North

A flowerpot of Nerine flexuosa. This kind has pale pink flowers. The edges of the petals are wavy.

America, Nerines can be grown out of doors. The best position is a sunny, well-drained border. The site is prepared by taking out the soil to the depth of 12 in.; a layer of broken bricks, 4 in. in depth, is placed in the bottom and this is covered with pieces of fibrous turf. The hole is then filled with sandy loam, and the bulbs are planted 3 in. deep in August. Once planted they must not be disturbed for many years, until, in fact, they show signs of deterioration. The bed is protected from November to April with a layer of dry litter, and is mulched in spring with leaf mold.

The chief kinds are N. sarniensis, salmon-pink; N. curvifolia, scarlet; N. curvifolia variety Fothergillii, scarlet; N. Bowdenii, pink; N. flexuosa, pale pink; N. flexuosa alba, white; and N. undulata, flesh-pink. There are many named varieties of garden origin.

NERIUM—*Oleander* (Ne′rium). Tender evergreen flowering shrubs which are found wild in the Orient. They belong to the Periwinkle family, Apocynaceae. The name Nerium is derived from *neros*, humid, and refers to the kind of place favored by the shrub.

The Oleander, as it is popularly called, is an old-fashioned shrub. It grows 20 ft. in height. All parts are poisonous if eaten. It is a favorite for outdoor cultivation in the far South, and as a tub plant there and elsewhere. The leaves, which are lanceolate (lance-shaped), average 6 in. in length and 1 in. in width. They are in whorls of three, are deep green in color and leathery in texture.

The flowers, which are produced in summer, are borne in clusters at the tips of the shoots. They are tubular at the base, but open out salver-shaped at the tips and are either single, semidouble or double, and red, pink, apricot or white.

Outdoor Culture of Oleanders. In Florida and in southern California, Oleanders are splendid shrubs for cultivating in the open. They are most excellent subjects for planting as lawn specimens, for setting along boulevards, for informal hedges, and as screens. They are well adapted for planting in city parks and in towns.

These beautiful shrubs begin to bloom from March to May, depending upon the local climate, and continue more or less continuously until fall.

Oleanders need full sun to give of their best and they appreciate a well-drained soil; they thrive in sandy areas. Pruning consists of cutting out dead, crowded and unwanted growths in late winter, before new growth begins. At that time, too, it is a good plan to give them a dressing of fertilizer. If it is possible to keep the roots mulched with manure or compost, that will be of great benefit. Outdoor specimens are easily propagated by layering.

How to Grow the Oleander Indoors. Oleander requires a minimum winter temperature of 45 degrees, and the best soil compost consists of two parts of sandy loam and one part of equal portions of well-decayed manure and leaf mold or peat moss with sand added freely. Repotting of small plants is done in March–April. Older plants growing in large pots or tubs are not repotted each year, but are kept growing vigorously by annual spring top dressing with fresh compost. After repotting, the plants are shaded from strong sunlight and the foliage is syringed twice a day until they are established.

When the weather is warm and settled, and all danger from frost has passed, plants in large pots are set out of doors in prominent positions where the beauty of their flowers is displayed to the best advantage. They are useful for decorating terraces, etc.

Why Oleanders Fail to Bloom. During the summer Oleanders need abundance of water, and it is often the practice to stand the pots in saucers of water to ensure that they have an unlimited supply. When the flower buds are expanding, the young shoots which develop at the bases of the flower trusses must be removed or the buds may not open. Failure to do this is a common cause of the plants failing to bloom.

Pruning is done as soon as the flowers have faded, the shoots of the previous year's growth being shortened by two thirds or more. Less water is needed after they have been pruned, but when new shoots are forming freely, the supply must be gradually increased to induce them to make as much growth as possible before the winter.

In early autumn, the plants are returned to the greenhouse, sunroom or other light storage place where they are to overwinter. Very little water is required during the winter, sufficient only to keep the leaves from shriveling.

Propagation. These plants are increased principally by cuttings 3-6 in. in length made from firm shoots which are cut off in summer. The cuttings are prepared for insertion by removal of their lower leaves and cutting of the bottom of the stem cleanly across just beneath a joint (node). The shoots are then inserted in a bottle or jar of water with their bases just beneath the surface of the water. The bottle may be placed in a sunny greenhouse or on the window sill.

Cuttings may also be rooted in sand, a mixture of sand and peat moss, or in vermiculite. A bell jar or mason jar is placed over them until roots are formed.

Cuttings, whether rooted in water or in any of the other mediums indicated, are potted singly in 3-in. pots, and subsequently in larger pots. To obtain bushy plants, the tips of the shoots are removed as soon as the plants are rooted in the 3-in. pots, and the subsequent side shoots are similarly treated when the plants are established in 5-in. pots.

The chief kinds are N. Oleander, red, and its varieties: album plenum, double white; Henri Mares, rosy-pink, double; splendens, double red; variegatum, red flowers and variegated leaves; Apple Blossom, shell pink; Scarlet Beauty, vivid red; Mrs. Roeding, double salmon pink; and Soeur Agnes, double white. N. indicum and its varieties, some of which are double-flowered, have very fragrant blooms. They do not usually exceed 8 ft. in height. The flowers vary, according to variety, from white to rosy pink.

NERTERA—*Fruiting Duckweed* (Ner'tera). Nertera depressa is a tender perennial plant with ornamental berries. A native of South America, New Zealand and Tasmania, this dainty little plant, which is of creeping habit, has miniature ovate green leaves, small greenish flowers, and orange-scarlet berries in summer and autumn. It is not commonly grown in the United States and Canada. It belongs to the Madder family, Rubiaceae. The name Nertera is from the Greek word meaning lowly and refers to the habit of growth.

A Beautiful Berried Plant. In mild localities, where summers are not excessively hot, Nertera may be grown out of doors, but elsewhere during the winter it should be sheltered in a greenhouse. It may be also grown in flower pans or pots but does not thrive where hot summers prevail. The plants, when smothered with orange-scarlet berries, are very attractive.

Nertera, when grown indoors, requires a minimum winter temperature of 45 degrees, and a soil compost of equal parts of good loam and leaf mold, with sand freely added.

Plants are raised from seeds sown thinly in a pan of fine compost, in March. A pane of glass is laid over the pan, which is placed in a greenhouse with a temperature of 55 degrees. The glass is wiped on the underside each morning to prevent the condensed moisture from dropping on the seedlings and setting up decay.

As soon as the seedlings appear, the glass is removed and they are given a well-lighted position, but shaded from sunlight. When large enough to handle, the seedlings are pricked out in little clusters in well-drained pans of compost, and are kept moist and shaded until large enough to be potted separately in 3-in. pots; several plants may be set in a wide seed pan.

How to Ensure a Crop of Berries. When they are established, the plants are placed on a shelf near the glass in a cool greenhouse. They must be shaded from bright sunlight and the soil kept moist throughout the summer. By this method of cultivation, flowers, and eventually fruits, will be freely produced. During the winter less water is required, but the soil is not allowed to remain in a dry condition.

Young plants can also be produced by division in March or April. The clumps are divided into small pieces, which are placed singly in 3-in. pots, or several in a seed pan, and treated as advised for seedlings.

Planting in the Rock Garden. Plants well rooted in 3-in. pots are planted out of doors in May. Ordinary light but rich soil is required and a moist, semishaded position. The plants are best suited for the rock garden, where the berry-laden shoots are displayed to the best advantage. Nertera may also be used as edging for summer flower beds, where the soil and situation are suitable. The soil must be kept moist during the summer, or few berries will be produced.

NETTLE, CHILE. Loasa, which see.

NETTLE, DEAD. See Lamium.

NEVADA, GARDENING IN. See Regional Gardening.

NEVIUSIA ALABAMENSIS—*Alabama Snow Wreath* (Neviu'sia). This is a leaf-losing shrub, allied to the Spiraeas, 4-6 ft. high, with numerous erect stems and spreading branches, wreathed with white flowers in April and early May; the flowers have no petals, but showy clusters or bunches of white stamens. This shrub is a native of Alabama and belongs to the Rose family, Rosaceae. It is hardy as far north as central New York and southern New England, provided it is given a somewhat sheltered location. The name commemorates the Reverend R. D. Nevius, of Alabama, who discovered the plant in 1858.

Planting and Pruning. Neviusia thrives in ordinary well-cultivated garden soil, which the gardener should prepare by mixing with it generous amounts of organic matter. Planting may be done in autumn or spring. If planted in good soil and kept well watered during dry weather, Neviusia is a very attractive shrub. Pruning should be done after flowering, the old shoots being cut out to encourage the development of strong young growths.

Propagation is by division of the clumps, or removal of suckers; the best time for either of these operations is early in fall. Cuttings, 3-4 in. long, may be made from young side shoots in June or July. These are inserted in a frame which must be kept close, or in a greenhouse. Slight bottom heat is advantageous.

NEW HAMPSHIRE, GARDENING IN. See Regional Gardening.

NEW JERSEY, GARDENING IN. See Regional Gardening.

NEW JERSEY TEA. Ceanothus americanus, which see.

NEW MEXICO, GARDENING IN. See Regional Gardening.

NEW YORK, GARDENING IN. See Regional Gardening.

NEW ZEALAND BUR. See Acaena.

NEW ZEALAND CLEMATIS. See Clematis indivisa.

NEW ZEALAND DAISY BUSH. See Olearia.

NEW ZEALAND FLAX. See Phormium.

NEW ZEALAND GLORY PEA. See Clianthus.

NEW ZEALAND SPINACH. This vegetable is cultivated for the tips of the shoots, which provide an excellent dish during the summer months, when the weather is too hot to favor the growth of ordinary Spinach. The plant's botanical name is Tetragonia expansa and it

New Zealand Spinach is an easily grown hot-weather vegetable crop.

belongs to the family group known as Aizoaceae.

As the plant is not hardy, it can be grown as a garden crop during the summer months only. It is easy to cultivate.

How to Sow Seeds. Because the seeds germinate erratically, it is well to pour hot water over them and allow them to soak for 24 hours before sowing. Sow the seeds out of doors as soon as the weather is warm enough to plant Corn. This plant needs rich soil and a sunny place; compost or well-decayed manure should be mixed with the ground before seeds are sown. Small groups of seeds should be sown in hills 3 ft. apart, but only one seedling is allowed to remain in each group or hill, as the New Zealand Spinach grows vigorously and requires room.

The tips of the leafy shoots should be picked frequently, even though not required for use, to cause fresh shoots to develop, for these only are of value.

NEW ZEALAND TREE FERN. Dicksonia antarctica, which see.

NICANDRA—*Apple of Peru, Shoo-fly Plant* (Nican'dra). Nicandra Physaloides, the only species, is a vigorous annual. It forms a branching plant up to 4 ft. in height, with soft, fleshy stems, and the blue flowers are borne singly in the axils of the leaves. They are succeeded by berries surrounded by a papery, five-winged envelope. The leaves are oval, deeply lobed, crenate (toothed at the margins), and 4-5 in. in length. Nicandra is a native of Peru and belongs to the Potato or Nightshade family, Solanaceae.

The blue-flowered annual Nicandra Physaloides, the Apple of Peru.

The flower formation of the annual Nicandra.

Its name honors Nikander of Colophon, who wrote on botany and medicine in the second century A.D.

Sow Seeds Out of Doors in Spring. This plant requires a sunny, open location and does well in ordinary garden soil. Seeds are sown in April or May, in hills (clusters of 4-5 seeds) 2 ft. apart, the seedlings being thinned out so that the strongest only remains in each hill. The plants need staking.

Earlier flowers can be obtained by sowing seeds in flats of soil in a greenhouse in March. The seedlings are pricked out 3 in. apart in other flats of soil and are kept growing in a greenhouse until it is nearly time to plant them outdoors, then they are gradually hardened off before being set in the garden in May or June.

NICODEMIA (Nicodem'ia). A group of 3 species that are natives of Madagascar and the Mascarene Islands and belong in the Logania family, the Loganiaceae. One, N. diversifolia, has been introduced into cultivation in the United States and is grown as a house plant and in greenhouses. It should prove adaptable for outdoor culture in the far South.

Nicodemia diversifolia is an evergreen shrub with small, neat leaves which, because of their shape and texture, are reminiscent of those of many Oaks. For this reason the plant is sometimes called Indoor Oak. Of easy cultivation, Nicodemia diversifolia thrives in any well-drained, moderately fertile soil that is kept evenly moist but not constantly saturated. It needs a temperature of 60-70 degrees and full sun for its best growth. The shoots may be pinched occasionally to induce a compact, bushy habit. Propagation is by cuttings.

NICOTIANA—*Tobacco Plant* (Nicotia'na). Annual, perennial and tender shrubby plants, chiefly natives of America, though a few are found in Australasia and on islands in the Pacific Ocean. The plants belong to the Potato or Nightshade family, Solanaceae. Nicotiana was named after Jean Nicot (1530-1600), a French consul.

This is a large group of plants containing many kinds, some of which are of botanical interest only. N. Tabacum is commercially important as the source of tobacco. Several annual kinds are decorative and useful for growing as pot plants in greenhouses for winter and spring flowering, and for growing outdoors in summer. Of these decorative kinds Nicotiana alata grandiflora, better known as N. affinis, and N. Sanderae are very beautiful. Several others make luxuriant growth and have handsome leaves for producing bold effects in flower gardens.

When to Sow Seeds. All these plants are raised from seeds. These may be sown in light soil in February or early March in a warm greenhouse, temperature 55 degrees. However, where the growing season is sufficiently long, seeds may be sown directly outdoors in early spring.

The white-flowered Nicotiana affinis.

As soon as the seedlings from seeds sown indoors are large enough to be handled, they should be pricked off in flats filled with sandy, fertile soil, a space of 2 in. or so being allowed between them. When the leaves touch, which will be very soon, the seedlings should be potted singly in 3-in. pots or be planted, if all danger of frost has passed, in the open garden. Nicotianas thrive best in fairly light, rich soil.

White and Colored Flowering Tobacco Plants. Nicotiana alata grandiflora (affinis), which for many years was almost the only Flowering Tobacco plant grown in our gardens, is essentially a flowering plant for summer evenings. During the day the long-tubed, white flowers hang down as though they were wilting on account of drought, but in the late afternoon they become large, milk-white stars yielding a most delicious fragrance. As well-grown plants will reach fully 3 ft. in height and bear spreading heads of bloom, specimens should be set 18 in. apart.

During recent years crimson, scarlet and pink varieties of Nicotiana alata grandiflora have been raised, which are very attractive. There is also a strain which keeps its blooms open throughout the day.

Nicotiana Sanderae, a hybrid which was raised towards the end of last century, has reddish flowers; these were at first of rather weak colors, but the seedsmen soon improved them and now the best strains are of rich tones. Unlike varieties of N. alata, they are day-flowering and are thus of even greater decorative value in the garden, though, unfortunately, they are scentless. The varieties of N. Sanderae are fully as luxuriant as those of alata.

Sweet-scented and Night-blooming. There are a number of other Tobaccos which are worth growing for their flowers. Among them are Nicotiana acuminata, a handsome annual which bears white flowers 3 in. in length; N. Bigelovii, a night-flowering annual of the western United States that is known as Indian Tobacco and has white flowers; and N. longiflora, native from Texas to Argentina, which has flowers that are white at first but become purplish.

N. noctiflora, a Chilean plant, produces white flowers which are stained with purple outside, and are very fragrant during the evenings. N. suaveolens, from Australia, is another sweetly scented sort; its fragrant white flowers are borne in loose heads. N. sylvestris is a handsome, large-leaved kind with fragrant, white, drooping flowers in large terminal clusters. It is an excellent border plant, a native of Argentina.

The flowering Tobaccos are generally self-supporting, though sometimes short stakes are required to keep the plants upright; the more robust kinds, which are grown for their ornamental leaves, should be staked securely, especially in exposed places.

The Tobacco of Commerce. Nicotiana Tabacum, which supplies the tobacco of commerce, was introduced to Britain from America in 1570, and the story of Sir Walter Raleigh as the first smoker in England is a matter of history.

The typical plant will reach a height of 5 ft.; it has large handsome leaves, and bears rose-pink flowers which have swollen corolla tubes, and are downy on the outsides. The whole plant is downy and somewhat clammy when handled. It is a good subject for subtropical gardening, as also is N. wigandioides, from Colombia, which bears yellowish-white flowers in large, drooping panicles.

Plants for the Greenhouse. Few tall-growing annuals are more attractive in the greenhouse than Nicotiana alata grandiflora and N. Sanderae, and their varieties. The plants are raised from seed in the manner already described for producing young plants for flowering in the garden. The seedlings required for the greenhouse should be potted firmly. When the 3-in. pots are filled with roots, the plants are transferred to 6-in. pots; plants from early sowings may later be moved to 7-in. or even 8-in. pots. For this last potting, a suitable soil mixture is made of three parts loam and one part leaf mold, with a handful of bone meal and sufficient coarse sand to keep the soil porous.

Seeds sown in September provide good plants for spring bloom. A sunny greenhouse with a night temperature of 50 degrees suits them well. If you want the plants to remain decorative for a long time, give them regular supplies of dilute liquid fertilizer, or a sprinkling of dry fertilizer from time to time, and remove the fading flowers.

[7—12]
Evening Primrose
(Oenothera)

[7—12a]
Sourgum
(Nyssa sylvatica)

[7—13]
Odontoglossum pulchellum

[7—13a]
Oncidium sphacelatum

NIDULARIUM (Nidular'ium). A group of tender, tree-perching (epiphytic) Brazilian plants that are grown for their attractive foliage and the ornamental bracts that surround the flower heads nestling down among the leaves. These plants belong to the Bromelia or Pineapple family, Bromeliaceae. The name is derived from *nidus,* a nest, and alludes to the location of the flower clusters.

Nidulariums are well adapted for growing in a warm, moist greenhouse and for cultivating in terrariums; under reasonably favorable conditions, they also serve well as house plants.

Advice on Culture. These plants require a minimum temperature of 55 degrees, and 5 or 10 degrees warmer is advantageous. In summer the temperatures should be higher. A moist atmosphere is necessary for their best development and they need an abundance of water from spring through fall—somewhat less in winter. Plants that have filled their pots with healthy roots benefit greatly from weekly applications of dilute liquid fertilizer from spring through fall, and biweekly applications in winter.

Repotting Is Done in Spring. The potting compost may consist of a mixture of orchid peat (osmunda fiber), coarse leaf mold, peat moss and sand with a little charcoal added—or the plants may be potted, in the same manner as many Orchids, in osmunda fiber alone. The pots must be exceptionally well drained; they may be filled to one quarter or one third of their depth with crocks.

Propagation is chiefly effected by suckers which develop from the bases of the old plants. These are taken off in spring and potted in the same compost that is used for mature plants. Natural species (kinds that occur wild in nature) may also be readily raised from seeds sown in a mixture of peat moss and sand in a moist atmosphere in a temperature of 70-80 degrees. The young plants should be pricked off in flats of peat moss and sand as soon as they are large enough to handle, and later may be transferred individually to small pots containing the regular potting mixture.

Kinds. N. fulgens, flowers white and violet, leaves light green, conspicuously spotted with dark green, center of rosette red; N. Innocentii, flowers white, leaves purplish beneath and sometimes above, central part of rosette orange-red (variety Francois-spa with a maroon center is offered); N. purpureum, flowers red, leaves strongly flushed with purple or claret-brown; N. striatum, flowers white, leaves with narrow white longitudinal lines on a green background—sometimes regarded as a variety of N. Innocentii.

NIEREMBERGIA — *Cupflower* (Nierember'-gia). Hardy and tender perennial flowering plants of which there are two types. Some kinds are of dwarf or trailing growth and are suitable for the rock garden; others are taller and of upright growth and are grown in flower beds or borders. All are suitable for cultivation in pots. They are natives of South America and belong to the Nightshade family, Solanaceae.

The stems are slender and clothed with small, smooth, green leaves, $\frac{1}{2}$-1 in. long. The cup-shaped flowers are 1-2 in. across, and white, blue, lilac or violet. They are borne singly on the ends of slender side branches. The tallest kinds do not usually exceed 18 in. in height.

The hardiest of the Cupflowers is Nierembergia rivularis. Here it grows in a moist crevice between flagstones.

The name Nierembergia commemorates Juan E. Nieremberg, a Spanish natural historian.

Treatment of Hardy Kind. Plants well rooted in 3-in. pots, which have been raised from seeds or cuttings, are planted in their permanent positions out of doors in spring. A sunny, moist situation in the rock garden is selected, and the best soil compost consists of equal parts of loam and leaf mold.

During the summer the soil must be kept moist.

The most popular kind is N. rivularis, which grows about 3 in. in height and forms a carpet of green foliage, dotted with cup-shaped, creamy white flowers, streaked with purple, 1½ in. in diameter. This plant is not reliably hardy as far north as New York City, although in sheltered locations it persists through most winters. It appreciates light shade and needs moist soil.

The tender kinds are grown in greenhouses in the North or they may be planted out of doors during the summer; in the South they may be

The beautiful half-hardy, blue-flowered Nierembergia frutescens.

A bed of the dainty Nierembergia frutescens at The New York Botanical Garden.

grown outdoors the year around as perennials. Plants raised from seeds or cuttings are planted in the rock garden, or the tallest kinds near the front of the herbaceous border. N. frutescens, 18 in., lilac, is the best for the border; it may also be used as a summer bedding plant.

A bed of the compact-growing, lavender-blue Nierembergia caerulea.

In the autumn the plants are lifted from the soil, trimmed back, potted and kept in a cold frame or greenhouse during the winter.

When to Sow Seeds. Propagation is by seeds or cuttings. Seeds are sown in March in well-drained pots in a sandy soil in a temperature of 55 degrees. When about 1½ in. high, the seedlings are pricked out 2 in. apart in well-drained seed flats filled with light soil.

Until established, the seedlings must be shaded and syringed lightly every day. Subsequently they are potted singly in 3-in. pots and eventually planted out of doors for the summer. Or they may be potted in 5 in. pots for decorating the greenhouse or window garden. A compost of two parts sandy loam, a little well-decayed manure, and a sprinkling of sand is used for the final potting. When well rooted, the plants are freely watered and set in a sunny, well-ventilated position to flower.

After flowering, less water is required, and during the winter the soil is moistened only at intervals when it becomes moderately dry.

When to Take Cuttings. Young plants may also be raised from cuttings in spring. Shoots 2 in. in length are taken off, the lower leaves are removed, and a cut is made just below the bottom node. The cuttings are then inserted in sand or vermiculite in a greenhouse propagating bench and, when rooted, are treated as seedlings.

Nierembergia frutescens makes an excellent summer-flowering plant for the window garden and greenhouse, where its light blue blooms prove very attractive. If grown for this purpose, it should be potted in 5-in. or 6-in. pots in spring in a compost of loam, leaf mold and sand. White Queen is an attractive variety.

Nierembergia caerulea (hippomanica) is a lovely kind from the Argentine. It is perennial, grows about 9 in. high, and bears blue-violet flowers in summer. It is suitable for the rock garden and also makes an excellent pot plant. It is not reliably hardy in the North.

The chief kinds are: *Hardy*—N. rivularis, of creeping habit, white, tinged with yellow or rose. *Tender*—N. frutescens, 18 in., blue; N. calycina, creeping, white and yellow; N. caerulea, 6-12 in., blue-violet; N. Veitchii, creeping, lilac.

NIGELLA — *Love-in-a-Mist, Devil-in-a-Bush* (Nigel'la). Favorite annual plants which grow wild in southern Europe, northern Africa and Asia Minor. They belong to the Buttercup family, Ranunculaceae. The name is derived from *niger*, black, and refers to the seeds.

These plants are useful in borders and as cut flowers. The flowers are surrounded by very finely divided stem leaves, which add considerably to their charm. Those commonly grown have blue or white flowers. They provide a charming show of bloom in the garden during the summer months.

Love-in-a-Mist is grown principally in the herbaceous or hardy flower border, where, if sown in groups towards the front, it is very beautiful for several weeks. It is also a useful annual to grow in the greenhouse. From seeds sown in September excellent specimens in 5-in. or 6-in. pots may be had in bloom in spring.

When to Sow Seeds. The cultivation of Nigella

A favorite blue-flowered hardy annual, Nigella Miss Jekyll, a variety of N. damescena.

is perfectly simple: the plants flourish in ordinary, well-cultivated garden ground. The seeds are usually sown outdoors in early spring to furnish flowers from July onwards. The chief causes of failure are sowing the seeds too thickly and omitting to thin out the seedlings to give them room for development. The plants reach a height of about 12 in., and after the final thinning the seedlings ought to be 4-5 in. apart. Well-grown plants will bear finer blooms and remain in flower for longer than those which are overcrowded. They need no support.

Fall Sowing. Love-in-a-Mist may also be sown outdoors in fall to provide flowers in May and June. This practice is only to be recommended to those whose garden soil is light or well-drained; on heavy, clayey soil autumn sowing is less satisfactory, for the losses among the seedlings during winter months will probably be heavy. If, however, sand and light compost or leaf mold are dug into the ground preparatory to sowing the seeds, a sufficient number of the seedlings may survive.

Autumn-sown plants are more vigorous than others raised in spring, because they have a longer season of growth, and it will be necessary to thin them out so that they are 5-6 in. apart.

The final thinning must not be done until spring, for some of the seedlings are certain to perish in winter.

The seeds should be sown where the plants are to bloom: Nigella seedlings, especially those raised in spring, do not transplant satisfactorily, but if the work is done with care, so that the roots suffer the least possible damage, those raised in autumn may be transplanted in early spring.

In the Greenhouse. Nigellas are easy to grow in a sunny greenhouse where night temperature is maintained at 45-50 degrees. Seeds may be sown from September to January to give a succession of flowering plants from March to June. They may be grown in pots—the 5-in. size is large enough for single plants—or in deep flats or in benches.

A light, fertile, well-drained soil is ideal. Great care must be taken when transplanting the seedlings, as these plants do not recover readily if their roots are seriously damaged or disturbed. At the first transplanting the plants should be set in small pots, and from these should later be transferred to larger pots or to benches.

Watering must at all times be done in moderation. An excessively wet condition of the soil, especially in winter, is a frequent cause of failure; on the other hand, extreme dryness is to be avoided, as it soon causes yellowing of the foliage. Plants that have filled their pots with healthy roots, or that have nearly exhausted the nutrients in the soil in a bench, will benefit from weekly applications of dilute liquid fertilizers.

The favorite kind is Nigella damascena, which bears blue flowers: the typical kind, however, has been superseded by the variety named Miss Jekyll, which has blooms of richer blue. There is a white variety, also.

Nigella hispanica, the Fennel Flower, 18 in., blue, and the varieties alba, white, and atropurpurea, purple-blue, are others of which seeds can be purchased. One named Nigella orientalis, with yellow, red-spotted flowers, is occasionally offered by seedsmen.

NIGER. The Latin for black: this word is used as the specific or species name of some trees and plants, e.g., Populus nigra.

NIGHT-BLOOMING CEREUS. The popular name of certain plants, members of the Cactus family, the flowers of which open in the evening. The principal ones are Hylocereus triangularis, H. undatus, Acanthocereus pentaganus, Selenicereus grandiflorus, S. Macdonaldiae, S. pteranthus and Nyctocereus serpentinus, which see.

NIGHT-FLOWERING PLANTS. Flowers which open only at night are chiefly white or light-colored, and sweetly scented, and are therefore easily located by night-flying insects. In most cases the flowers are tubular, so that the nectar at the bases of the tubes can only be reached by those moths and other insects which are provided with very long tongues. The following are the principal night-flowering plants:

Evening Primrose (Oenothera). Most of these have yellow flowers which open at night, although several kinds—for example, O. glauca variety Fraseri—open their blooms during the daytime.

Tobacco (Nicotiana). The most popular kind, N. alata grandiflora, is night-flowering. It is an annual with tubular, sweetly scented white flowers.

Thorn Apple (Datura). D. Stramonium, a hardy plant, rarely cultivated except for its medicinal properties, has large white trumpet-shaped flowers.

Night-scented Stock (Mathiola bicornis). This annual is very drab-looking by day, but in the evening the lilac-colored flowers expand and emit a most delicious perfume.

Catchfly. Several of the Silenes, especially S. noctiflora, S. vespertina and S. longiflora, do not expand their blooms until the evening.

Night-flowering Cacti. The climbing kinds of the Cereus group, and some of the nonclimbing kinds, have large, showy, white flowers which open in the evening and fade the next morning. To prevent the blooms from fading so quickly, they may be cut when they are fully expanded, and placed in water. See Hylocereus, Nyctocereus and Selenicereus.

Honeysuckle. Many of these free-flowering, hardy, climbing shrubs open their blooms more widely at night and emit their delicious perfume.

Other night-flowering plants include

Zaluzianskya (Star Balsam), an annual from South Africa; Night-flowering Jasmine (Cestrum nocturnum), a tender shrub, 5 ft. in height, which bears creamy yellow flowers, very fragrant, at night; and Marvel of Peru (Mirabilis Jalapa), a tender herbaceous plant which, in summer, bears funnel-shaped white or red and yellow-striped flowers, which open only in cloudy weather or late in the afternoon, and close in the early morning.

NIGHT-SCENTED STOCK. See Mathiola bicornis.

NIGHTSHADE, DEADLY. See Atropa. Solanum Dulcamara is often misnamed Deadly Nightshade.

NIGHTSHADE, MALABAR. See Basella.

NIGHTSHADE, WOODY. Solanum Dulcamara, which see.

NIKKO FIR. Abies homolepis, which see.

NINEBARK. Physocarpus, which see.

NIPA (Ni'pa). A single species of feather-leaved Palm from tropical Asia, the Philippines and Australia. It belongs to the Palm family, Palmaceae, and may be grown outdoors in southern Florida. The name is the Moluccan one for this plant. In parts of the tropics the leaves of this palm are extensively used for thatching, and the plant is a source of sugar, toddy, vinegar and other products.

Nipa fruticans has leaves 20-30 ft. long that arise directly from the branching rootstock; it has no erect trunk. It thrives best in moist or wet soils, especially where the water is slightly brackish.

NIPPLE CACTUS. Mammillaria, which see.

NIPPON BELLS. Shortia uniflora, which see.

NITRATE OF LIME. This is obtained from the union of atmospheric nitrogen with lime in a special manner. See Fertilizers.

NITRATE OF POTASH. See Fertilizers.

NITRATE OF SODA. This, one of the oldest nitrogenous fertilizers, is a natural salt obtained in certain localities. The bulk of the natural supply comes from the deserts in the north of Chile. It is also manufactured synthetically. See Fertilizers.

NITRIFICATION. Organic matter that is added to the soil undergoes certain changes and eventually, after a longer or shorter time, depending upon temperatures, soil aeration and other factors, is reduced to salts and other chemicals, some of which are important plant nutrients.

Among the early products of this process of decay are ammonium salts. These salts contain nitrogen and are transformed by certain tiny soil bacteria into nitrates, one of the most valuable plant foods; the transformation is called nitrification. This process is continually going on in all fertile soils when the temperature is high enough, and it is intimately connected with the soils' fertility and ability to produce satisfactory crops.

To encourage the microscopic organisms that cause nitrification it is essential that the soil be kept in suitable condition for them by providing good drainage and by such cultural operations as liming, digging, cultivating and the addition of organic matter. Soil that does not contain enough nitrifying bacteria is "dead" and unable to produce the finest crops.

In the process of nitrification, part of the organic matter is first of all reduced to ammonia; the ammonia is then transformed into nitric acid. The nitric acid then unites with potash, soda, and lime already in the soil, and nitrates are ultimately produced. The nitrates, when dissolved in soil moisture, become available for plants at once.

The humus content of soils must be maintained by the use of natural manures or other organic material at intervals, preferably annually, so that the process of nitrification may go on continuously. Lime is also essential in many soils, and digging and working the soil in which crops are grown must be practiced to admit air.

While moisture is required for the process of nitrification, excess of soil water prevents the bacteria from working; this explains the necessity for good drainage. Heat is also required. Nitrification is always faster in summer when plants are in growth and able to use up the fertilizing nitrates formed; in winter it slows down as the soil becomes cold, but revives with the warmth of spring. Turning over the soil in spring accelerates the process of nitrification, and thorough cultivation at all times aids crops indirectly in a similar manner.

NITROGEN. Although four-fifths of our atmosphere is composed of nitrogen, the gas is of no use to plant life in that free state, yet, when combined with other elements, it is the most important of all plant foods. Nitrogen is as necessary to the cultivated crops as sunshine and moisture, and analysis shows that the roots, stems, leaves, flowers, and fruit all contain nitrogen.

In the natural process of decay, when plants die and form humus in the soil, the nitrogen which they contain is rendered available for future plants by the assistance of soil bacteria; this process is called nitrification. Since the amount of nitrogen in manure form in most soils is too little to yield the heavy crops desired in cultivation, gardeners add to the store available by applying as a fertilizer such nitrogenous manures as the nitrates, sulphate of ammonia, urea and so on.

The legume family, which includes Peas, Beans, etc., have nodules on their roots that are the homes of nitrifying bacteria. These are engaged in preparing nitrates in a suitable form for the plants, and it is not usually necessary to give such plants much fertilizer nitrogen. See Fertilizers.

NIVEUS. A botanical term meaning pure white, sometimes used as the specific or second scientific name of plants.

NOBLE FIR. Abies nobilis, which see.

NODE. A term in common use by gardeners to denote the place on a stem or shoot from which leaves develop; the word "joint" has the same meaning.

In gardening, the use of these words arises chiefly in connection with the work of taking cuttings; the instruction is usually, when making a cutting, to sever the shoot just beneath a node or joint. The reason for this is that a callus or ring of tissue, which develops before roots are seen, forms more certainly and quickly just beneath a node than between the nodes.

NODULE. When a healthy Bean, Lupine, Vetch, or Pea plant is dug up and the roots are examined after being washed, they are found to be covered with a number of warts or nodules. These, at first sight, may seem to indicate disease, but the reverse is the case; they are the home of countless tiny organisms or bacteria, engaged in fixing atmospheric nitrogen for the good of the plant.

NOISETTE ROSE. A name given to a number of vigorous climbing Roses, raised by M. Noisette more than 100 years ago; they bear large clusters of flowers. Few of them are now grown in gardens; they have been largely superseded by the newer climbing and rambler Roses. See Rosa Noisettiana.

NOLANA—*Chilean Bellflower* (Nola'na). Annual flowering plants from Chile and Peru, which belong to the family Nolanaceae. They are of prostrate growth, have elliptic leaves, 2-6 in. in length, and produce light or dark blue, bell-shaped flowers, 1-2 in. in diameter, singly in the axils of the leaves, in summer. The name Nolana is derived from *nola*, meaning a little bell, and refers to the bell-shaped flowers.

Especially Suitable for Seaside Gardens. In their native habitats these plants are found growing chiefly in maritime districts, and are therefore particularly suitable for cultivating near the seaside in this country. They like a sunny, open position and light, well-drained soil. If the soil is infertile, a little well-decayed manure should be dug into the ground in the spring.

When to Sow Seeds. In spring, as soon as the ground is sufficiently dry, the surface is made

The Chilean Bellflower, Nolana atriplicifolia, a charming annual. The flowers are blue with a white central zone.

smooth and even with a small-toothed rake. The seeds are then scattered thinly on the surface and raked in by drawing the rake gently backwards and forwards over the soil. When 1 in. in height, the seedlings are thinned out 6 in. apart.

During the remainder of the summer the plants need very little attention, except that the soil must be kept free from weeds and stirred occasionally with a Dutch hoe, hand fork or cultivator, to allow air to enter. Owing to their prostrate habit of growth, these plants are particularly suitable for growing in a sunny rockery.

The chief kinds are N. prostrata, pale blue; N. tenella, light blue; N. atriplicifolia, blue and white.

NOLINA (Noli'na). Tender ornamental foliage plants of little horticultural value. They are found wild in Mexico and the southwestern United States and belong to the Lily family, Liliaceae. Nolina is closely related to Beaucarnea, and some of the species are included by botanists in that genus. They form thick, woody stems surmounted by tufts of drooping lanceolate (lance-shaped), dracaena-like leaves, up to 3 ft. in length. The flowers are inconspicuous. The name Nolina commemorates P. C. Nolin, a French author. As outdoor plants, Nolinas are of value only in warm desert and semidesert regions.

Ornamental-leaved Plants for a Greenhouse. Nolinas are sometimes cultivated in greenhouses by fanciers of succulent plants. When they are so grown, a minimum winter temperature of 50 degrees is required, and the best compost consists of fibrous loam two parts, leaf mold one part, and a sprinkling of sand. Repotting is done in March; the crocks and loose soil are removed from the roots with a pointed stick and the plants are set in pots two sizes larger.

After repotting, the plants are carefully watered until the pots are filled with roots, and during the remainder of the summer the soil is kept moist. From September to March very little water is required, sufficient only being given to prevent the leaves from withering.

When to Sow Seeds. Seeds are sown in March in well-drained pots filled with a sandy compost. The pots are covered with panes of glass and set in a propagating case in the greenhouse until germination takes place. When the seedlings are 2 in. high, they are potted separately in 3-in. pots and subsequently into larger sizes.

Taking Cuttings. Cuttings of side shoots are also taken in March. The lower leaves on these shoots are removed, and a cut is made below the bottom joint. The shoots are then inserted in pots of sandy soil and plunged in a propagating case. When sufficient roots are formed, the cuttings are potted separately and treated as advised for the seedlings.

The chief kinds are N. longifolia and N. Parryi.

NOMENCLATURE. See article entitled Names of Plants.

NOMOCHARIS (Nomo'charis; Nomochar'is). These hardy bulbs, which produce strikingly handsome flowers, are natives of China and belong to the Lily family, Liliaceae. The flowering stems are 1-2 ft. in height and bear numerous bell-shaped flowers up to 3 in. in diameter. They are white or rosy-purple and are blotched in the center with purple or maroon, the segments being spotted with reddish-purple or maroon. The leaves are in whorls or scattered on the stems. The name is from *nomos,* pasture, and *charis,* charm.

Nomocharis Farrerri, a very choice bulbous plant from northeastern Burma, with flowers of delicate pink, lightly spotted with red at the base of the inner segments. It is closely related to N. pardanthina and requires similar treatment.

Nomocharis pardanthina, a beautiful bulbous plant closely related to the Lily. The flowers are rose-purple, with maroon blotch at base.

Planting the Bulbs Out of Doors. The treatment which is given to the majority of hardy Lilies will suit these bulb plants in regions where they are likely to thrive, but, unfortunately, that does not include most of the United States. They are high-mountain plants that need cool summers. In parts of the Pacific Northwest they may be cultivated. Where they may be grown, they are planted in October–November or February–March, when soil and weather conditions are suitable. A position which is shaded from the sun at midday is best. Very heavy or light soils can be improved by incorporating liberal quantities of leaf mold.

To plant the bulbs, dig a hole 6 in. in depth and of sufficient area to accommodate the bulbs when set 6 in. apart. If the soil is heavy, place a layer of sand around each bulb before putting it in position. Then fill the hole with the excavated soil and mark the site with a label, so that you can avoid damaging the bulbs when digging near them before they send up their shoots in the spring. A summer mulch of leaf mold or well-decayed manure is beneficial.

Once planted, the bulbs should not be disturbed until the vigor of the plants shows signs of deterioration. Then they are lifted in the autumn and are replanted in freshly prepared soil.

Cultivation in Pots in the Greenhouse. In favored regions these fine plants may also be grown in pots in a cool greenhouse. Large pots, 7 or 8 in. in diameter, are best. These must be well-drained with crocks, which are covered with a layer of rough siftings from the compost. A compost of fibrous loam two parts, leaf mold one part, and a scattering of sand, is used. Enough of this is placed in the pots so that, when the bulbs are placed in position, their tips will be 2 in. below the rim. Three bulbs are set in a 7-in. pot and are covered, all but the tips, with compost. The pots are placed in a cold frame or greenhouse until they start into growth, and are then transferred to a greenhouse having a minimum temperature of 45 degrees.

Summer and Winter Treatment. From the time of potting up to the commencement of vigorous growth, the soil is kept moist, but care must be taken to prevent a waterlogged condition or the bulbs will rot. Later on, when the plants are growing freely, more moisture is required, and when the flower buds commence to show, an occasional watering with liquid fertilizer is beneficial. Towards the end of May the plants are placed out of doors and, as the foliage dies down, less water is given. In the following autumn the plants are turned out of their pots, the best bulbs selected for potting, and the offsets saved and planted out in a spare bed as a means of increasing the stock.

Propagation by Seed. The seeds are sown in well-drained pans filled with sandy soil in February or March. They are set in a temperature of 50-55 degrees and the soil is moistened only when it becomes moderately dry. When the seedlings are large enough to handle, they are pricked out into well-drained flats or pans, in a mixture of equal parts of loam and leaf mold with sand added freely. During the summer they are grown in a cold frame and the soil is kept moist. When the foliage dies down, water is withheld until growth recommences in spring.

They are then planted 3 in. apart in rows 1 ft. apart, in a spare border.

The Chief Kinds. N. pardanthina, 2 ft., rosy-purple, spotted externally with deep maroon blotches at the base; N. saluenensis, 2 ft., rosy-purple and white; N. Mairei, 18 in., satiny white, spotted with reddish-purple, the edges frilled and crimped; N. Farreri, 2½ ft., soft pink, spotted with red; and N. aperta, similar to N. Mairei but less frilled.

NOPALEA (Nopa'lea). A small genus of Cacti, family Cactaceae, similar to Opuntias in their flattened joints, and previously included in that genus.

The principal kind is Nopalea cochenillifera, a treelike Cactus with large, oblong, sparsely spiny joints, which was once cultivated extensively in tropical America as a host plant for the cochineal bug. The flowers are red, with pink stamens. N. dejecta has larger joints, yellow spines, and dark red flowers. It requires the same culture as Opuntia, which see.

NOPALXOCHIA (Nopalxoch'ia). Two species of Cactus, family Cactaceae, that are natives of Mexico. The name is from the Aztec.

These plants are closely related to Epiphyllum and require the same cultural care. In gardens they are often grown under the name Epiphyllum and sometimes under the names Phyllocactus and Zygocactus. N. Ackermannii (Epiphyllum Ackermannii, Zygocactus Ackermannii) grows about 3 ft. tall and has large scarlet and carmine flowers; a white-flowered variety has been described under the name candida. N. phyllanthoides (Epiphyllum phyllanthoides) has rose or red flowers and is the parent of many garden hybrids.

NORDMANNIA. The hardy herbaceous plant sometimes known as Nordmannia cordifolia is Trachystemon orientale, which see.

NORFOLK ISLAND PINE. See Araucaria.

NORTH CAROLINA, GARDENING IN. See Regional Gardening.

NORTH DAKOTA, GARDENING IN. See Regional Gardening.

NORWAY MAPLE. See Acer platanoides.

NORWAY SPRUCE. See Picea Abies.

NOTHOFAGUS—*Antarctic Beech* (Nothofa'-gus). The Antarctic or southern Beeches are natives of South America and Australasia. They belong to the Beech family, Fagaceae, and are the representatives in the Southern Hemisphere of the Beech of the Northern Hemisphere. The Antarctic Beeches include both evergreen and deciduous trees. The name is from *nothos,* false, and *fagus,* Beech.

Not Suitable for Cold Climates. The South American kinds are hardier than those from Australasia; however, as is only to be expected in view of the climatic conditions in which they grow naturally, the Antarctic Beeches are not suitable for planting in cold climates.

The two kinds most likely to be cultivated are the typical Antarctic Beech, Nothofagus antarctica, found in South America from Tierra del Fuego to Chile, where it grows to a large timber tree, and N. obliqua, a tree 100 ft. or more in height in Chile.

Three other Southern Beeches are cultivated in European gardens, all of them natives of South America. They are N. procera, a deciduous kind; N. Dombeyi, usually evergreen, but semi-deciduous in cold winters; and N. betuloides, evergreen.

Suitable for Mild Districts. The following Australasian Beeches are cultivated in the mild climate of the south and west of England and Wales, the southwest of Scotland, and in Ireland, and are suitable for cultivation on the Pacific Coast: Nothofagus cliffortioides, the Mountain Beech of New Zealand; N. Cunninghamii, a native tree of Tasmania; N. fusca, also from New Zealand, and N. Moorei, the Australian Beech, a native of New South Wales. These are all evergreen trees.

Propagation. Antarctic Beeches are propagated by layering the lower branches in autumn. Cuttings made of the ends of the young shoots will sometimes root if inserted in a frame in July. They may also be raised from seeds. The trees thrive best in deep and well-drained loamy soil to which plenty of organic matter and coarse grit has been added.

NOTHOLAENA—*Gold and Silver Maidenhair Ferns* (Notholae'na). Mostly tender Ferns. They belong to the family Polypodiaceae, and are natives of Australia, New Zealand, South Africa, tropical America, North America and Asia. These Ferns do not exceed 12 in. in height, and have bipinnate fronds which, in some kinds, are coated with silvery or golden waxy powder. Others have woolly, hairy or scaly fronds. The frond stems are thin and wiry, and the rhizomes are covered with scales. The name Notholaena is derived from *nothos,* spurious, and *chlaina,* a cloak, and refers to the covering of the spore cases. Except in mild or warm regions, they are suitable only for greenhouse culture. Some are more tender than others; here we shall refer to these as hothouse kinds, and to the rest as greenhouse kinds. Among the latter is included N. Fendleri, a native of an area extending from Colorado to Arizona and Texas.

Hothouse and Greenhouse Ferns. The hothouse kinds require a minimum winter temperature of 55 degrees, and the greenhouse kinds one of 45 degrees. The best soil compost consists of equal parts of loam, peat, leaf mold and sand. Repotting is done in March, or as soon as the new fronds commence to uncurl. Well-rooted plants are taken out of their pots, the crocks and loose soil are removed from the roots, and the plants are set in slightly larger pots, which are nearly half-filled with crocks. Plants which have not filled their pots with roots are not disturbed until the following spring.

In cases where the roots have decayed, the plants are removed from their pots, and the crocks and all the compost are washed away from the roots. They are then cut back to live portions, and the plants placed in pots just large enough to hold them.

Summer and Winter Management. After repotting, the plants are shaded from sunlight, and the atmosphere is kept moist, but the fronds must not be syringed. When well rooted, they are given a light, dry position, where moisture cannot collect on the fronds.

Watering must be done carefully at all times of the year, as the roots quickly decay if the soil is waterlogged. Much more water is required in summer, when the soil dries up quickly, than in winter, when the temperature is lower and the plants are at rest.

Raising Gold and Silver Ferns from Spores. Propagation is by spores and division. The spores may be sown as soon as they are ripe, or they may be stored in seed packets and sown at a later date. To ascertain if the spores are ripe, a frond' is gathered on which they are brown in color. This is placed in a paper bag, which is hung in a dry room or shed for 48 hours; the ripe spores will then be found at the bottom of the bag in the form of a brown powder. For advice on their treatment, see Ferns.

Dividing the Old Ferns. Division, which is done in the spring at potting time, consists of separating the plants into small pieces, each piece containing a portion of rhizomes furnished with roots and fronds. The divided portions are potted in small pots and treated as previously advised.

The Chief Kinds. *For the greenhouse:* N. (Pellaea) dealbata, 4 in., fronds covered with white powder; N. Fendleri, 9 in., fronds white beneath; N. Hookeri, 9 in., fronds covered with white powder; N. vellaea (lanuginosa), 9 in., woolly fronds. *For the hothouse:* N. sinuata, 12 in., fronds covered with rusty-brown scales; and N. trichomanoides, 12 in., the fronds covered with white powder. The measurements refer to the length of the fronds.

NOTHOLIRION (Notholi'rion). Bulbous plants from northern India, upper Burma, Tibet and western China, closely related to the Lily and belonging to the family Liliaceae. As they tend to bloom early in the year, they are, except in fairly mild climates, best grown in a cool greenhouse, in a compost of peaty soil, with plenty of moisture while in active growth. The name is from *nothos,* spurious, and *leirion,* lily.

In favored localities the Notholirions can be grown successfully in semishady positions out of doors. Increase is by seed, treated in the same way as advised for Lilies, or by bulbils, the latter being produced as the old bulb dies after flowering.

Four kinds are known: N. campanulatum, 4 ft., bearing many bell-shaped, dark red, green-tipped flowers; N. hyacinthinum, 3 ft., funnel-shaped flowers, lavender to rosy lilac, tipped green; N. macrophyllum, 3 ft., funnel-shaped, pink-mauve flowers; and N. Thomsonianum, 3 ft., fragrant, pink, funnel-shaped flowers.

NOTHOPANAX (Notho'panax; Nothopan'ax). Tender evergreen trees and shrubs that occur naturally from Malaya to New Zealand. They are grown in climates such as that of California. Nothopanax belongs to the Ginseng family, Araliaceae. The name is derived from *nothos,* spurious, and Panax, a genus of plants.

These plants may be propagated by seeds or cuttings, and by air layering.

A great deal of confusion exists as to the correct identification of many of the plants in this group, particularly because (1) some do not bloom in cultivation and (2) the character of the foliage often varies with the age of the plant and sometimes with the parts of the same plant. Among kinds that may be grown are N. anomalum, 12 ft., much branched; N. arboreum, a rounded tree to 25 ft. tall; N. Colensoi, shrub or tree to 15 ft. tall; N. lineare, shrub, 5-10 ft. tall; N. simplex, shrub or tree to 25 ft. tall.

NOTHOSCORDUM—*False Garlic* (Nothoscor'dum). A small group of summer-flowering bulbs, suitable for planting in sunny, well-drained borders or in the rock garden. Division of the offsets in September provides the best means of increase. The bulbs should be planted 2 in. deep in September. Nothoscordum is allied to the Onion (Allium) and belongs to the Lily family, Liliaceae. The name is derived from *nothos,* spurious, and *skordon* or *skorodon,* Garlic.

The principal kinds are N. fragrans, 2 ft.,

Nothoscordum bivalve is a summer-blooming bulbous plant.

Notocactus mammulosus, with golden-yellow flowers, is easy to grow.

with flowers yellow: N. floricomus, N. Mueller-Melchersii, N. Leninghausii, N. Ottonis, N. pampeanus, N. submammulosus, N. apricus and N. mammulosus.

NOTYLIA (Noty'lia). A small group of Orchids found wild in Central America. They have small pseudobulbs and evergreen leaves. The racemes are often pendent and thickly set with small flowers. All are summer or autumn flowering. The name is derived from *notos,* the back, and *tylus,* a lump, and is applied on account of a little hump on the back of the column formed by the pollinia.

Small pans or Orchid baskets which can conveniently be suspended suit these plants better than pots. The compost should consist of two parts of osmunda fiber and one part of sphagnum moss. Repotting is not required every year. Shade is necessary, particularly during the growing season, and the plants require water throughout the year, but it must be given carefully in winter. A greenhouse with a temperature of about 60 degrees in winter and with a considerable rise in summer suits these Orchids.

The chief kind is N. bicolor, with inflorescences about 4 in. long; the flowers are white, sometimes flushed with lilac. Other kinds, sometimes grown in collections, are N. albida, N. bipartita, and N. Bungerothii.

NUDICAULIS, NUDICAULE. A botanical term meaning naked-stalked, which is sometimes used in technical names of plants. The Iceland Poppy, Papaver nudicaule, provides an example.

NUPHAR—*Yellow Pond Lily, Spatterdock* (Nu'phar). Hardy aquatic perennial flowering plants, natives of North America, Japan, and Europe. These plants belong to the Water Lily family, Nymphaeaceae. They have floating leaves which resemble those of the Water Lily, and chiefly yellow flowers. The five or more sepals which constitute the showy part of the flower are concave, while the numerous petals are inconspicuous and resemble stamens. They are more compact than the Nymphaeas (Water Lilies). The name Nuphar is derived from *naufar,* the Arabic name for Nymphaea.

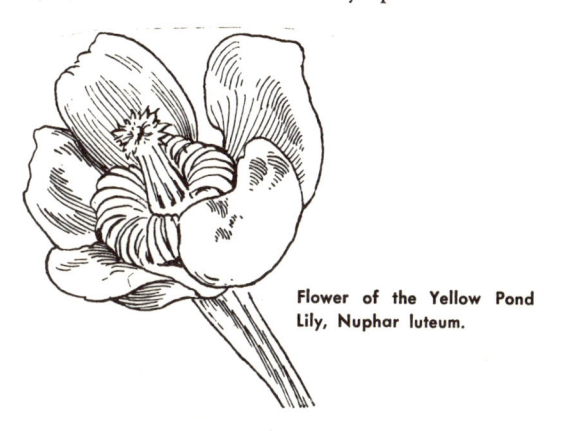

Flower of the Yellow Pond Lily, Nuphar luteum.

For the Margins of Ponds or Large Tanks. Nuphar should be planted in spring and a compost of two parts of rich loam and one part of well-decayed cow manure is used. The roots are placed in shallow wicker baskets, which are filled with the compost, or they are enclosed in pieces of burlap with compost around the roots. They are lowered into the water, which should be 12 in. in depth, and are kept in place with a few stones. Eventually the plants root through the sacking or basket and establish themselves in the mud. Once planted, they need no further attention, except that their growth should be restricted to the allotted space.

Propagation is by division of the roots at planting time or seeds may be sown in pans of soil, which are immersed in a tank of water. The seedlings are afterwards transplanted into a shallow tank or left in the pan until large enough to plant out in their permanent positions.

The Chief Kinds are N. luteum, yellow; N.

microphyllum (Kalmianum), yellow; N. advenum, yellow; N. japonicum, golden-yellow; N. pumilum, tiny yellow flowers; and N. polysepalum, yellow. N. advenum is the common Spatterdock of North America.

NURSE GRASS. A quick-germinating and quick-growing grass, such as Redtop, is used in lawn seed mixtures to provide a rapid ground cover and help to crowd out weeds during the early development of the more permanent grasses such as Kentucky Blue Grass. The latter may take two or three years to reach their full development; under favorable circumstances they gradually crowd out the nurse grasses.

NURSERY. An establishment in which trees, shrubs and plants are propagated by seeds, cuttings, grafting or in other ways, and are "grown on" until they are large enough to be offered for sale. The term nursery or nursery

In this combination nursery and cut-flower garden, biennials, perennials and shrubs are raised for transplanting elsewhere.

border or nursery bed is also often used to describe a spare or reserve border in which seedlings and cuttings are raised, or in which young plants are grown until they are large enough to be set out in their permanent places.

NUTMEG. The common and commercial name for the seed of Myristica fragrans, a tree growing 30-40 ft. high. A native of the Moluccas, and other East Indian Islands, the tree is also widely grown in other tropical countries.

The fruit of the Nutmeg tree resembles a large golden or orange-colored plum. It is usually oval in shape, but in different forms may be round or pear-shaped. When ripe, the fleshy outer part bursts open and discloses the brown seed covered by a crimson net, aril or arillus. This arillus is easily separated from the seed. It is dried and constitutes the spice called Mace, the brown seeds being also of considerable value as spice.

NUTTALLIA CERASIFORMIS. Osmaronia, which see.

NUX VOMICA. The common name for the tree Strychnos Nux-vomica, and for a drug obtained from the seeds. S. Nux-vomica is a small tree widely distributed in India, Ceylon, Australia, etc. It bears orange-like fruits, among the flesh of which several thin, flattened, disclike seeds are embedded. These seeds are ½-¾ in. across, and have a satiny, grayish surface, owing to the presence of numerous, tiny, closely appressed hairs.

The seeds have little or no odor, but have a very bitter taste, and are highly poisonous. The chief poisonous constituents (2-3 per cent) of the seeds are strychnine and brucine. There is also a small quantity of strychnine in other parts of the tree. From these seeds, with those of S. Ignati, much of the strychnine of commerce is obtained. See Strychnos.

NYCTANTHES—*Tree of Sadness* (Nyctan'-thes). A jasmine-like shrub or small tree that is sometimes also known as Night Jasmine. It is a native of India and adaptable for outdoor cultivation only in Florida and southern California in the United States. This plant belongs to the Olive family, Oleaceae. Its name is derived from *nyktos,* night, and *anthos,* flower, and has reference to the fact that the flowers open only from nightfall to dawn.

Nyctanthes Arbor-tristis grows well in a variety of soils and situations. It may be increased by means of cuttings in early summer and by seeds.

This plant may also be grown in greenhouses in a fertile, peaty soil in well-drained pots. It needs a moist atmosphere and a minimum winter temperature of 60 degrees. Old plants are pruned back, repotted and started into new growth in late winter or early spring. They need watering freely from spring to fall, more moderately in winter. Regular applications of dilute liquid fertilizer are beneficial during the season of active growth.

NYCTERINIA. Zaluzianskya, which see.

NYCTOCEREUS (Nyctocer'eus). A group of slender, erect or vinelike Cacti that are natives of Mexico and Central America. They are night-bloomers. They belong to the Cactus family, Cactaceae. The name, which has reference to their flowering habit, is derived from *nyktos,* night, and Cereus, a genus of Cacti. For their cultivation, see Cacti.

Kinds include N. guatemalensis, flowers red or yellow outside, white within; N. Hirschtianus, flowers pale pink to white; N. serpentinus, flowers white with tips darker. The last-named is commonly cultivated outdoors in mild climates, in greenhouses and as a house plant.

NYMPHAEA or WATER LILY
Full Instructions on How to Grow These Lovely Aquatics

Nymphaeas or Water Lilies are true aquatics. They grow with their roots in soil and their leaves floating on the surface of the water. The flowers of some kinds float, those of others are carried on stout stems well above the water. About 40 wild species of Nymphaea are known. They are natives of the Northern Hemisphere, the tropics, Australia and South Africa. From these wild species horticulturists have raised a large number of hybrid kinds which are the ones

A well furnished garden pool in a delightful setting. Water lilies and other aquatic plants keep it gay with bloom throughout the summer.

most commonly grown in gardens at present.

Horticulturally, Nymphaeas are the most important group of all aquatic plants. They are much admired by gardeners, and few water gardens would be considered complete without one or more included in the planting. Nymphaeas provide a succession of handsome blooms over a period of many weeks and their foliage is decidedly attractive; in some varieties the leaves are green, in others green marked with chocolate or purple blotchings, and in yet others the foliage is rich maroon.

The cultivation of Water Lilies is simple. They are well adapted for growing by amateur gardeners, and few other plants give such splendid or sure returns for so little expenditure of cost or effort. Water is, of course, essential, and because many varieties require considerable space for their full development a pool or pools of considerable area would be required to accommodate a really large collection. But a few Water Lilies can be grown easily in a pool of modest size, and the small-growing varieties which dealers call Pygmy Water Lilies can even be cultivated and flowered successfully in a miniature pool or tub garden.

Miniature Water Lily pools or tub gardens may be made by sinking into the ground, almost to their rims, tubs or cut-down barrels, 18-20 in. deep. In the bottom of each of these a layer of soil 9-12 in. in depth is placed and one Water Lily plant is set in the center. After planting, an inch of clean sand is spread over the soil surface and the tiny pool is then filled slowly with water. It is better not to use manure in soil mix-

A beautiful hardy Water Lily.

tures that are used in miniature pools; good topsoil with bone meal mixed in at the rate of 1 qt. to each bushel gives the best results. The decorative value of a miniature pool is enhanced if its margins are planted with bog or waterside plants.

For miniature pools, select only varieties of Water Lilies that are restrained in their growth. These include both hardy and tropical kinds. In dealers' catalogues they are often classified as Pygmy Water Lilies. Among the best of the hardy varieties are: Aurora, Joanne Pring, N. tetragona (White Pygmy) and N. tetragona helvola (Yellow Pygmy). Among the best of the small-growing tropicals are Patricia, Royal Purple, Colorata and Daubeniana. In addition to the Water Lily, a selection of other aquatic plants, such as Water Hyacinth (Eichoria), Water Poppy (Hydrocleys), Water Lettuce (Pistia) and Parrot's-Feather (Myriophyllum) may be planted in a tub garden. These kinds grow well together, and with them delightful effects can be obtained.

Classification. For garden purposes, the Nymphaeas may be divided into two separate classes: the tropical kinds, which have tubers and carry their flowers well above the water; and the hardy varieties, which have fleshy rhizomes and flowers that normally float on the surface of the water, but which may be raised above the water somewhat if the plants are old and overgrown (in need of dividing), so that the foliage is much crowded.

A day-blooming tropical Nymphaea.

[7—14]
Neillia sinensis

[7—15]
Fennel Flower
(Nigella hispanica)

[7—15a]
Tobacco
(Nicotiana Tabacum)

[7—15b]
Cup Flower
(Nierembergia caerulea)

[7—15c]
Cholla Cactus
(Opuntia)

Hardy Water Lilies

These are among the easiest plants to grow. They luxuriate in any moderately shallow pool, lake, pond, or slow-flowing stream, provided they receive ample sunshine. The water should be sufficiently deep to cover the crowns (rhizomes) of the plants to a depth of 8-15 in. Only the very strongest varieties thrive in deeper water. If planting is to be done in definitely running water, select only the most vigorous kinds and, if possible, make "bays" away from the current, where the flow of water will be slowed and so be more favorable to the growth of Water Lilies.

How to Plant. The roots of hardy Water Lilies may be confined to tubs or other containers of soil submerged in a suitable place or the Lilies may be planted where their roots can grow directly into soil forming the bottom of a pond or pool. If the plants are confined to containers, a pool 2-2½ ft. deep is most satisfactory (see Water Garden), but miniature varieties can be successfully cultivated in shallower water.

The best method of establishing hardy Nymphaeas in soil-bottomed ponds or streams is to plant them in soil-filled wicker or wire baskets, lacing a few sticks across the basket tops so that the rhizomes will not float out of the soil, and then sink these baskets at suitable places.

The sulphur-yellow N. tetragona helvola.

Each basket should contain approximately 1 bushel of soil. The soil should be rich, consisting of good topsoil, two thirds, and well-decayed manure, one third. The addition of bone meal at the rate of 1 pint to each bushel is advantageous.

If the pool has a concrete bottom, it is better to plant the Water Lilies in tubs, one plant to each. Each tub should hold a minimum of 1 bushel of soil; 2-4 bushels is better, especially for strong-growing varieties. After planting, the surface of the soil should be covered with an inch or two of sand before submerging the plants. This prevents bits of leaves, manure and other debris from floating to the surface.

When to Plant. The best and safest time to plant hardy Water Lilies is in spring, just before they start to grow, though they will succeed if planted later, provided care is taken not to injure the roots. At no time must the plants be permitted to become dry. When purchased plants are received, they should be at once submerged; if this cannot be done, they must be placed in the shade and covered with wet leaves, straw, burlap or similar material.

Although the leaves are leathery in texture, they wilt and curl very quickly when the plants are taken out of the water.

General Care. Once planted, hardy Water Lilies need little care. Throughout the summer, dead leaves and faded flowers should be removed at regular intervals. The plants benefit if they are fertilized once or twice during the summer. This may be done by taking pieces of cheesecloth and tying in each about an eggcup full of general garden fertilizer, such as a 5-10-5 (see Fertilizers), of a kind that is not rapidly soluble, and carefully planting four or five of these packages among the roots of each Water Lily plant.

Hardy Water Lilies may be left outdoors over winter, provided there is a sufficient depth of water over them to keep their rhizomes and roots from freezing. It is advisable to drain small pools of water in the fall in regions where much freezing takes place. The Water Lilies may be left in the drained pools and covered with a sufficient depth of leaves, straw, hay or some similar material to prevent them freezing, or they may be moved—in the containers in which they are planted—into a cool but frost-free basement, garage or shed. In any case the soil must be kept moist at all times. To prevent undue drying, it is well to cover the soil surface with peat moss, leaves or wet burlap.

Once hardy Water Lilies are established in tubs or other containers of adequate size, it is not necessary to disturb them until they become crowded and show signs of producing inferior and fewer flowers and poorer foliage. When this occurs, the roots should be dug up, divided and replanted in fresh soil in early spring. If the plants are in large containers, such replanting will normally be necessary every 3-4 years; plants in smaller tubs may need replanting every second year or even every year.

Propagation. Hardy Water Lilies are propagated by dividing the clumps of rhizomes (roots) just before new growth begins in spring. This should be done at least every three or four years, at which time the plants are taken up and set in new soil if they are growing in tubs or other containers. Seeds may be used to increase natural species, but improved garden varieties do not breed true from seeds.

Seeds of Water Lilies are sown in pots or pans of sandy soil with a 1-in. covering of sand over the seeds. After sowing, the seed containers are immersed in water so that they are covered to a depth of 2-3 in. For hardy kinds the water temperature must be maintained at about 60 degrees. As soon as the seedlings form floating leaves, they are transplanted individually to small pots.

Hardy Species. Among hardy Water Lilies that occur naturally wild in some parts of the world, as distinct from the improved or hybrid kinds developed by horticulturists, a number are worth growing in gardens. These include:

The European White Water Lily, Nymphaea alba. This is a vigorous grower, with leaves up to 12 in. across which are reddish when young, and flowers that measure 4-5 in. in diameter. The blooms are white and open by day. In the variety candidissima, the flowers are at first yellowish.

The Fragrant Water Lily, Nymphaea odorata. This is a common native of the eastern United States. Its leaves are not quite as large as those of N. alba, measuring usually up to about 10 in. across. The flowers, which open by day, are 3-5 in. in diameter and white. In variety gigantea the flowers are larger. In variety sulphurea (which is possibly a hybrid between N. odorata and N. mexicana) the flowers are pale yellow and the foliage is marked with brown splashes.

The Pygmy Water Lily, N. tetragona (White Pygmy). The smallest Water Lily in cultivation, this is a native of eastern Asia and of North America from Idaho to Ontario. Its flowers are $1\frac{1}{2}$-$2\frac{1}{2}$ in. in diameter and open in the daytime. They are white. The leaves measure 3-4 in. across and are reddish beneath. N. tetragona variety helvola (Yellow Pygmy) has yellow flowers and its foliage is blotched with brown; it may be a hybrid between N. mexicana and N. tetragona.

The Magnolia or Tuberous Water Lily, N. tuberosa. A native of North America, this kind has white flowers with little or no fragrance, that open by day. They measure 4-9 in. across.

The Best Hardy Hybrids. *White:* Marliacea albida (offered as Marliac White), flowers sparkling white, continuous blooming and of moderate growth; Gladstone, large, pure white flowers, but not too free a bloomer; Gonnere, very double flowers; Hermine, of moderate growth with pointed petals.

Red Shades: Attraction, large garnet-red flowers; Escarboucle, very large, continuous flowering, scarlet-crimson; Gloriosa, early, free-blooming, fragrant; James Brydon, free-blooming, amaranth-rose.

Pink and Rose Shades: Marliacea carnea (offered as Marliac Flesh), flesh-colored; Marliacea rosea (offered as Marliac Rose), deep pink; Joanne Pring, a sport of N. tetragona helvola, deep pink, excellent for small pools; Gloire de Temple-sur-Lot, opens pink and fades to white; Lustrous, rose-pink with a silvery sheen; Esmeralda, pink and white variegated; Lucida, soft rose-pink deepening to rosy red as flowers age.

Yellow and Apricot Shades: Marliacea chromatella, bright yellow, leaves blotched brown; Sunrise, large flowers, bright yellow; Aurora, coppery rose, opening to salmon and wine-red; Comanche, rich apricot changing to coppery bronze.

Tropical Water Lilies

The tropical Nymphaeas are chiefly natives of Egypt, the East Indies, Mexico, India and Australasia. One named Nymphaea thermalis is the Hungarian Lotus; it has white flowers which often emit a vinous odor. Most of those grown in gardens are hybrids.

In regions of cold winters most amateurs do not attempt to carry over their tropical Water Lilies from year to year but prefer to purchase new young plants from specialists each spring. The young plants must not be set in outdoor pools until warm weather has become settled and the water is at a temperature of about 70 degrees. Cold water is especially harmful to tropical Water Lilies, and for this reason they are not likely to do well if fountains or streams of water play into the pool.

Culture of Tropical Water Lilies. These plants need a rich loamy soil enriched with one third part by bulk of rotted manure or other organic matter and with a generous amount of bone meal added. If rotted manure is not available, a 5-10-5 fertilizer (see Fertilizers) or one of approximately similar analysis should be added to the mixture at the rate of a pound to each bushel of the mixture. The fertilizer should be of a kind that releases its nutrients slowly rather than one that contains rapidly soluble nutrients.

It is important that the tropicals be located in

Tropical Water Lilies carry their blooms on stems that lift them well above the surface of the water.

full sunshine. The best planting depth is one which allows a water depth of 6-8 in. above the soil level.

When planted in containers, strong-growing tropical Water Lilies need at least one third of a cubic yard of soil each, and more is advantageous (a third of a cubic yard is contained in a tub measuring 3 ft. square and 1 ft. deep); less vigorous-growing kinds will get along with about half this amount of soil (they may be grown in tubs measuring 2 ft. square and 1 ft. deep or their equivalents).

Summer care is very simple. It is necessary to remove faded blooms and yellowing leaves once or twice a week and to make sure that the plants are not crowded by the growth of their neighbors. Once they are well established and their containers are filled with roots, these Water Lilies benefit from being fertilized in the manner described above for hardy Water Lilies.

Propagation of Tropical Water Lilies. At the end of the growing season it is usual to discard the old plants of tropical Water Lilies, although it is sometimes possible to carry them over stored in moist sand in a warm greenhouse; this plan, however, is not recommended. Where facilities exist, the most usual methods of propagating tropicals are by tubers and, in the case of those kinds that produce young plantlets on the stems, by leaf propagation. Seeds may be used for natural species, but named garden varieties do not breed true from seeds. The seeds are sown in the same way as recommended above for hardy Water Lilies but the water temperature should be higher; from 70 to 80 degrees is suitable.

Leaf propagation consists of removing the young plants that form on the leaves, each with a small piece of stalk attached, when the mother leaf begins to turn yellow, and potting each in a small pot. The young plants may be set in the outdoor pool in the summer, but they should be removed to a tank of water in a warm greenhouse before frost comes.

To effect tuber propagation, the small tubers that form around the base of the old one are carefully removed in late August or early September and are rested by being stored in barely moist sand in a closed tin or a glass container for two or three weeks. At the conclusion of this period they are planted individually at the bottom of small pots in an indoor tank, in water heated to 80 degrees.

New shoots soon appear; as soon as each of these has formed two leaves, it is pinched off at the point where it joins the tuber and is potted in a small pot and returned to the tank. The tuber, which is left undisturbed in the pot, will continue to produce a succession of these young shoots over a long period, and each may be treated in the way described. The young plants are kept in the greenhouse tank until planting-out time the following year.

In a variation of this method, stock plants of the Water Lilies to be propagated are grown in 4-in. pots, without ever being transplanted to a larger size. Such plants form small, hard tubers which may be taken in August or September and stored until the following January or February in containers of scarcely moist sand. Early in the year they are planted and started into growth, and treated exactly as advised above for tubers taken from around the bases of old plants in fall.

Tropical Species. Many of the best tropical Water Lilies are hybrids or garden varieties that have been developed by horticulturists. The best of these are listed below under the headings Day-blooming Varieties of Tropicals and Night-blooming Tropical Varieties. Despite the magnificence of the hybrids many of the wild species and their forms are well worthy of cultivation. A selection of the more interesting follows.

Nymphaea stellata, the Blue Lotus of India, is one of the finest blue-flowered Water Lilies. It is day-blooming. Its rich blue flowers stand well above the water. The Cape Blue Water Lily, N. capensis, is one of the most intensely colored of the blue-flowered Water Lilies. It is a native of South Africa. N. capensis zanzibariensis has deep blue flowers that measure to 12 in. across. Both N. capensis and its variety are day-bloomers. Nymphaea gigantea, from Australia, has lovely blue flowers fully 6 in. across. It, too, is a day-bloomer.

The Egyptian Lotus, Nymphaea Lotus, is the Lotus Flower of the Ancient Egyptians which was sacred to the goddess Isis, and occasionally the flower was engraved on their coins. The seeds and roots were often dried and ground to meal and made into a sort of bread by the ancient Egyptians. The flowers of this species open on four successive nights and are white, shaded with pink or red. The variety dentata of N. Lotus is a vigorous form with large milk-white flowers, the sepals of which are edged with red.

Nymphaea mexicana (flava), native from Florida to Mexico, is a day-bloomer. It has a slender rhizome and small flowers of canary yellow color.

Day-blooming Varieties of Tropicals. Many magnificent hybrid varieties of tropical Water Lilies have been developed, notably by American plant breeders. These include the following kinds which open their flowers during the daytime and close them at night:

Blue-flowered Varieties: Blue Beauty, a fine shade of blue; Blue Bird, clear blue, free-flowering, Colorata, a miniature variety suitable for restricted areas; Daubeniana, light blue, fragrant flowers and small leaves, easily reproduced by plantlets which form on the leaves, and a good kind for small pools; Henry Shaw, dark blue; marmorata, leaves streaked and mottled with brown; Mrs. Edward Whitaker, huge lavender-blue flowers.

Pink-flowered and Red-flowered Varieties: Castaliflora, pale pink with mottled leaves; Cleveland, rich rose-pink flowers, foliage mottled and streaked with brown; Patricia, flowers crimson, growth moderate; Peach Blow, pale pink flushed with yellow at the bases of the petals.

White-flowered Varieties: Alice Tricker, a fine, strong-growing kind; Isabelle Pring, of compact growth, flowers pure white: Mrs. George H. Pring, largest of the white-flowered day-bloomers.

Purple-flowered Varieties: August Koch, free-blooming, flowers medium-sized; Director Moore, a fine variety of compact growth; Panama-Pacific, a moderate grower, very desirable for small pools: Royal Purple, suitable for small pools, flowers glowing purple.

Yellow-flowered Varieties: Saint Louis, large light yellow blooms; Sunbeam, large flowers, clear yellow; Golden West, yellow and pink, attractive foliage that is streaked and mottled.

Night-blooming Tropical Varieties. Garden varieties of tropical Water Lilies that open their flowers at night and keep them closed by day include the following:

Red-flowered Varieties: Devonshire, bright rosy-red; Emily Grant Hutchings, amaranth-rose, free-blooming; Frank Trelease, dark crimson with mahogany stamens; H. C. Haarstick, dark copper leaves, brilliant red flowers; Pride of California, free-flowering, flowers large, vermilion red.

Pink-flowered Varieties: Mrs. George Hitchcock, clear rose-pink; Sturtevant, bright pink.

White-flowered Varieties: Missouri, a spectacular flower with fine flowers and attractive foliage; Juno, white with saffron-colored stamens.

NYMPHOIDES—*Floating Heart* (Nymphoid′-es). Hardy and tender aquatic plants, natives of Europe, Asia, North America and the tropics. They have a perennial rootstock and floating leaves which are ovate, heart-shaped at the base and 2-4 in. in diameter. The flowers are white or yellow and about 1 in. in diameter. The name Nymphoides is derived from Nymphaea and the suffix *oides,* resembling; it refers to the similarity of the leaves of Nymphoides and Nymphaea. These plants belong to the Gentian family, Gentianaceae and are closely allied to Villarsia; they are named Limnanthemum by some botanists.

Culture of Hardy Kinds. These are grown in the same manner as hardy Water Lilies (see Nymphaea). They may be planted in the soil at the bottom of natural pools or in large pots or tubs with the surface soil 3-9 in. beneath the water. A rich soil is desirable and, if the plants are to be grown in containers, it is a good plan to cover the soil—after planting, and before submersing—with an inch of clean sand. This prevents the soil from making the water muddy and prevents leaf fragments, etc., that may be contained in the soil, from floating to the surface.

Planting should be done in spring just before new growth begins. When grown in containers, the plants should be divided, and replanted every 3-4 years. These plants need exposure to full sunshine.

Culture of Tender Kinds. In frost-free or

nearly frost-free climates tender Nymphoides may be grown outdoors the year round in the way that is recommended for hardy kinds. In colder climates they may be grown permanently in a tub in the greenhouse or in a tub which is kept in the greenhouse in the winter and outdoors in summer. Alternatively, they may be planted in tubs or large pots which are submersed in outdoor pools in the summer and are kept in water indoors in winter.

The rootstocks are planted in a tank or tub which is set in a greenhouse with a minimum winter temperature of 45 degrees. The tub or tank should be not less than 2 ft. in depth, and a layer of soil consisting of equal parts of loam and leaf mold, peat moss, or well-rotted manure is placed in the bottom. After the roots are planted, the water is added gently so as not to disturb the soil, and is replenished from time to time as it evaporates. When the tub or tank becomes overcrowded, it is emptied and replanted.

When used for summer decoration of outdoor pools, young plants are set in large pots, pans or tubs of rich soil in late spring or early summer, after the weather is warm and settled and the water is fairly warm, and are submersed a few inches beneath the water. Their culture and care is essentially the same as that of tropical Water Lilies (see Nymphaea).

The Chief Kinds. Of the approximately twenty kinds that are known to botanists, the following are likely to be cultivated: N. indicum, Water Snowflake, a tender kind that is a native of the tropics, flowers white; N. lacunosum (cordatum), Floating Heart, a native of eastern North America from Newfoundland and Quebec southwards to South Carolina and Louisiana, flowers white or cream-colored; N. peltatum, Water Fringe, a native of Europe that is naturalized to some extent in the northeastern United States, flowers bright yellow.

NYSSA—*Tupelo* (Nys'sa). A small group of deciduous trees consisting of six kinds, four of North America and two from Asia. The name Nyssa is the Greek name of a water nymph, and alludes to the trees' growing in swampy and moist ground. Nyssa belongs to the family Nyssaceae, and is allied to the Cornus or Dogwood.

Leaves Color Well in Autumn. These ornamental trees are of distinctive growth, with handsome lustrous foliage which changes to rich scarlet and crimson in autumn. They thrive best in moist, lime-free soils in low-lying ground and by the waterside; but one, Nyssa sylvatica, will thrive under more varied conditions; however, like the others, it must have an acid soil. Well-developed trees are most difficult to transplant successfully; they should be planted in their permanent positions while quite small.

Propagation is by seeds. They should be sown, as soon as ripe, in sandy soil in a cold frame. Special kinds may be increased by an alternative method of propagation, which is to graft them on seedling trees of Nyssa sylvatica grown in pots under glass. Increase may also be secured by layering.

Planting should be done in early spring or fall.

No pruning is necessary except to train a leading shoot to form a straight trunk and to remove the lower branches as the trees grow in height.

The best-known kind is Nyssa sylvatica, the Tupelo or Pepperidge Tree of eastern North America (it is also known as the Sour Gum and Black Gum). The leaves of seedling trees vary considerably in shape, and some have a shining surface, while that of others is dull.

Nyssa sylvatica grows 60-100 ft. high with a trunk up to 5 ft. in diameter. The obovate or elliptical leaves are 3-6 in. long and half as wide. In June and early July the small greenish male and female flowers appear, and the latter are followed by small, egg-shaped bluish-black fruits.

A variety of N. sylvatica called N. sylvatica biflora occurs from North Carolina to Florida and Louisiana. It is distinguished by having leaves that are mostly blunter than those of N. sylvatica and by the fact that the stones contained in the fruits are much-flattened and ribbed.

Other American species of this group of trees are N. aquatica, the Cotton Gum or Tupelo Gum, which occurs naturally from Virginia to southern Illinois, Florida and Texas; and N. Ogeche, the Ogeechee Lime, which grows naturally from South Carolina to Florida. N. aquatica grows to 10 ft. tall and inhabits swamps and wet places. It is not hardy in the North. N.

Ogeche is probably less hardy than N. aquatica. It attains a height of 60-70 ft. and has red fruits larger than those of N. sylvatica.

The Chinese Tupelo, N. sinensis, attains a height of 20-40 ft. It was introduced to cultivation from central China in 1902 by the late Dr. E. H. Wilson ("Chinese" Wilson). It is not hardy in the North and is rare in cultivation.

OAK. Quercus, which see.

OAK APPLES. A term applied to galls which appear on Oak trees. The galls are caused by various insects. They do no particular harm.

OAK FERN. See Dryopteris.

OAK-LEAVED FERN. See Polypodium quercifolium.

OAK-LEAVED GERANIUM. Pelargonium quercifolium, which see.

OATS, ANIMATED. See Avena sterilis.

OBELISCARIA (Obelisca'ria). Perennial flowering plants from northwestern America, now included in the genus Lepachys, which see.

OBERONIA (Oberon'ia). Orchids which are found wild throughout the Orient, from India to Australia; they are of little horticultural value. They have evergreen foliage and no pseudobulbs. Their attractiveness lies in the inflorescences, which are tail-like and thickly set with small brownish or yellowish flowers, produced at various times but generally in the summer. The name is said to be derived from Oberon, the Fairy King, an allusion to the odd and variable forms assumed by the plants.

The kinds with firm-textured leaves withstand a slightly lower temperature and require less water than those with leaves of softer texture, but most of them need a winter temperature of 60 degrees, and a tropical atmosphere in the summer. The compost should consist of three parts of osmunda fiber to one part of sphagnum moss, with rather more moss for the smaller kinds. Orchid pans may be used or the plants can be attached to pieces of wood.

The chief kinds are O. Myosurus and O. ensiformis.

OBLATE. Flattened at the poles, or ends, as is a Tangerine Orange.

OBOVATE. A term used in describing simple leaves which are wider above than below the middle.

OCHNA (Och'na). Tropical evergreen flowering shrubs which are grown for their ornamental fruits. These plants are chiefly cultivated in southern California and in Florida and, occasionally, in greenhouses. They are natives of tropical Africa and India, and belong to the family Ochnaceae. The shrubs' name is from *ochne*, an old Greek name for Pear, which they somewhat resemble in the shape of the leaves.

Ornamental Evergreens. The shrubs grow about 5 ft. in height, have oblong leaves, 3 in. in length, with serrate (toothed) edges. The flowers, which are yellow, are borne in a raceme on the ends of the side branches in spring, and are not very showy. After they have faded, however, the sepals change from green to bright red and, in combination with the black seeds embedded in the fleshy, red receptacle, form a feature of special interest.

Hints on Management. When grown indoors, these plants require a minimum winter temperature of 55 degrees and a soil compost of equal parts of peat, loam and leaf mold with sand added freely. Repotting is done in February. The shoots are first shortened by two thirds, and the plants syringed three or four times a day to induce new shoots to form. They are then taken out of the pots, the crocks and all loose soil removed from the roots, and set in pots one or two sizes larger.

The new pots must be well drained and the crocks covered with a layer of rough siftings from the compost. The compost is made firm with a potting stick and the plants are frequently syringed and shaded from sunlight until the roots have entered the new compost. The plants are then placed in a well-lighted part of the hothouse and only shaded from the fiercest rays of the sun.

After repotting, water is applied to the soil only when it becomes quite dry, but when the plants are established the soil is kept moist for the remainder of the summer. During the winter the compost is moistened only when it becomes fairly dry. When the plants are in flower, syringing is discontinued until the flowers have set. When planted outdoors in mild climates, the Ochna seems to thrive in any reasonably good soil.

Propagation is by inserting cuttings of side shoots, 2-3 in. long, in spring or summer, in a propagating case with a bottom heat of 70-75 degrees. The case is kept close except for a few minutes each morning, when the glass is lifted to change the air, and to get rid of condensed moisture.

When roots are formed, the cuttings are potted separately in 3-in. pots, and subsequently in larger ones. The tips of the main shoots are removed, and the side branches are similarly treated to ensure bushy plants.

The chief kind is O. multiflora, with yellow flowers and red and black fruits.

OCIMUM—*Sweet Basil* (O'cimum). Annual and perennial plants, the leaves of which are used for flavoring salads, stews and soups. They are natives of tropical Asia and belong to the Mint family, Labiatae. These aromatic herbs grow 12 in. tall, have ovate leaves, about 1 in. in length, and terminal spikes of small white labiate flowers in summer. The name is a modification of the ancient Greek name, *okimon*, which referred to these plants.

The chief kinds are O. Basilicum (Sweet Basil), 12 in., and O. minimum (Bush Basil), 6-12 in. For details of cultivation, see Basil.

OCONEE BELLS. Shortia galacifolia, which see.

OCOTILLO. Fouquieria splendens, which see.

OCTOMERIA (Octomer'ia). Free-flowering but not showy Orchids which grow wild from the West Indies to Brazil. Stems take the place of pseudobulbs and the flowers are generally in small clusters set near the junction of the stems and the thick, fleshy evergreen leaves. The plants vary in height; some are small, others are 12 in. or more high. The prevailing color of the flowers is yellow and, as they are often produced from the old as well as from the new shoots, there is no definite flowering season. The name comes from *okto*, eight, and *meris*, a part —there are eight pollen masses in the flowers.

Easily Grown Orchids. All are of easy cultivation in a greenhouse with a winter temperature of 50 to 60 degrees and a summer temperature somewhat higher. A moist atmosphere is needed. The compost should consist of osmunda or Tree Fern fiber or of Fir or Redwood bark. Drainage must be free, and the plants should be repotted, if necessary, about February or March.

The chief kinds are O. diaphana, with white flowers; O. graminifolia and O. juncifolia, with yellow flowers.

ODONTIODA (Odontio'da). A name given to hybrid or crossbred Orchids raised between Odontoglossum and Cochlioda. The Cochlioda most used in crossbreeding is the scarlet C. Noezliana. The first hybrids—for example, O. Vuylstekeae, O. Bradshawiae and O. Charlesworthii—are of brilliant coloring, but the flowers are rather small. Further cross-fertilization between those and Odontoglossum has increased the size of the blooms, of the offspring and in many kinds the rich coloring has been retained. These Orchids need the same treatment as Odontoglossum.

ODONTOCIDIUM. Orchids which have been raised by crossbreeding between Oncidium and Odontoglossum.

A graceful hybrid Odontoglossum with attractive flowers of rich coloring.

ODONTOGLOSSUM (Odontoglos'sum). An important group of Orchids; most kinds have handsome flowers on long arching scapes. They are found wild in Central America, Ecuador, Mexico, Guatemala and Colombia, at fairly high altitudes. Great variation exists in the size, shape and coloring of the flowers and the appearance of the plants. Some kinds are small; others are comparatively large; but nearly all have attractive flowers, often of considerable size, with spreading sepals and petals. All are epiphytes or semi-epiphytes.

In recent years a large number of hybrids has been raised between O. Harryanum, O. crispum and others; these add to the color variation and prolong the flowering season.

The name Odontoglossum is derived from *odon,* a tooth, and *glossa,* a tongue, an allusion to the shape of the lip and the teethlike projections of hair found on the crest near the base of the lip. These plants belong to the family Orchidaceae, which is the Orchid family.

Beautiful Orchids for a Cool Greenhouse. In a large group such as this, slightly different treatment must be meted out to the various kinds, but generally all Odontoglossums are hill plants, and resent high temperature. For this reason they are generally difficult to grow well in many

Odontoglossum maculatum has soft yellow flowers with red-brown markings.

Odontoglossum Andersonianum, a natural hybrid of O. crispum and O. gloriosum. The flowers are yellowish, with red markings, but vary considerably in their coloring.

parts of North America. They need a greenhouse with a cool, moist atmosphere and a temperature as near 60 degrees as possible throughout the year; the temperature will, of course, rise during summer and may decrease somewhat during winter. Ventilation, damping, and shading are necessary during hot weather to keep the greenhouse cool and moist. Modern techniques, including the provision of air-cooling apparatus in greenhouses, makes it far easier to grow good Odontoglossums than was once the case.

In winter no attempt should be made to force the temperature beyond 55 degrees by artificial warmth; occasional falls of temperature to 50 degrees do no harm.

Free Ventilation Is Necessary. Air must be admitted freely whenever possible, but drafts must be avoided.

Shading Is Important. The plants enjoy light, but strong sunlight, particularly when the growths are tender, may cause injury. In late autumn and winter the plants must be exposed to as much light as possible. A very slight reddish tinge on the matured foliage in autumn shows that sufficient light has been admitted.

In warm weather the greenhouse should be moistened thoroughly. If the temperature falls to 50 degrees in winter, or if such a fall is anticipated, the greenhouse should be kept moderately dry, certainly free from superfluous moisture. The syringe may be freely used in summer over the plants, but not too heavily; the growths must not be filled with water.

Suitable Potting Composts. Odontoglossums may be grown in osmunda fiber, in Tree Fern fiber or in Fir bark or Redwood bark. Drainage must be ample, and the plants potted moderately firmly.

Repotting need not be done every year if the compost is not sour (worn out); the usual time for the work is in February or March, or very early in September. The better time is whenever fresh growth is seen. Avoid repotting in the warm or the cold months.

Watering. Water must be freely given to Odontoglossums in spring and summer. O. crispum and its varieties should be watered during the winter, but less frequently than in summer. At no time must the compost be allowed to get sodden. Kinds with hard (firm) pseudobulbs, like O. grande and O. pendulum require a decided rest in the winter.

The Chief Kinds. In addition to the hybrids, many beautiful species or wild types are known. One of the chief kinds is O. crispum, which has white flowers 3-4 in. across; 12-13 flowers may be borne on one arching stem. Color variations are innumerable. Spring is the chief flowering season.

O. Harryanum, from Colombia, has large, chestnut-colored flowers marked with white and purple, the sepals tipped with yellow. O. triumphans, O. luteo-purpurum, and O. Hallii resemble O. crispum in growth, but have flowers of very different colors. O. nobile (Pescatorei) resembles O. crispum, but has branching panicles and the flowers are smaller and more rounded. O. grande, O. Insleayi, O. Schlieperianum and O. Williamsianum have harder (firmer) leaves and pseudobulbs; they flower later and require a decided rest in winter.

O. pendulum, flowering in May, has pendent inflorescences with many rounded, fragrant flowers, white flushed with rose. O. Rossii and O. Cervantesii are smaller in growth, and flower in winter; they are better suited to cultivation in pans than pots.

Others of note are O. Uroskinneri, a strong-growing kind; O. coronarium, O. gloriosum, sweet-scented; O. cirrhosum and O. pulchellum.

ODONTONEMA (Odontone'ma). Tropical subshrubs or herbaceous plants suitable for planting outdoors in the very warmest parts of the United States and for greenhouse cultivation. They belong in the Acanthus family, Acanthaceae. The name is derived from *odon*, a

Odontonema Schomburgkianum, a native of tropical South America, has slender drooping panicles of red flowers.

tooth, and *nema*, a thread. These plants are often grown under the names Thyrsacanthus and Justicia. They are closely related to Eranthemum and are also sometimes confused with that genus.

Odontonemas thrive without difficulty in any fairly good garden soil. The two kinds mentioned here form shrubs that have a maximum height of about 6 ft.

Greenhouse Cultivation. A minimum winter temperature of 55 degrees and a compost of equal parts of loam, peat, leaf mold and sand are required. To produce well-developed plants by midwinter, cuttings are rooted in March. Small side shoots are taken off, trimmed and inserted in a close, warm propagating case and, when rooted, are potted singly in 3-in. pots. When well rooted, they are repotted in 5-in. pots, or extra vigorous specimens in 6-in. or 7-in. pots.

To induce a bushy form of growth, the tips of the shoots are pinched out until August, when they are allowed to develop unchecked. When well rooted in their final pots, they are watered once a week with diluted liquid fertilizer until the flowers commence to open. After the flowers have faded, less water is given and the soil is kept on the dry side until February, when the shoots are pruned back to a few inches. When new shoots develop, they are removed as cuttings, or the old plants are shaken out and repotted in larger pots.

The chief kinds in cultivation are O. Schomburgkianum (Thyrsacanthus rutilans), a native of British Guiana, and O. strictum (Justicia coccinea), from Central America. O. Schomburgkianum has slender, erect stems clothed with lanceolate leaves, 2 in. in length, and bears slender, pendulous flower racemes, 10 in. or more in length, from near the tops of the shoots. The flowers are scarlet, narrow and tubular, about 1½ in. long, and are produced in winter. O. strictum has leaves to 6 in. long, and long, erect spikes (technically thryses) of bright red flowers in spring.

ODONTONIA. Orchids raised by crossbreeding between Miltonia and Odontoglossum.

OENOTHERA—*Evening Primrose, Sundrops* (Oenothe'ra). A large group of hardy perennial, biennial and annual plants, some of which are of great horticultural value. They are natives chiefly of North and South America and belong to the family Onagraceae. The name is an old Greek one.

Most of the Evening Primroses and Sundrops flourish in ordinary well-cultivated garden soil and need no special attention. Some of them are suitable for planting in the wild garden, others are admirable plants for the herbaceous border or for the rock garden. Evening Primroses mostly are night-bloomers; Sundrops are day-bloomers.

The Common Evening Primrose, Oenothera biennis, is the most familiar kind. It grows 3-4

Oenothera acaulis, with white flowers, is a good subject for the rock garden.

ft. high and bears large, delicately scented, yellow flowers which do not expand until the evening; then, however, they are very attractive.

This plant is unattractive during the day, and for that reason it is not suitable for conspicuous positions in the flower garden, but, if set among shrubs, on the outskirts of the formal garden, or in open spaces in woodland, it is beautiful in the summer evenings. It is a biennial; that is to say, the plant blooms in the year following that in which seed is sown, and perishes after having flowered. Seeds should be sown in a nursery border, or where the plants are to grow, in June; if raised in a nursery border, the seedlings should be set out finally in autumn.

Once a few plants of the common Evening Primrose have been grown in a garden, self-sown seedlings are likely to spring up in large numbers; they ought to be transplanted, if necessary, while small, for it is difficult to move large plants without serious damage to the roots. Oenothera Lamarckiana is showier than O. biennis. Several variations of it are sometimes grown.

One of the best of the perennial Oenotheras for the herbaceous border is Oenothera glauca Fraseri. It grows about 2 ft. high and bears golden-yellow flowers during many summer weeks; the red buds add to its charm. O. glauca is native from Virginia and Kentucky southward. This and the following kinds are day-blooming. It is increased by seeds in a frame, or in a prepared seed bed out of doors, in May or June; the seedlings are set out in autumn where they are to remain. Another method of propagation is to detach rooted pieces in September, or to lift the plant out of the soil at this time and

The rich yellow-flowered Oenothera fruticosa Youngii is a showy dwarf plant for the herbaceous border.

separate it into rooted pieces for replanting.

O. fruticosa, a native of eastern North America, is also a most excellent kind for the perennial border; it grows 1-3 ft. high and has showy yellow flowers. O. fruticosa variety Youngii is an even finer plant, of stockier growth and with larger blooms. O. fruticosa variety major is of bushy growth and bears its yellow blooms very freely.

Oenothera speciosa is a very beautiful plant, 2 ft. high, which bears white flowers in summer. There is a pretty pink variety named rosea.

For the Rock Garden. Several Oenotheras are attractive flowering plants for the rock garden, where they are easily grown in light or well-drained soil in a sunny position. Plants may be

Oenothera missouriensis is a low-growing kind suitable for rock gardens and the fronts of perennial borders.

planted in early autumn or in spring. O. acaulis, the Dandelion-leaved Sundrop, is of low trailing growth and in summer bears large white flowers which become tinged with rose as they age. O. missouriensis is another admirable rock-garden plant, about 1 ft. high and with very large yellow flowers, which open in the evening.

O. caespitosa, which grows about 12 in. high and bears white flowers, is suitable for the rock garden or for the front of the border. So, too, is O. rosea, with blooms of pale rose coloring. The smallest kind is one named O. perennis; it grows only about 4-5 in. high and bears yellow flowers. All bloom in summer and are most easily propagated by sowing seeds in May or June in fine soil in a cold frame.

OFFSET. A name loosely used by gardeners for the small bulbs produced by mature ones; for the small rooted pieces of herbaceous plants

A healthy Narcissus bulb with an offset (in this case a bulblet) growing from its base.

which are detached and replanted to increase the stock; and for short runners, terminated by plantlets, of rosette-forming plants like Sempervivum, etc.

OHIO, GARDENING IN. See Regional Gardening.

OHIO BUCKEYE. Aesculus glabra, which see.

OKLAHOMA, GARDENING IN. See Regional Gardening.

OKRA. Hibiscus esculentus, an annual plant, native to the tropics of the Old World. It is grown for its immature pods, which are known as Okra or Gumbo and are used in soups and stews, and for other culinary purposes.

Okra is essentially a crop for warm climates, although it can be successfully grown wherever it is practicable to cultivate Cucumbers and Melons outdoors. It thrives in a variety of soils, and attains a height of 3-7 ft.

Seeding should be delayed until the weather is definitely warm and settled. The seeds should be sown a few inches apart and about an inch deep in rows spaced 4-5 ft. apart. The plants should be thinned to stand 2-3 ft. apart. These distances are intended for tall varieties; dwarf varieties, which bear less prolifically, may be spaced more closely. Frequent cultivation through the summer should be practiced. The pods should be harvested while still young and tender. A long succession of picking is provided through the summer and until the coming of frost.

OLD MAN. Artemisia Abrotanum, which see.

OLD-MAN'S-BEARD. Clematis Vitalba, which see.

OLD WOMAN. Artemisia Stellariana, which see.

OLEA—*Olive* (O'lea). Evergreen trees or shrubs, native to the Mediterranean region, tropical and central Asia, various parts of Africa and other regions. They are not hardy in the North. O. europaea is the hardiest kind, but it can be grown out of doors only in the milder parts of the United States. For fruit production it generally can be relied upon in the Pacific Southwest and in Arizona, although it is grown as an ornamental on the Gulf Coast and in some other parts. Olea belongs to the Olive family, Oleaceae, and the name is the old Latin name for the European Olive.

For decorative purposes the value of Oleas lie in the evergreen leaves, as the flowers are small and uninteresting. The fruits of some kinds, particularly O. europaea, are rich in oil. This is one of the most favored of the edible oils, and has a considerable commercial value.

The wood of most kinds is very hard, heavy, and close grained, prettily marked with various shades of light and dark brown, and sometimes with yellow. It is used for turnery and for articles of cabinetwork and furniture.

The most important kind is Olea europaea. It is a very widely distributed tree throughout the Mediterranean region, and has been cultivated from ancient times. It is mentioned by the oldest writers of botanical and agricultural works, is often referred to in the Bible, and is one of the trees of which fragments are found in ancient Egyptian tombs. The ancient Greeks and Romans used the branches with those of the Sweet Bay for decorative purposes, and to crown the victors in their sports.

It is thought that the Greeks may first have taken the trouble to cultivate trees, but that is not definitely known. It is, however, certain that for hundreds of years the Olive has been an important standard crop throughout the Mediterranean region, and in more recent times cultivation has extended to the United States, South Africa and Australia. Olive trees live to be very old.

The culture of the Olive presents no especial difficulty. It thrives in a wide variety of soils but will not tolerate poor drainage. To ripen fruit, it requires a long, hot growing season and, because of this, commercial fruit production in the United States is practically limited to the warmer parts of California and Arizona. The tree may be grown as an ornamental in other warm parts, such as the Gulf States. It is injured by temperatures lower than 15 degrees F. Early fall frosts are a hazard to the maturing fruits; hot dry winds may be harmful during the period when the flowers are open and the young fruits are setting.

To encourage the production of large-sized fruits, moderate pruning is practiced and, for the same purpose, thinning out (reducing the number of) the young fruits is done. Irrigation is definitely helpful in increasing the quality of the fruit, but only on very poor soils is it considered profitable to use fertilizer.

The fruits are harvested by hand and several pickings are necessary because not all the fruits ripen at one time. The picking season extends from October to December.

Olives are propagated by cuttings, suckers and grafting. Stocks on which to graft superior varieties are obtained by sowing seeds.

Varieties. Among the kinds favored for fruit production are: Ascolano, Barouni, Mission, Manzanillo and Sevillano. The varieties Ascolano, Barouni and Sevillano produce the large fruits called Queen Olives.

OLEANDER. Nerium, which see.

OLEANDER, YELLOW. Thevetia nereifolia, which see.

OLEARIA—*Daisybush* (Olear'ia). Evergreen shrubs which are often of great beauty. Very few are generally grown, and those chiefly in California. They are found growing wild in many parts of New Zealand and Australia.

These shrubs grow well near the sea and are useful alike as flowering plants and evergreens. However, they do have a shortcoming: after flowering, the dead flower heads may detract from the appearance of the plants unless one takes the trouble to cut them off. Olearia belongs to the Daisy family, Compositae; the name, taken from *Olea,* Olive, refers to the fact that some kinds have olive-like leaves.

When to Take Cuttings. Propagation by means of cuttings is satisfactory for most kinds; a few, however—O. insignis, for example—should be raised from seed whenever it can be obtained. Cuttings of all the smaller-leaved kinds may be made 4-5 in. long during summer, and inserted in a bed of sandy peat in a propagating frame. Cuttings of the common Daisybush, O. Haastii, root very well if placed in a cold frame in July. Rather longer cuttings of the large-leaved kinds may be inserted in a slightly warm frame.

Seeds should be sown in a frame in light, sandy soil as soon as possible after being gathered; if kept long, they will germinate slowly.

Advice on Culture. The Olearias succeed in a great variety of soils, but they dislike ground which contains much lime. Most give excellent results in gardens near the sea for they are not averse to a salty atmosphere. They should be planted in permanent positions when small, for they do not transplant very well after they have attained considerable size and age. As they grow freely, they should be given plenty of room for development; if, after 3-4 years, the plants appear to be too close together, it is better to take a few out rather than allow them to crowd each other.

The New Zealand Daisy Bush, Olearia Haastii, in full bloom.

How to Prune the Daisybushes. A slight amount of pruning is necessary in the earlier stages in order to encourage a dense, bushy habit, but many of them grow into shapely bushes with little pruning. When plants are becoming too big for their positions they may be cut hard back to force the growth of new shoots from the old wood, though severe pruning is not advocated. When pruning is necessary, early spring is a good time for the work. A little pruning may be done as soon as the flowers fade.

Hedges of Daisybushes. Very attractive hedges can be made with some of the more vigorous kinds. O. macrodonta may be used for this purpose. O. Haastii also forms a very serviceable hedge 3-4 ft. high.

Several kinds are useful for the rock garden, where they look well growing in crevices between large blocks of stone. It is wise to plant them while they are small, instead of trying to insert large plants from pots for an immediate effect.

The Most Useful Kind. O. Haastii is the most generally useful kind. It is comparatively hardy, and usually forms a shapely bush, 4-5 ft. high, although it may grow much taller. As with most of the other kinds, the branches and undersides of the leaves are covered with dense grayish down. The leaves are thick and leathery, dark green above, silvery beneath, $\frac{1}{2}$-1 in. long and about $\frac{1}{2}$ in. wide. They are produced with great freedom and form a very good setting for the numerous clusters of starlike, white flowers which open during July and early August.

For seaside gardens this is an excellent bush, for it withstands a good deal of exposure and always looks well.

Other Kinds. O. macrodonta is not so hardy as O. Haastii, although an excellent shrub. At its best it is seen as a shapely bush 12-15 ft. high and equally wide. The leaves are 2-5 in. long and ½-1½ in. wide, with wavy edges. They are thick and leathery, dark green above and silvery beneath.

The flowers are white and borne in flattened heads up to 6 in. across; the flowering time is May to July. O. macrodonta is a native of New Zealand.

O. stellulata is a Tasmanian shrub and different from the two last named. At its best it may grow 8-10 ft. high, but it is more frequently seen as a bush, 3-5 ft. high, with a mass of slender branches covered with narrow leaves, ½-1½ in. long and scarcely more than ¼ in. wide. The white starlike flowers are produced freely in large heads in early summer. In the form called splendens the flowers are in shades of pink and mauve.

O. albida is a vigorous bush from New Zealand with leaves 2-4 in. long and ½-1 in. wide, and white flowers borne in large, dense heads in summer. It is moderately hardy.

O. argophylla is a native of Tasmania and Australia, where it grows into a tree with a gnarled trunk, 12-15 in. through. The leaves, when crushed, have a musky odor, as has also the newly worked wood.

Olearia insignis is one of the most interesting kinds. It is a native of New Zealand, where it is a mountain plant found on rocky ledges and in dry crevices. The leaves are large, thick and leathery, often 6 or more in. long and 4 in. wide. Single heads of flowers 2½-3½ in. across are carried on stalks 6-9 in. long; the ray florets are white, the disc florets yellow. A well-drained position is desirable.

A few other kinds worth noting are O. furfuracea, O. avicenniaefolia, O. ilicifolia, O. paniculata (Forsteri), O. myrsinoides, O. myrsinoides variety erubescens, O. odorata, O. Traversii and O. virgata.

OLEASTER. See Elaeagnus.

OLIVE. The common name of Olea europaea, and, with one or another prefix, for other kinds of Olea and for a few other plants. The European Olive is a very definite feature in the landscape, not only of southern Europe, but of other parts of the Mediterranean region. It is prominent on the sides of hills and mountains, both wild and cultivated, and often attains a venerable age and appearance, old trees having gnarled trunks and branches, grotesque heads and hollow trunks. See Olea.

OMPHALODES — *Navelwort* (Omphalo'des). A small group containing a few exceptionally beautiful annual and perennial hardy plants which belong to the Borage family, Boraginaceae. The name is derived from *omphalos,* the navel, and *eidos,* resemblance, and refers to the shape of

The Creeping Forget Me Not, Omphalodes verna, a very charming little spring-flowering plant for the rock garden.

the seeds. The Navelworts are natives of Europe, North Africa, western and central Asia and Japan.

These plants may be propagated by seeds sown in spring in pots of light soil in a cold frame. The seedlings should be pricked out into flats of similar soil when large enough to handle; later they are potted or planted in their permanent quarters. They may also be increased by careful division of the roots in spring. All grow best in cool places, in light shade, where the soil is not excessively dry.

With Blue Flowers. Omphalodes cappadocica is a perennial of tufted habit, growing 9-12 in. high, with ovate, pointed, dark green leaves, grayish on the underside, and graceful sprays of flowers of an intense pure azure-blue, like those of the Forget-Me-Not, in spring and early summer. It is a charming and showy plant for a cool, half-shady position in the rock garden in light and fairly rich soil. It is propagated by simple division of the roots.

A Charming Rock-Garden Plant. Omphalodes Luciliae is one of the aristocrats of the rock garden and the alpine house, and a plant of exquisite beauty. The spoon-shaped leaves are glaucous (blue-gray) in color, and are most attractive, and the flowers, like very large Forget-Me-Not blossoms, each about ½ in. across, are carried in loose, straggling sprays. The color of the flowers is lavender-blue of a most exquisite tone and purity, and the contrast between them and the pearl-gray leaves is very beautiful.

How to Grow Omphalodes Luciliae. Omphalodes Luciliae has the reputation of being difficult to cultivate, but given a sunny, well-drained position in the rock garden, and light, sandy loam, in which is mixed a liberal allowance of old lime rubble, it will, where the climate is favorable, flourish vigorously and flower abundantly in summer.

This plant is a native of Asia Minor and seems to appreciate moderate warmth.

The best means of propagating O. Luciliae is by seeds. These should be sown as soon as they are gathered. A flower only produces four seeds, never more, often less. They are large and flat, and fall from the plant at an early stage. They may be kept for a week or two to dry and should then be sown thinly in light, sandy loam in a greenhouse or cold frame. Grow the seedlings undisturbed until the earliest are fairly large and begin to crowd one another, and then pot them singly in 2-in. pots.

Old clumps may also be lifted and carefully divided in early summer, and it is possible to strike cuttings taken off with a "heel," but this is neither easy nor very satisfactory, and seeds or simple division offers the better ways. O. Luciliae may be grown to great advantage in the dry wall garden. The white variety alba is also very choice.

A Charming Hardy Annual. O. linifolia, Venus's Navelwort, is an annual, and a native of southern Europe. It is easy to grow, and a plant of the greatest charm. Of erect, wiry, slightly branched habit, and 9-12 in. high, the plant is clothed with smooth leaves of silver-gray color; the large milk-white Forget-Me-Not-like

A Tasmanian Daisybush, Olearia stellulata.

flowers are in numerous loose racemes and are open from June until the coming of really hot weather. Seeds may be sown in the open in September, where the plants are to flower the following summer. The seedlings should be thinned out to 6-9 in. apart. Or they may be sown in April, to flower the same year from July onwards.

Autumn-sown seeds usually make sturdier plants than those raised in spring. This very pretty annual is all too little known and can be recommended to all who have never tried it. It is extremely pretty if grown in irregular groups in the mixed flower border, and it is a useful cut flower for the house, lasting well in water.

O. lusitanica (nitida), from Spain, is a clump-forming perennial for cool places in the rock garden. It grows about 12 in. tall, and has sprays of small, bright blue flowers in summer. It may be increased by simple division of the roots in spring or early summer.

Creeping Forget-Me-Not is the name given to

O. verna from southern Europe. It is a deservedly popular hardy perennial. Of prostrate trailing habit, it spreads by means of "runners" rather in the manner of a Strawberry, and in early spring—March to May—it produces its lovely sprays of handsome flowers like large azure Forget-Me-Nots, white-eyed and brilliant. This species is a fine plant for the woodland and for shady, cool places in the rock garden, and as ground cover under shrubs. It is easily increased by simple division of the roots in spring or autumn.

There is a white-flowered variety, O. verna alba, which, though attractive, lacks the brilliance and special charm of the typical kind.

OMPHALOGRAMMA (Omphalogram'ma). A small genus of perennial herbs from western China, which bear solitary flowers on stout scapes rising from rosettes or tufts of foliage. They are little known in North America. Closely related to Primula, they belong to the family Primulaceae. The name is from *omphalos,* navel, and *gramma,* writing, and alludes to the flattened, winged seeds. These plants are difficult to grow successfully, being best suited to cultivation in pans in the alpine house, with treatment similar to that for the rarer Chinese Primulas.

Omphalogramma vinciflorum has violet flowers on 6-in. scapes. Other kinds are O. Delavayi, deep purple; O. Elwesianum, violet; and O. Souliei, blue-violet.

ONCIDIODA. Orchids raised by crossbreeding between Oncidium and Cochlioda.

ONCIDIUM (Oncid'ium). A large and varied group of Orchids, closely allied to Odontoglossum, and which contains many kinds of great horticultural value. All are epiphytal and evergreen, and in a wild state are distributed from the West Indies to the south of Brazil, some being found throughout Central America. The kinds that are from high elevations are intolerant of high temperatures.

Many kinds have hard (firm) pseudobulbs with narrow, glossy leaves resembling those of Odontoglossum in shape. In some kinds the pseudobulbs are set at intervals on the rhizomes or rootstock; in others they are in clusters. The prevailing color of the flowers is yellow.

The flower stems, which often need support,

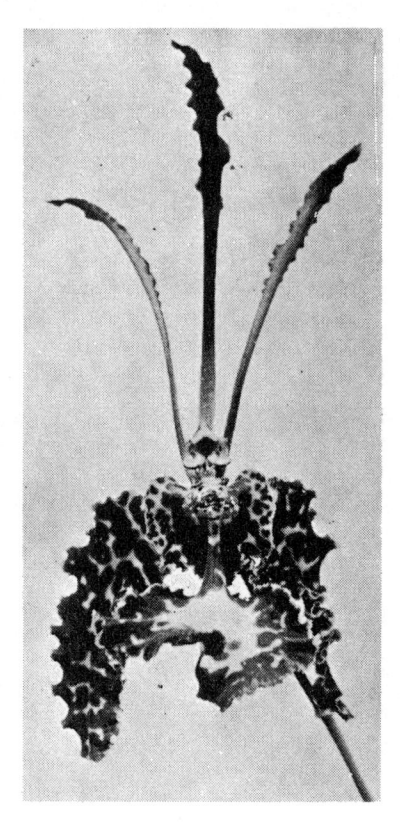

Oncidium Papilio, the Butterfly Orchid.

may be branching and many-flowered, or erect with the flowers in dense clusters. The sepals and petals are usually much smaller than the lip, but are not always so. The name is derived from *onkos,* a Greek word meaning a tumor, and refers to the crest on the lip. Oncidium belongs in the Orchid family, Orchidaceae.

Orchids for a Warm Greenhouse. A great number of Oncidiums come from fairly high altitudes and, as many of these have hard, pseudobulbs which mature in the autumn, they can be wintered in a greenhouse having a night temperature of 50-55 degrees, similar to that required by Odontoglossum. However, as they can be kept for much longer intervals without water, the temperature need not be so regular.

Individual study and treatment of each kind is the best means to success. All Oncidiums require a moist atmosphere when in full growth, and most of them need free ventilation. Those with hard bulbs should be exposed to as much light as possible when growth is complete.

The time to repot varies from February to

April; repotting should be done when young growths appear. A few plants may have to be potted later, but the work should never be deferred until late autumn. A suitable compost is osmunda fiber, Tree Fern fiber, Fir bark or Redwood bark. The smaller kinds, are better grown in flower pans than pots. Even the moderate-sized kinds may be grown in flower pans, as these are more convenient for suspending near the glass in autumn to expose the plants to full light. Free drainage is essential and every care must be taken not to maintain the potting compost in such a constantly saturated condition that the roots rot.

The Best Kinds. There are many kinds of Oncidiums which deserve the attention and interest of the grower. Especially noteworthy for their beauty are those now to be described.

O. macranthum has pseudobulbs 4-6 in. high and stems 10-12 ft. long, bearing large flowers with yellowish-brown sepals, yellow petals and white, purple-marked lip. It should be grown under the same conditions as Odontoglossum, as it can never be really rested, large plants often having flower spikes and new growths at the same time. With it may be grown O. superbiens, O. loxense, O. serratum and O. falcipetalum.

From the Organ Mountains in Brazil comes O. Marshallianum, flowering in May, from the matured pseudobulb; the flowers are yellow marked with red and are borne on tall branching panicles. O. crispum, O. praetextum, and O. Gravesianum are autumn-flowering. O. Forbesii, with rich chestnut flowers marked with gold, blooms usually in the autumn or winter.

O. varicosum and its variety Rogersii, both of which have tall, many-flowered panicles of bright yellow, reddish-centered flowers in late September, need cool conditions in the winter and a moderately warm atmosphere in the summer. This treatment also suits O. tigrinum, from Mexico, a November-flowering kind with striped sepals and petals and a large golden-yellow lip. The blooms emit a fragrance of violets.

O. concolor bears yellow flowers in spring; O. cheirophorum has small, yellow, scented flowers in late autumn and winter. O. dastyle is called the Parson in the Pulpit Orchid from the curious arrangement of the lip tubercles. The Flying Dove Orchid, O. candidum, also known as Palumbina candida, needs the same conditions as Odontoglossum.

Oncidium sphacelatum and O. altissimum, which are very similar, have tall branched spikes of yellow and brown flowers in summer. O. pulvinatum and O. divarcatum have tall, branching stems and bear yellow and brown flowers, O. bicallosum is chestnut and green, and O. Cavendishianum has yellow flowers; these should be kept in a warm greenhouse in the winter, in a temperature of 60 degrees.

Oncidium Papilio, the Butterfly Orchid, and O. Kramerianum, which is very similar in flower shape, but with smaller, brighter yellow flowers, are attractive. Both are small-growing, with prettily mottled brownish leaves. They are sometimes attached to pieces of cork, but it is better to grow them in small pans. They should be grown in a warm greenhouse; so, too, should the broader lipped variety, O. tigrinum splendidum, a Christmas-flowering kind.

Other good Oncidiums are O. sarcodes, O. Schlimii, O. phymatochilum, O. ornithorhynchum, and O. incurvum.

ONION: THERE ARE MANY DIFFERENT TYPES
A Complete Guide to the Cultivation of These Important Vegetables

Few vegetable garden crops are of greater importance than the Onion, a hardy biennial which is a native of western Asia. Its botanical name is Allium Cepa; it belongs to the Lily family, Liliaceae.

The ordinary Onion is represented by many types and numerous varieties, which vary greatly in size, shape and coloring. It is generally raised every year from seeds, sown either out of doors or under glass; but it is also often grown from small bulbs called Onion sets. These are raised from seeds sown in the summer of the previous year; under good cultivation they will yield fair-sized bulbs by the end of the season, but Onions

A fine crop of Onions grown in an amateur's garden.

obtained in this way are seldom so fine as those from first-year seedling plants and they do not keep well. Onion sets are excellent for producing an early crop of Scallions.

Other types of Onion sometimes grown in gardens are the Potato Onion, which forms single bulbs or a cluster of bulbs beneath the soil, and the Top or Egyptian Onion, which bears small bulbs at the tops of stems above the ground. The Shallot and Garlic, both quite closely related to Onions, are dealt with in this work under their respective headings.

Preparing the Onion Bed. Large Onions can be grown only on deeply dug and manured soil and in a sunny position.

Dig or plow the site of the Onion bed deeply and add animal manure or compost in generous amounts. This preparatory work should preferably be done during the autumn, and the surface left rough so that it will be exposed to frost, snow and wind; these have a beneficial effect on garden ground. In early spring a scattering of wood ash should be applied to the surface of the Onion bed, together with 3 oz. of a good general fertilizer per square yard, and these should be forked into the top 9 in. of the bed.

The seed bed must be made firm by treading the soil when it is reasonably dry; it must also be well raked to remove all lumps and stones, and to provide a "fine" and level surface for sowing. On light soils it pays to roll the bed to consolidate it.

A bed of deep, rich soil is required to assure the most successful results; on poor, shallow ground the Onions will be small.

White Sweet Spanish is a popular variety of Onion.

Sowing Onions Out of Doors. Onions can be grown from seeds sown out of doors in a bed of soil prepared in the way already recommended. Drills, ½ in. or so deep, are made 1 ft. apart; the seeds are sown thinly, covered and firmed. Finish off with a light raking.

The best time to sow the seeds out of doors is early spring, as soon as the soil is reasonably dry and can be made "fine" by forking and raking, and firm by treading or rolling. Skilled gardeners lay great stress on the provision of a fine and firm surface soil for an Onion bed.

As soon as the seedlings are well through the soil, the hoe must be plied between the rows to keep down weeds, though, in cultivating, care is necessary not to work so near the seedlings as to loosen them. Weeds which come up in the rows among the plants should be pulled carefully by hand.

Thinning the Seedlings. When the seedlings are a few inches high the first thinning is done; the superfluous plants must be pulled up gently to avoid disturbing the remainder.

At the next and subsequent thinnings, the seedlings which are pulled up will be large enough to be used as scallions. The work of thinning must be continued until the Onions average about eight per foot of row.

Occasional applications of nitrate of soda or of a commercial fertilizer, ½ oz. per yard of row, during the growing season, help the plants by encouraging free growth. During the summer months Onions need little attention, but the soil between the rows must be hoed often to be kept free from weeds. Dilute liquid fertilizer may be given once a week with advantage when the bulbs are developing. Careful watch must be kept for thrips and other pests, and prompt remedial measures taken. (See Pests and Diseases.)

In August, when the growth of the bulbs is nearly complete, it is a good plan to draw the soil away from them to expose them as much as possible to air and sunshine, and to assist their ripening.

When the leaves begin to turn yellow they should be bent down with the back of a rake, the leaves of adjoining rows being turned towards each other; thus one side of each row will be left clear of leaves.

Lifting and Storing Onions. When the leaves have died, the bulbs should be lifted and set out to dry in a sunny, airy place for a few days if the weather is dry, or under cover if it is wet. Leaves and soil are then removed and the Onions are stored in a cool place for use in winter.

Sowing Onion Seeds Under Glass. Those who grow Onions for exhibition sow the seeds in late January or early in February in a sunny greenhouse in which a minimum temperature of 60 degrees is maintained. As soon as the seedlings are 1 in. or so high they need a lower temperature—one of 50 degrees is high enough, for it is necessary that they grow into sturdy plants. The finest possible results are obtained by potting the plants separately in 3-in. pots.

The more usual practice is to transplant them to flats 4-5 in. deep, filled with loamy soil with which a little leaf mold, decayed manure and sand have been mixed. They are set 2 in. apart, care being taken not to place them so deeply in the soil that the tiny bulb is covered. Careful watering is necessary; the soil should be moistened only when it is fairly dry.

When the Onions are well rooted and danger of frost has passed, they should be hardened off in a cold frame and planted out of doors 6 in. apart. Onions raised in this way are likely to make fine exhibition specimens but they usually do not keep well in storage.

Planting Seedling Onions Out of Doors. When

To ensure a good crop of Onions it is important that weeds be kept down by frequent surface cultivation.

When Onions have completed their growth, their tops may be pushed over with the back of a rake to hasten ripening of the bulbs.

After they are pulled up, Onions should be left on the ground or in some other sunny, airy place to dry.

Ripening the bulbs may be completed by spreading them in trays and leaving them until they are thoroughly dry. Then they are stored away.

planting seedling Onions which were raised under glass, great care must be taken not to plant them deeply or thick-necked Onions, which do not keep well, will result. The plants should be set out so that the small bulb rests on the soil, or is only partly covered—in fact, only just deep enough to hold them upright.

Onions need light and air to ensure their proper development and to provide bulbs which will keep well when stored. Hoeing too near the plants during the summer months, so as to loosen the soil there, may result in the bulbs being covered.

Skilled growers of exhibition Onions lay stress on the need for keeping the soil firm alongside the bulbs, though it must be loose and crumbly between the rows. If weeds appear among the rows of Onions, no attempt should be made to hoe them out. They should be uprooted by hand when the soil is moist.

Sowing Onion Seeds Out of Doors in August. Another way of raising Onions where winters are not too severe is to sow the seeds out of doors in a reserve border during August.

The seedlings remain undisturbed except for a slight thinning out if they are overcrowded,

Transplanting young Onions.

until the following March or April, when they are set out finally in a bed of rich soil prepared in the way advised previously. Those which are not required for planting may be used as Scallions.

The Best Varieties of Onion. There are numerous varieties of Onion, and often good and indifferent strains of the same variety exist. The varieties are listed and described in the catalogues of seedsmen. Among the most popular are Ebenezer, Early Yellow Globe, Southport Red Globe, Southport White Globe, Southport Yellow Globe, Sweet Spanish, White Portugal or Silverskin, White Sweet Spanish and Yellow Globe Danvers.

Pickling Onions may be grown by sowing seeds thickly on rather poor ground in April or May. The site needs little cultivation but it should be dug over, weeds thus being destroyed, and made firm by treading or rolling. The seeds may be sown broadcast or in drills about 8 in. apart; the latter method is to be preferred because it enables hoeing to be done conveniently for the purpose of keeping down weeds. Varieties listed as suitable for pickling should be selected for this purpose.

Onion Sets are small bulbs which are sold for planting in spring; they are raised from seeds sown in the previous summer. Those who find it impossible, or very difficult, to raise Onions from seeds sown out of doors in spring, owing to the ravages of the Onion fly maggots, and have no heated greenhouse in which to raise the seedlings, would do well to give Onion sets a trial. They are certainly less liable to suffer from the Onion fly than seedlings. There is a possibility that some of them may "run to seed" —that is, produce flower stems instead of serviceable bulbs—but most of them may be expected to succeed, and a crop of Onions of moderate size will result.

Planting Onion Sets. The sets should be spaced about 4 in. apart in rows 10 in. from each other; they are merely pressed into the soil, not buried. The only attention required during the summer months is to hoe frequently between the rows but not near the bulbs. In due course, they must be lifted and harvested in the way already explained.

Onion sets spaced along a shallow drill and just pressed into the soil.

Onion sets are sold by seedsmen and are listed in seed catalogues.

The Potato Onion or Underground Onion is not commonly grown and cannot be regarded as of the same value as the ordinary Onion, which is raised from seed. Like all other types, the Potato Onion thrives best in rich firm ground, and this should be prepared by digging and manuring in the way previously described, though scarcely such thorough soil cultivation is needed as when preparing an Onion bed.

When to Plant Potato Onion Bulbs. The bulbs may be planted in earliest spring as soon as the soil is in a suitable condition. The bulbs are pressed into the soil, like Onion sets. In due course, a cluster or group of bulbs will form around the old bulb beneath the ground. In summer it is a good plan to draw away the soil from the bulbs and expose them fully to light and air to assist in the ripening process. The bulbs of the Potato Onion are usually ready to be lifted, dried and harvested in July.

The Top or Tree Onion. This curious plant, known also as Egyptian Onion, is quite distinct

A clump of the Tree or Egyptian Onion.

from the ordinary Onion, for it bears a bunch of small bulbs at the top of the stems instead of a head of flowers as in the familiar kind. The bulbs are chiefly of value for pickling. They should be planted in early spring in the way advised for the management of Onion sets, in well-dug and manured ground.

Top Onions are planted 5-6 in. apart in rows 10 in. from each other. During the summer months the only attention needed is to keep the ground free from weeds by hoeing frequently. The Top Onion, like all other kinds, must be planted in an open, sunny position in the garden. It does not flourish in shady places.

To make sure stems bear clusters of bulbs at their tops, full-sized bulbs must be planted; the small ones will not yield a crop the first season.

Welsh or Perennial Onion. Still another kind of Onion which may be grown is the Welsh Onion, Allium fistulosum; it is curious in that it produces no true bulbs, but is grown for the sake of its leaves and stems, which are used chiefly for flavoring purposes. It is increased by division, the clumps being split into small clusters and planted 6 in. apart in early spring.

ONION, FLOWERING. See Allium.
ONION, SEA. Urginea maritima, which see.
ONION, TREE. See Onion.
ONION, WELSH. See Onion.
ONOCLEA—*Sensitive Fern* (Onocle'a; Onoc'-lea). A hardy deciduous (leaf-losing) Fern, native to the North Temperate Zone, including North America. It belongs to the Polypody family, Polypodiaceae.

In addition to the ordinary fronds, which are infertile (do not produce spores), Onoclea has fertile (spore-bearing) fronds. These are constricted in growth, thickly covered with sporangia (spore-bearing structures), and are formed in the centers of the plants. The name Onoclea is from the Greek, meaning closed vessels, and refers to the constricted sporophylls (spore-bearing fronds).

For Shady Places. Onoclea is of coarse appearance and has but limited use in gardens. It requires a semishaded moist position, and is suitable for growing on the margins of ponds or streams, at the edge of a shrubbery, or in a moist border. The best soil is one that contains an abundance of organic matter. Planting is done in spring, when the crowns are set 2-3 ft. apart and the soil thoroughly moistened if at all dry.

Plants growing by ponds or streams need little attention, as their roots have access to plenty of moisture, but those which are planted in shrubbery borders must be kept moist by frequent watering in dry weather. The dead fronds must not be removed until spring, as they form a natural protection for the crowns during the winter.

Sowing Spores. Propagation is by spores or stolons (runners). Spores are sown as soon as ripe in summer or they may be stored in seed packets and sown at a later date. To ascertain whether the spores are ripe, a frond, on which the spores are brownish in color, is selected and placed in a paper bag. This is hung in a dry, airy shed or room for 48 hours, when the ripe spores are found at the bottom of the bag, in the form of a fine brownish powder. For advice on the treatment of these spores, see Ferns. Young plants may also be obtained by detaching the rooted runners in spring.

ONONIS—*Restharrow* (Ono'nis). An interesting group of plants belonging to the Pea family, Leguminosae, and comprising about sixty tender and hardy herbs and shrubs, annual, biennial and perennial. They are natives of Europe, western Asia, and northern Africa.

Although the Restharrows are beautiful plants, only some eight or ten kinds are known to cultivation, and probably not more than four or five are obtainable at the present time. The name Ononis is the old Greek name for the plant given by Theophrastus.

Restharrows are most easily propagated by means of seeds sown in pots of light, sandy soil in spring, in a cold frame or greenhouse. The seedlings are pricked off when large enough to handle, and finally potted before being planted out. All the hardy kinds should be planted in fullest sun in light, well-drained soil.

For the Rock Garden. Ononis aragonensis is a tender shrub from Spain, growing 1-2 ft. tall, and bearing yellow flowers in May, June and July.

Ononis cenisia is an alpine or subalpine plant of the utmost charm and beauty, but of doubtful hardiness. It is not found at Mont Cenis, as its name would lead one to suppose, though it is abundant in the neighborhood several thousand feet lower down. It is a small, prostrate plant, making specimens 6-12 in. across, with a mass of beautiful little Pea flowers of rose and white.

In the rock garden, Ononis cenisia should be given light, well-drained soil or planted in the moraine or scree; as sunny a position as possible should be chosen for it. The plant is also suitable for the alpine house.

Handsome Dwarf Flowering Shrubs. Ononis fruticosa is a hardy shrub, 2-3 ft. high, with trifoliate leaves and handsome pink pealike flowers, arranged in threes. It should be given a warm, sunny position and light, well-drained soil. Seeds may be sown in pots of light, sandy soil in a cold frame in spring; the seedlings are potted off singly in small pots and planted out later in the summer. This shrubby Restharrow is an exceedingly ornamental plant and one of the best of the family.

Ononis hispanica, a native of Spain, is a tender dwarf shrubby kind with yellow flowers. It grows 1½ ft. tall. Ononis minutissima from southwestern Europe is a biennial of compact habit. It grows only 3 in. high and has yellow flowers.

Rarely Seen in Gardens. Ononis Natrix, or Goatroot, is a perennial herb from southern Europe. It grows 1½-2 ft. tall, and bears golden pealike flowers veined with red. This handsome plant is seldom seen in gardens, but it makes a fine summer show in the rock garden or choice flower border. It must have a very sunny position and light, well-drained soil. It is best propagated by seeds sown in a cold frame or cool greenhouse in spring.

A Shrub for the Rock Garden. Ononis rotundifolia is a most beautiful hardy dwarf shrub for the front of the shrub border or for a sunny location in the rock garden. It grows 2-3 ft. tall, and bears quantities of rose-pink pealike flowers. It is easily raised from seeds sown in a pot in the cold frame in spring. The seedlings should be potted in small pots and planted out in their permanent quarters later in the summer.

Ononis viscosa is a handsome annual from southern Europe, growing 1½-3 ft. tall; the flowers are yellow, with purple-striped standards.

ONOPORDUM—*Cotton Thistle, Scotch Thistle* (Onopor'dum). Hardy perennial and biennial herbaceous flowering plants of little horticultural value. They are natives of Europe and Asia and belong to the Daisy family, Compositae. The name Onopordum is derived from *onos*, an ass, and *porde*, wind, and refers to the plant's supposed effect of producing flatulence in the ass. This plant is the Thistle which was selected by James V as the emblem of Scotland.

Onopordum Acanthium, the principal kind, is typically thistle-like in appearance. It grows 4-5 ft. in height, has stout, branching stems and lanceolate (lance-shaped) prickly-edged leaves. The stems and leaves are covered with a white cottony substance. The branches are terminated by small heads of purple flowers.

These plants show to advantage when they are planted in close proximity to dark-leaved evergreens, against which their cottony whiteness is well displayed.

Planting and Propagation. These Cotton Thistles require a sunny position and well-drained, ordinary soil. Planting is done in spring or fall when the soil is in a workable condition. For the best effect they should be planted in irregular groups at unequal distances apart.

Propagation of the perennial kinds is by division of seeds; of the biennials, by seeds only.

Seeds are sown in a drill, 1 in. deep, out of doors in April or May. The seedlings, when 3 in. high, are pricked out, 12 in. apart in a nursery bed, and are planted in their final positions in autumn or spring.

ONOSMA—*Golden Drop* (Onos'ma). A large group of hardy plants native to southern Europe, northern Africa and western central Asia. Among them are annual, biennial and perennial herbs, the latter often subshrubby at the base. The flowers are yellow, white or purplish. The plants belong to the Borage family, Boraginaceae. The name is derived from *onos,* an ass, and *osme,* smell; the scent of the plant was supposed to be liked by asses.

Flowering shoot of the Golden Drop, Onosma stellulatum variety tauricum.

Although there are about seventy known kinds of Onosma, only five or six are in cultivation, and this is the more surprising because many are of considerable beauty.

Taking Cuttings. These plants may be raised from seed—when this is obtainable—sown in pots of light soil in a cold frame in spring. The better way, however, is to root cuttings of nonflowering shoots taken off with a "heel" during summer, and set in sand in a cold frame, kept close. They should be potted as soon as rooted, kept shaded for a time, and then hardened off before being planted out of doors in late summer; or they may be wintered in a frame and planted outdoors during the following spring.

For the Rock Garden. All the Onosmas described here are excellent plants for the rock garden, and should be given a sunny, well-drained position in light soil, well raised up among the larger rocks. They also make beautiful subjects for a wall garden facing south or west.

Onosma albo-roseum, 6-8 in., is a very beautiful plant, a native of Asia Minor. It has blunt leaves, hoary white with rough hairs, and bears curled heads of fine tubular flowers that are white, tinged with pink and crimson. It likes a warm, well-drained location in the rock garden, and makes an attractive specimen in a pan or planted out in the alpine house.

Onosma stellulatum, 6 in., is a variable plant, many forms of which have, at one time or another, been given variety names and have also been distinguished as species. It is a native of Greece and Asia Minor. The flowers are white, yellow or citron and appear in spring.

With Almond-scented Flowers. Onosma stellulatum variety tauricum, Golden Drop, is a native of southeastern Europe and is the most beautiful and satisfactory Onosma in cultivation. The base of the plant is woody, the narrowish leaves are gray-green and rough-textured. In early summer the lovely Golden Drop flowers appear, borne on 6-9 in. stems in forked, curled heads. Each corolla is an elegant drop-shaped tube of rich amber color. The flowers are deliciously almond-scented.

Onosma echioides, 1-1½ ft., resembles O. stellulatum variety tauricum in general appearance. The flowers are soft yellow on very short stems.

ONYCHIUM (Onych'ium). A small group of hothouse and cool greenhouse Ferns (family Polypodiaceae) from tropical America, Malaya and Japan. They are closely related to Pteris but have more finely divided fronds, somewhat resembling those of Davallia. They grow 12 in. in height and form elegant tufts of light and graceful greenery. The spores are borne on separate fronds which are similar in appearance to the barren ones. The name Onychium is derived from *onyx,* a claw, and refers to the lobes of the fronds.

Summer and Winter Management. The

hothouse kinds require a minimum winter temperature of 55 degrees and the cool greenhouse kinds one of 45 degrees. Repotting is done in February or March, or as soon as new fronds appear in spring.

The best soil compost consists of equal parts of peat, loam, leaf mold and sand. The plants are turned out of their pots, and the crocks and all loose soil removed from the roots with a pointed stick. The plants are then repotted in slightly larger pots. These must be well drained with crocks, which are covered with the rough siftings from the compost. The soil should be pressed firmly around the roots, and sufficient space left at the top of the pot for watering.

After potting, the plants are shaded from sunlight and the atmosphere is kept moist by frequently damping the floor and benches. The compost is not watered until it becomes fairly dry, but then it is thoroughly saturated. This procedure is followed until the pots are filled with roots, and then the compost is kept moist throughout the summer. During the winter much less water is required; enough only is given to prevent the fronds from withering.

Propagation is by spores (see Ferns), and by division, which is accomplished by removing the plants from their pots, washing the soil from the roots, then splitting them into smaller portions, which are potted in 3-in. pots.

The chief kinds are O. japonicum, 12 in., semi-deciduous, and O. siliculosum (auratum), 12 in., evergreen.

OPHIOGLOSSUM — *Adder's-Tongue Fern* (Ophigloss'um). Hardy deciduous Ferns, natives of the Northern Hemisphere. They are of little horticultural value and are grown in gardens as a curiosity or for botanical interest.

O. vulgatum, a native of North America, Europe and Asia, consists of an underground rhizome or rootlike stem; from this there rises, in spring, a single leaf, which is entire (undivided), oval, and 16 in. long. It is pea-green in color and is borne on a slender petiole (leafstalk) 3-4 in. in length. This leaf is infertile: the spores are produced on a narrow, tongue-shaped structure rising from the base of the leaf blade.

O. Engelmannii has 2-5 leaves each to 9 in. long. It is a North American kind.

For a Shady Corner. These Ferns require a shady, moist position. In their native habitats they are found growing in damp meadows, where they are shaded from the glare of the sun by the tall herbage, and in damp woods. A shady position at the base of a rockery or at the edge of the woodland suits them best. When preparing the site, dig in liberal quantities of leaf mold to conserve the moisture. The rhizomes, or rootlike stems, may be planted in autumn or spring, and are lightly covered with soil. Plants found growing wild are not easy to transplant and establish in gardens.

These plants belong to the family Ophioglossaceae; their name is derived from *ophis,* a serpent, and *glossa,* a tongue, and refers to the tongue-shaped sporophyllum (spore-bearing structure).

OPHIOPOGON—*Lily Turf* (Ophiopo'gon). Ornamental foliage and flowering plants, from Japan, which belong to the Lily family, Liliaceae. These plants have short, thick rhizomes (rootlike stems), and the sessile leaves (joined to the rhizomes without stalks) are linear (long and narrow), 1-3 ft. in length, green or striped with white or yellow. The flowers, which are small and not very conspicuous, are violet-purple, blue or white, and are arranged in dense spikes.

Although some kinds are hardy, at least as far north as New York City, these plants are principally grown in pots in the greenhouse in the North. In the South they are valuable ground-cover plants. The name Ophiopogon is from *ophis,* a snake, and *pogon,* a beard, and probably refers to the flower spike. These plants are sometimes cultivated under the name Mondo.

Cultivation in Pots. The plants require a minimum winter temperature of 40 degrees; the best soil compost consists of two parts of loam, one of leaf mold or peat moss and a small quantity of decayed manure and sand. Repotting is done in April. The plants are knocked out of the pots, the crocks and all soil removed from the roots. They are then divided into pieces, each piece bearing several leaves, and the pieces are potted separately in 5-in. pots. This procedure is usually adopted each year, as the plants are most useful when grown in small pots.

After repotting, the plants are set close

together in a warm corner of the greenhouse and are shaded from bright sunlight. The atmosphere is kept moist by damping the floor and benches, and the leaves are syringed twice a day. Water is very carefully applied to the soil until roots are forming freely, then the soil is kept moist during the remainder of the summer. During the winter the soil is only moistened when it becomes fairly dry.

For a Border. When grown out of doors, the plants require light, rich soil. They thrive in sun or partial shade. The roots are planted in clumps in April and are not disturbed until they show signs of deterioration or it is desired to increase the stock. They should then be lifted at planting time, divided into small clumps, the soil enriched by digging in decayed manure or compost, and the pieces replanted, and watered if the soil is dry.

For Summer Beds. Plants grown in pots are sometimes used as an edging for flower beds in summer. For this purpose they are grown in 3-in. or 4-in. pots, from which they are planted in the beds as soon as the weather is warm and settled. In the autumn they are lifted, divided, potted in 3-in. pots, and kept in a cool greenhouse or sunroom through the winter.

The Chief Kinds: O. intermedius, 18 in., flowers lilac, leaves margined with white; O. Jaburan, 18 in., leaves green, flowers white; O. Jaburan variegatus, 18 in., flowers white, leaves striped green and white; O. japonicus, 18 in., flowers white, leaves green (striped yellow in variety variegatus). O. japonicus is an excellent sod-forming plant. Both O. Jaburan and O. japonicus and their varieties are hardy as far north as New York City.

OPHRYS—*Bee Orchis, Spider Orchis, Fly Orchis* (Oph'rys). Hardy terrestrial Orchids which are found wild chiefly in Europe, northern Africa and Asia Minor. They are closely related to Orchis, but the flowers of most kinds are without a spur. The plants have underground tubers, and erect, leafy flower stems with large leaves near the ground. All are leaf-losing (deciduous). The flowers have equal, spreading sepals, smaller petals and a large lip, sometimes with two fleshy "horns" near its base. Great variation exists in size and color.

(Right) The Bee Orchis, Ophrys apifera. *(Left)* The Fly Orchis, O. muscifera.

The most beautiful is O. apifera, the Bee Orchis, so called from the resemblance of the lip to a bee. The stem attains a foot or more in height, and bears five or six comparatively large flowers in July; the sepals are pinkish, the narrow, downy petals greenish, and the velvet-like lip is dark brown marked with yellow. The Bee Orchis, in nature, seems to prefer chalky pastures. There is a white variety.

The Spider Orchis. O. sphegodes (aranifera), the Spider Orchis, resembles O. apifera in growth; it blooms in April or May, the sepals and petals being greenish and the lip dull brown. It likes dry, chalky pastures, and is more easily cultivated than O. apifera.

The Fly Orchis. O. muscifera, the Fly Orchis, has narrow leaves and a slender stem bearing three or four yellowish-green flowers. It is often found in rather dry, chalky meadows, but grows larger in damp pastures.

These Orchids may be grown in loamy, limy soil in a sunny place in the rock garden.

OPHTHALMOPHYLLUM (Ophthalmophyll'um). A curious group of small succulent plants of the Carpetweed family, Aizoaceae, natives of South Africa. The name is from *ophthalmos*, an eye, and *phyllon*, a leaf, and refers to the fact that the fleshy leaves of the plants are transparent ("windowed") at their tips. Some are night-flowering.

In cultivation these plants should be rested by being kept quite dry in April and May. For details of their cultivation see Mesembryanthemum, in which genus they were previously included.

A few interesting kinds are O. Friedrichiae, 1-2 in. high, flowers purplish or white; O. Herrei, similar in height, flowers white or rose; O. Maughanii, 1 in. tall, flowers white; O. Schlechteri, similar to O. Friedrichiae but smaller; O. Schuldtii, 1 in. tall, flowers creamy white.

OPIUM POPPY. See Papaver somniferum.

OPLISMENUS—*Variegated Grass* (Oplis'menus; Oplisme'nus). Tender perennial trailing plants with ornamental foliage. They belong to the Grass family, Gramineae, and are natives of tropical countries. The principal kind, O. hirtellus variegatus, has slender procumbent stems which bear lance-shaped alternate leaves running to a point at the tips. The leaves are beautifully striped with white and pink, and are the most ornamental feature of these plants. The flowers are inconspicuous. Oplismenus is grown in pots in the greenhouse or in hanging baskets. The name is derived from *oplismenos*, which is Greek for armored, and refers to the appendages of the seeds.

Greenhouse Plants. Under greenhouse cultivation these plants require a minimum winter temperature of 50 degrees, and the best soil compost consists of equal parts of loam, leaf mold or peat moss and sand. Plants in 4-in. or 5-in. pots being the most useful, it is not customary to repot them in larger pots each year.

How to Plant Cuttings. A supply of small plants is maintained by taking cuttings in spring or summer. Shoots about 2 in. in length are cut off, the lower leaves removed and a clear cut made below the bottom node (joint). A sufficient number of 3-in. pots are then prepared. Crocks to a depth of 1 in. are arranged in the bottom; these are covered with a thin layer of rough leaves, moss, or rough siftings from the compost. They are then filled with the soil mentioned above, but it is first sifted through a ½-in. sieve. A layer of sand is sprinkled on the surface and the cuttings are inserted to half their depth, around the edge of the pots. The soil is watered and the pots placed in a propagating case.

The cuttings are shaded from strong sunlight and the glass case is kept close except for a few minutes each morning, when the cover glass is raised to change the air. The condensed moisture is also wiped from the underside of the glass to prevent drops of water from falling on the cuttings and setting up decay.

When roots have formed, more air is admitted each day and eventually the plants are placed in the open greenhouse. In a week or so each potful of rooted cuttings is repotted, without being separated, in 5-in. pots. By this method bushy plants are obtained more quickly than by potting the cuttings singly.

Water is sparingly applied to the soil until the plants are well rooted, when it is kept moist at all times, although much less water is required in winter than in summer. When well established in 5-in. pots, the plants are attractive for decorative purposes. To maintain an unbroken display, it is necessary to have a number of young plants always in reserve to replace the older ones as they become worn out.

For Hanging Baskets. Prepare the baskets by lining them inside with a thick layer of moss and filling them with the potting compost recommended. Small plants are planted a few inches apart at the top of the basket. They may also be inserted all around the outside of the basket with the end of a dibble pushed through the moss into the compost. After planting, the baskets are hung in a shaded position, well watered and syringed frequently until the shoots have become established, and are growing freely, when they are suspended in their permanent positions.

The chief kind is O. hirtellus variegatus, which is often grown under the name Panicum variegatum. It has leaves that are green with white and pink stripings. In O. hirtellus albidus the leaves are mainly white with a central green stripe.

OPLOPANAX HORRIDUM — *Devil's-Club* (Oplo'panax; Oplopan'ax). This native of the West Coast, from Alaska to California, is an American representative of a small group of chiefly Asiatic plants that belong to the Aralia or Ginseng family, the Araliaceae. The name is derived from the Greek for weapon, and Panax, a genus of plants.

Oplopanax horridum is hardy and handsome. It is attractive both in foliage and fruit. Its stems and leaves are prickly. It forms a shapely bush 10-12 ft. tall and is hardy in the North and of easy cultivation. Its fruits are scarlet.

Favoring rather moist soils, the Devil's-Club thrives well near the sea. It may be propagated by seeds, suckers and root cuttings.

Oplopanax horridum is sometimes cultivated under the name Fatsia horrida.

OPPOSITE. A term used in describing the arrangement of leaves when they are arranged in pairs and are thus opposite to each other on a stem.

OPUNTIA or PRICKLY PEAR
A Distinctive Group of Cacti for Outdoor and Indoor Cultivation

(Opun'tia). These are mostly tender, succulent plants that are natives of North and South America and the West Indies. Although they belong to the Cactus family, Cactaceae, they are distinct in appearance from the majority of Cacti. The name Opuntia is derived from Opus, a city in Greece, where other plants of cactus-like appearance were grown.

Opuntias vary greatly in size; they range from a few inches to 20 ft. or more in height. No true leaves are produced by most kinds. The stems are composed of a number of distinct

A group of hardy Opuntias growing outdoors at The New York Botanical Garden.

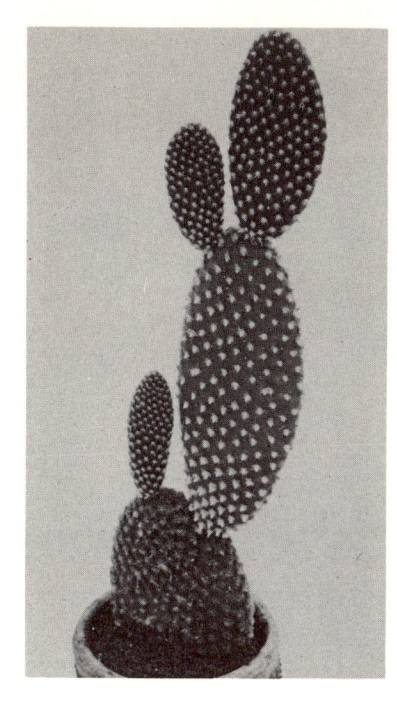

Opuntia microdasys is an interesting kind that has no long spines but bears many tufts of golden yellow bristles on its pads.

sections which, in some kinds, are flat pads of round or oval shape, and in other kinds are cylindrical or club-shaped.

Most Opuntias are armed with groups of sharp spines with tiny barbed hooks at their tips. If these penetrate the flesh it is difficult to extract them without lacerating the skin. In many warm, dry parts of the world selected kinds of Opuntias are planted as hedges; when so used, they form impenetrable barriers.

Under favorable conditions these plants spread rapidly. The smallest portion of a stem quickly takes root when it comes into contact with the soil, and the seeds, which are scattered by birds, germinate very quickly. Because of this, in some countries where these plants have been introduced, notably Australia, they have covered large tracts of ground, and have become a menace to farmers, who find great difficulty in exterminating them.

The flowers of Opuntia are cup- or saucer-shaped. They are borne singly towards the upper parts of the joints, have numerous petals and average 3 in. in diameter. They are mostly yellow, but some are purple, and others orange or red.

The fruit, which is pear-shaped and in some species is about the same size as a pear but in others is smaller, is really a swollen joint of the stem, into which the ovary grows after the ovules are fertilized as a result of the flower's being pollinated. The stem then changes into a pulpy mass of tissue. In many tropical countries the fruits of some kinds are an important article of diet. These fruits, known as Prickly Pears, are marketed in most parts of the United States.

Details of Indoor Cultivation. Opuntias, when grown indoors, require a minimum winter temperature of 50 degrees and a soil composed of two parts of sandy loam, one part of broken brick and one part of sand. Repotting is not done every year, as these plants can be cultivated in the same pots for several years. When it does become necessary, because the soil is worn out, or the plants cease to make fair growth, they are taken out of the pots in March or April. After the crocks and loose soil have been removed from the roots, the plants are repotted into slightly larger pots if their roots are healthy and plentiful, into pots just large enough to hold the roots without crowding if the root system is meager.

The soil is not watered until it becomes almost dry; then it is soaked and allowed to become nearly dry again before watering. This procedure is repeated until the pots become filled with roots, after which the soil is kept fairly moist throughout the summer. During winter the soil is only soaked occasionally—just often enough to prevent the stems from shriveling. In the depth of winter, a month or six weeks may elapse between the times of watering plants that are being grown in a cool greenhouse, sun porch or other location where the night temperature is about 50 degrees and the daytime temperature a little higher. Specimens grown under living-room conditions or in a greenhouse where the night temperature is about 60 degrees and the daytime temperature is higher, need more frequent watering. No shading is required and free ventilation must be afforded on all favorable occasions.

In summer, plants of Opuntia that are grown in pots may, with advantage, be placed outdoors. The best plan is to sink the pots to their rims in a bed of sand or ashes in a sunny spot; or they may be buried to the rims of their pots in a garden bed with some ashes beneath the pots to assure drainage and prevent the entry of worms.

Outdoor Cultivation. In mild climates, where desert or semidesert conditions prevail, Opuntias grow with the greatest ease; in fact, unless they are controlled, some species may become serious pests, as they have in Australia. They need very good drainage and sun.

Hardy Opuntias. In the northern United States, O. compressa may be grown outdoors without difficulty where the soil is well drained; it seems to thrive especially well in sandy places near the sea. Others of the more hardy kinds, such as O. arenaria, O. fragilis, O. imbricata, O. phaeacantha and O. polyacantha, can be grown outdoors in the North if a specially made bed with extremely good drainage is prepared against a south-facing wall. It is well to have the bed raised a few inches above the surrounding ground level. If, in winter, you can protect the bed from rainfall and snowfall by covering it with glass, cold-frame sash, or some similar device, more kinds will be likely to succeed.

Taking Cuttings. Pieces of stem of almost any size are detached and laid aside in a dry place for a few hours or days to allow the cut to heal. These cuttings are then planted in sand or very sandy soil in pots, flats or in a propagating bench. They are exposed to full sun and are not watered until the medium in which they are planted becomes quite dry. Subsequently, the rooting medium must be moistened regularly when it becomes nearly dry; it must not, under any circumstances, be kept constantly wet.

In favorable climates, cuttings root easily when they are set directly in soil outdoors.

How to Graft Prickly Pear. Grafting is only done to perpetuate monstrous forms such as cristate (crested) kinds and to produce curiosities as, for instance, when two dissimilar forms are grafted together.

Grafting is done during the summer when the sap is moving freely. To prepare the stock, cut it straight across the top and notch it in the center. Make the scion wedge-shaped at the base, and fit stock and scion together and hold them together by pushing through them a large spine taken from a Cactus. There is no need to remove this spine after stock and scion have united.

Raising Seedlings. Seeds are sown in spring or summer in well-drained pots of sandy soil. The pots are half-filled with crocks; these are covered with rough siftings from the compost; and the latter is made smooth and even on the surface. The seeds are sown thinly and covered with a little fine soil. The soil is then moistened and a pane of glass is laid over the pot.

The seed pot is set in a warm greenhouse or sunny window until germination takes place. The glass is then removed and the seedlings are exposed to full light and air. Sometimes germination is very irregular, but it is not wise to leave the glass on the pot once the seedlings are through the soil. If some of them are up in advance of the others, they may be pricked off in another pot, the seed pot being again covered with a pane of glass. The transplanted seedlings must not be disturbed until they are well rooted; then they are placed separately in small pots.

The Chief Kinds. There are numerous species and varieties of Opuntia, the chief kinds being the following: O. arenaria, red; O. aurantiaca, orange; O. basilaris, rosy-purple; O. compressa (Rafinesquei), yellow; O. cylindrica, red; O. Dillenii, yellow and red; O. Ficus-indica (the Indian Fig), sulphur-yellow; O. fragilis, pale yellow; O. imbricata (arborescens), purple; O. leucotricha, yellow; O. microdasys, yellow; O. Pentlandii (boliviana), yellow; O. phaeacantha, yellow; O. polyacantha, yellow tinged with red; O. Pottsii (filipendula), purple; O. spinosissima, orange; O. Tuna, reddish-orange, and O. Whipplei, red. The species commonly known as Opuntia cochenillifera is now included in the genus Nopalea, which see.

ORACH. See Atriplex.

ORANGE. Citrus, which see.

ORANGE, HARDY. See Poncirus.

ORANGE, JESSAMINE. See Murraea exotica.

ORANGE LILY. Lilium bulbiferum croceum, which see.

ORANGE, MEXICAN. See Choisya ternata.

ORANGE, MOCK. See Philadelphus.

ORANGE, NATAL. See Strichnos spinosa.

ORANGE, OSAGE. See Maclura.

ORANGE, TRIFOLIATE. Poncirus trifoliata, which see.